"*Beyond the Individual* is a challenging but accessible study which stresses the importance of the idea of the collective or whole in Stoic thought rather than that of unique individual personality. The book combines a wide-ranging study of Stoic ideas with suggestive readings of salient writings (including those of Epictetus, Hierocles, and Musonius) and will interest readers looking for life-guidance as well as more specialist scholars."

—**Christopher Gill**
Author of *Naturalistic Psychology in Galen and Stoicism*

"Modern Stoicism has become individualistic and sometimes devolves into an egoistic search for resilience against a harsh world. Will Johncock shows in this important counterweight in the growing Stoic literature that the ancient Stoics were, as Seneca says, the most sociable of the ancient philosophers, recommending that we prioritize our interconnectedness with others in order to live well ourselves, given the kinds of rational social creatures who we are."

—**Matthew Sharpe**
Author of *The Other Enlightenment: Self-estrangement, Race, and Gender*

"Stoicism is not, and has never been, a philosophy of self-help hacks. Stoicism is the art of living a life worthy of being lived. If you wish to learn how to paint your own journey to true happiness, Will Johncock's *Beyond the Individual* is an important addition to your bookshelf."

—**Kai Whiting**
Co-author of *Being Better: Stoicism for a World Worth Living In*

"Well-grounded in study of the ancient Stoic texts and thinkers, as well as recent academic and popular literature, this book provides persuasive re-interpretations of central Stoic themes, fleshing out their implications and significance for our contemporary settings. Johncock engages the reader with thought-provoking analyses of individuals and communities, rationality and freedom, materialism and metaphysics, cosmopolitanism and care for self and others, and the nature of genuine happiness."

—**Gregory Sadler**
Editor of *Stoicism Today*

Beyond the Individual

Beyond the Individual

Stoic Philosophy on Community and Connection

WILL JOHNCOCK

PICKWICK *Publications* · Eugene, Oregon

BEYOND THE INDIVIDUAL
Stoic Philosophy on Community and Connection

Pickwick Publications
An Imprint of Wipf and Stock Publishers
199 W. 8th Ave., Suite 3
Eugene, OR 97401

www.wipfandstock.com

PAPERBACK ISBN: 978-1-6667-5936-5
HARDCOVER ISBN: 978-1-6667-5937-2
EBOOK ISBN: 978-1-6667-5938-9

Cataloguing-in-Publication data:

Names: Johncock, Will, 1977–, author.

Title: Beyond the individual : Stoic philosophy on community and connection / Will Johncock.

Description: Eugene, OR: Pickwick Publications, 2023. | Includes bibliographical references and index.

Identifiers: ISBN 978-1-6667-5936-5 (paperback). | ISBN 978-1-6667-5937-2 (hardcover). | ISBN 978-1-6667-5938-9 (ebook).

Subjects: LCSH: Stoics. | Stoicism. | Philosophy, Ancient. | Ethics, Ancient.

Classification: B528 J64 2023 (paperback). | B528 (ebook).

VERSION NUMBER 020123

Contents

1 How a Social Philosophy Became Personalized | 1

2 Shared Minds | 23

3 Common Bodies | 51

4 Caring for the Self Is Caring for Others | 84

5 Knowledge, a Social Education | 113

6 Collective Happiness | 144

Bibliography | 179

1

How a Social Philosophy Became Personalized

A Philosophy about Our Interconnections

THE BENEFITS FOR INDIVIDUALS who adopt and practice features of Stoic philosophy have recently been much publicized. Stoicism has become synonymous with themes of personal well-being, with a seemingly limitless supply of Stoic commentaries during the last decade directing new devotees on how to apply its ancient principles to their own anxieties and concerns. For people experiencing adverse mental or emotional states, Stoicism has emerged as a standard prescription. The dispensers of this philosophical remedy furthermore instruct to use Stoicism daily to improve an individual's welfare. Therapists, business and marketing professionals, life coaches, academics, in fact all kinds of experts and practitioners recommend that we employ Stoic philosophy to help manage our own lives. If you have the appetite and discipline for self-improvement, the promise is that Stoic philosophy can help you.

These rewards for individuals are consistent with the ancient Stoic characterization of its philosophy as a practical project. Modern applications of Stoicism emphasize that the people who actively practice and enact aspects of the philosophy, rather than engage it as an intellectual exercise, will be the ones to gain from it. A focus on how we can personally, particularly psychologically, benefit from incorporating Stoic techniques and perspectives into our lives has duly seen the public awareness of the philosophy explode. The timing for many Stoic commentators in this regard could not have been more opportune. With a growing public consciousness and concern around themes of mental health, Stoicism has been positioned as a source of self-reflection that is consistent with current human needs. Stoicism's techniques have accordingly become known as tools that can help every individual to cope more resiliently with the mental and emotional provocations thrown at them by an overwhelming world. For people looking to take responsibility for enacting positive personal change in their own lives, the philosophies of the ancient Stoics are proving to be increasingly appealing.

What if we consider, though, that ancient Stoicism's priorities were more complex than the targeting of an *individual's* adversities, prosperities, goals, or outcomes? Within the frenzy of attention around Stoicism regarding how it can benefit us personally, how does our relationship with the philosophy change when we pause to appreciate that Stoicism was primarily concerned with something grander than an individual's pursuits? Given the currently fruitful intersection between Stoicism and self-help literature, it could be surprising to consider that using Stoic philosophy with the exclusive or even main intention of serving our own personal needs or goals might not straightforwardly cohere with the ancient Stoic project.

I am here opening the suggestion that in being interested in how Stoic philosophy can serve personal goals and positive psychological outcomes, we must firstly appreciate how the Stoics contextualize everything about us personally within grander, impersonal priorities. We must appreciate this in order that our era's, at times, feverish engagement with Stoicism's apparent suitability for self-development, is complemented with an awareness of the philosophy's repeated demand to avoid personalizing or individualizing intentions and outcomes. If Stoicism is reduced, for example, to a refrain regarding being resilient to both the actions of other people and to an uncertain world, we neglect that fundamentally the Stoics inversely ask us to direct our consciousness toward our interconnections with those people and that world. From these considerations, the need emerges for the kind of study I present in this book. Stoicism's understanding of all of us as dependent on each other, rather than as individually self-creating or self-determining, is a theme of this book.

The interpretation that Stoicism is a philosophy of collective purposes and ends, rather than of personal orientations, radiates from the Stoic identification that we each live according to three levels of commitments. The first commitment is to recognize ourselves as interconnected parts of a unified whole. To understand what that means, we will explore what the Stoics intend when they say we are each produced by a worldwide system of interrelated causes. This idea will present serious ramifications for suppositions that Stoicism is a toolkit via which we can individually author anything at all about our lives, even our psychological impressions of our lives. When the Roman Emperor Marcus Aurelius states that our every thought or action as Stoics must reflect that the world's happenings have already been ordered and determined via a successive chain of causes and effects, we need to ask where that leaves beliefs in subjective freedom. We might require an un-conventional understanding of personal liberty if for the Stoics we must perpetually be conscious, as Marcus states repeatedly in his *Meditations*, that "all that happens to you . . . was ordained for you from the beginning and spun to be your fate."[1]

This worldview contextualizes considerations of the next level of com-mitments for the Stoics, those involving (i) the shared conditions for our individual existences, and (ii) our duties to those shared conditions. Our considerations of what humans share will be based on the just noted Stoic understanding of the world as a system that causes and activates, or orders and determines, everything and everyone. This will require asking to what extent for the Stoics we are all bound to each other, given their belief that we are all shaped by the same physical, causal mechanism. If each of us is ordered according to this shared impetus (which might even be responsible for the characteristics of our "own" reasoning minds), individuals become understood as mutually bonded. From appreciations of what the Stoics de-scribe as these "kindred" conditions, we can ask whether a Stoic orients toward collective rather than personal outcomes because our thinking and acting never had individualized conditions to begin with. This will require determining whether *everything* about us for the Stoics is a trace of a fellow-ship, and if so, whether being a Stoic simply means living in service of that union.

It is only once we arrive at the third level of our existence for the Stoics that we can discuss what in a modern sense we refer to as the "individual." The Stoics are conscious of, and celebratory of, the benefits to individuals that arise from living "Stoically." I cannot think of an ancient Stoic work that does not refer to the betterment of individual lives that occurs from living in accordance with their beliefs. What is also clear though, is that if when thinking and acting we exclusively or predominantly hold a consciousness or anticipation of personal benefits, needs, adversities, goals, problems, or outcomes, we have missed not only the Stoic point but also the real advan-tages that Stoicism provides. An overly individualistic perspective might sound practical in terms of self-development, however we cannot define it as Stoic. We will consider whether instead, every thought or action only

1. Marcus Aurelius, *Meditations* (2011), 4.26.

occurs in accordance with our Stoic nature if it is engaging with communal and universal commitments.

The method via which this book studies these communal commitments does not need or intend to argue against publications, authors, or practitioners that are conversely occupied with the individualized or personalized benefits that living according to Stoic principles can offer. As I have indicated, concerns around individual well-being are not absent from ancient Stoicism. Outcomes for individuals are indeed a constant topic for the Stoics, which means that modern works focusing on the personal prosperities associated with Stoicism will to some extent always intersect with features of the philosophy. Rather than therefore attack any well-intentioned adaptations of Stoicism that attempt to help people's lives by focusing on their individual needs, the purpose of my book is to distinctively contribute to an era replete with such works by instead offering a recognition of Stoicism's principles around our social and interconnected natures. Many existing Stoic scholarly commentaries do in fact reflect on these features of the Stoic nature. I accordingly engage such works in the chapters that follow. I am not aware, however, of another single published work that shares this book's dedicated focus on the communal priorities of Stoicism.

While the ancient Stoics emphasize that a philosophically oriented life is a rewarding life for individuals, what demands our attention is the extent to which living according to Stoic philosophy requires different commitments than targeting personal rewards or goals. We will duly discuss ancient arguments of how thinking as a Stoic involves being conscious that we are embedded in a world and a group, rather than of being psychologically resilient to, or distinct from, the world and the people around us. This will require at times engaging plural recognized translations of ancient Stoic works, in order that we are able to consider a spectrum of modern interpretations of the same thinker and text. Such an approach will reflect how interpretations of ideas manifest via collective debate, and will therefore cohere with a theme of this book; Stoicism's commitment to collegially conditioned identities and meanings.

Stoicism's Recent Popularity

The nature of this book's reflection on Stoicism is timely given the resurgence of academic and public interest in the philosophy. Renowned philosopher of the Stoics, Anthony Long, reports that as recently as the mid-1960s academia had relatively ignored the Stoics.[2] It is conversely now not unusual

2. Long (in Holiday, "Stoic Scholar," para. 1) reports that his first encounter with

for professional philosophers who specialize in the ancient eras to enthusiastically engage the fragments of Stoic texts. The number of scholarly publications grows every year that not only integrate the Stoics within grander considerations of Plato, Aristotle, and their ancient contemporaries, but that are also dedicated to the Stoics.

Stoicism begins as an ancient Hellenistic school, originating around the turn of the third century BCE. To an extent it is therefore contemporaneous with Plato's Academy, Aristotle's Lyceum, and the Epicurean Garden. While names like Plato and Aristotle are well recognized (but not always well understood) outside academic circles, it is likely that no components of either's elaborate philosophical models have been discussed anywhere as much by the public as certain features of Stoic philosophy are right now. It is also possible that no form or school of philosophy has ever had the sheer number of minds occupied with it that Stoicism currently has. Bestseller books are one indication of this broader appetite for Stoic philosophy among non-academic audiences.[3] Beyond these works though, most new publications on Stoicism also explicitly broadcast the message that a daily "guide to better living" is available through the philosophy. Readers and practitioners are offered the idea that their modern lives can be improved by incorporating the wisdoms of ancient Stoic sages. Such works regularly attend to the interpreted intersection between Stoicism and modern mental health practices, especially around themes of resilience and inner peace. On the day I write this, Stoic related books in the top one hundred online sellers of "Greek and Roman Philosophy" feature titles or subtitles including: *Stoicism for Inner Peace*; *The Little Book of Stoicism: Timeless Wisdom to Gain Resilience, Confidence, and Calmness*; *Stoicism and the Art of Happiness*; *The Stoic Challenge: A Philosopher's Guide to Becoming Tougher, Calmer, and More Resilient*; *Stoicism: How to Use Stoic Philosophy to Find Inner Peace and Happiness*; *Mastering the Stoic Way of Life: Improve Your Mental Toughness, Self-Discipline, and Productivity with Ancient Stoic Wisdom*; *A Handbook for New Stoics: How to Thrive in a World out of Your Control*. The emphasis in these works is on personal development and therefore represents an admirably practical application of philosophy. This application typically links, to current contexts, the Stoics' ideas about how we might manage the adverse feeling of being buffeted around by an uncontrollable world.

This enthusiasm for new books that apply Stoicism to current psychological concerns is also reflected in complementarily increased sales for the

---

Stoicism in the mid-1960s occurred when an academic mentor advised him that "Stoicism is the most neglected field in ancient philosophy, why don't you look into that?"

3. Holiday, *Obstacle Is the Way*; Holiday and Hanselman, *Daily Stoic*; Irvine, *Good Life*; Pigliucci, *How to Be a Stoic*; Robertson, *Roman Emperor*.

original texts. Part of this trend is attributable to the COVID-19 pandemic. Penguin Random House reports that print sales of Marcus Aurelius' *Meditations* increased 28 percent in the first quarter of 2020 in comparison to that of 2019. Print sales of the Roman Stoic philosopher and statesperson Seneca's *Letters from a Stoic* rose 42 percent in the same period, which also saw the e-book version sales soar by 356 percent in one four-week period. The increase in sales of classical Stoicism is not solely attributable to the pandemic though. Penguin informs that sales of *Meditations* have been climbing for eight years. Sixteen thousand copies were sold in 2012, a figure that had risen to one hundred thousand by 2019. This prompts a representative from the publisher to note a "slightly mysterious year-on-year increase in our sales of the Stoic philosophers."[4]

A wave of mass media coverage over preceding years also illustrates the extent to which Stoic philosophy has outgrown a scholarly or academic readership and is now devoured by millions of public readers.[5] Much of this attention celebrates how Stoic philosophy can assist us with specifically modern problems. Terms such as "life hack" are employed in certain perspectives,[6] presenting Stoic philosophy as a set of ancient tricks via which we can filter or negate the anxieties and emotional intensities that we each internally and privately experience.

Portrayals of Stoic philosophy as a useful self-help guide for individuals are justified. Thousands of people report that integrating certain Stoic techniques does improve their personal well-being. We see this in accounts posted daily in the largest (currently over one hundred thousand members) Stoicism Facebook group, as well as in empoweringly titled articles such as: "How Learning Stoicism Helped Me in the Age of Anxiety";[7] "How Stoicism Helped Me Overcome Depression";[8] "Stoicism Saved My Life";[9] and "Marcus

---

4. Flood, "Dress Rehearsal," para. 4.

5. Alter, "Ryan Holiday"; Balkhi, "How Stoicism"; Batuman, "How to Be a Stoic"; Berry, "Why Stoicism"; Feloni, "11 Timeless Lessons"; Humphreys, "Five Lessons"; Irvine, "Greek Back into Stoicism"; O'Grady, "Lockdown Blues"; Pigliucci, "How to Be a Stoic"; Sharpe, "Stoicism 5.0"; Sharpe, "Life Gives You Lemons"; Sherman, "Stoicism for Life Hacks."

6. Love ("Revival of Stoicism") reflects on the integration of this terminology in modern applications of the philosophy. Also relevant is where Sherman ("Stoicism for Life Hacks") critiques recent reductive characterizations of Stoic philosophy. Additionally, see how Goodhill ("Silicon Valley," para. 1) details that "silicon valley tech workers are using an ancient philosophy [Stoicism] designed for Greek slaves as a lifehack," which means that "Stoicism is having a moment."

7. Derinbogaz, "How Learning Stoicism Helped."

8. Overby, "How Stoicism Helped."

9. Kennedy, "Stoicism Saved."

Aurelius Helped Me Survive Grief and Rebuild My Life."[10] Psychotherapists such as Tim LeBon and Donald Robertson report that Stoicism's principles underpin their clinical applications of cognitive behavioral therapies that positively impact people's lives.[11] All such accounts describe people's calmer states of mind, clearer definitions of themselves, and newly discovered disciplines for self-improvement that have ensued through adopting Stoic principles. The widespread public celebration of these practical outcomes is surely a significant part of the reason for the surge in the number of Stoicism's devotees.

Given that anecdotal evidence suggests that approaches using Stoicism for one's individual or personal ends are in fact serving or satisfying such ends, we might therefore pause to ask why the different focus that I propose in this book is necessary. Applications of Stoicism that are occupied with an individual's self-development and personal psychological benefits have reportedly produced positive results for the lives of a new generation of readers and adopters. If Stoicism is a philosophy concerned with practical outcomes, and practical outcomes are being realized, what does it matter if an author or practitioner primarily targets their own goals and outcomes when adapting and applying Stoicism?

In responding to this question, I must clarify that my motivation to instead highlight the communal and universal preoccupations of Stoicism does not restrict itself to intellectual and theoretical aspirations of simply doing justice to the original texts, to the exclusion of practical considerations. Yes, my intention is to present an engagement of Stoicism that is consistent with underlying ancient Stoic principles and theories. My work, however, is not an exercise in setting the record straight for purely academic purposes that steers us away from the practical and instead toward the intellectual. As stated, I am also not intending to identify and criticize authors or negate works that emphasize the personalized or individualized aspects of Stoicism's modern relevance. This is because the ancient Stoics *do* consider how living in accordance with what they call our "nature" will improve each of our individual lives.

My purpose is therefore not to invalidate our belief in the positive effects for individuals. Instead I plan to address where our focus should principally point for the Stoics, and to recognize the associated *practical* benefits of that refocusing. This concerns the Stoic investment in what is communal and shared, which needs to be highlighted, as does how the Stoics prioritize

10. Lombardi, "Marcus Aurelius Helped."

11. Lampert, "Interview"; LeBon, *Achieve Your Potential*; LeBon, "Interview"; Robertson, *Cognitive-Behavioural Therapy*; Robertson, *Art of Happiness*.

that investment before anything resembling individualized or personalized ends can be considered. Appreciating this difference has significant ramifications not only for how we read Stoic theory but also for how we practically live day-to-day with the philosophy.

This is not an incidental point, given that I just asked whether this book's intervention really matters if people already feel real benefits from engaging applications of Stoicism that are concerned primarily with one's own fortunes and development. My response to that question is that what matters about this book becomes apparent when we review how for the Stoics our most practical personal flourishing is associated not with an individually oriented existence, but instead with a consciousness of ourselves as collectively and universally interconnected and motivated minds and actors. We will consider in the coming chapters whether it is only by engaging Stoicism as a philosophy of grander stakes than an individual's personal prosperities, that we can ever experience the kind of personal well-being that people seek through it and that the Stoics intended from it.

This concerns the difference between living primarily with a consciousness of (a) our interconnections with other people and the world, versus a consciousness of (b) our personal borders and boundaries and needing to be resilient to a world outside our control. In this study I want to explore where and why the Stoics identify our individual well-being with position (a): our interconnected existences. Complementarily, we will need to examine how, when the Stoics instruct us to be indifferent and resilient to what is outside our control in apparent accordance with position (b), it is only ever to serve position (a).

Our Internal Psychological Lives

Reports of the psychological rewards for individuals who use certain Stoic techniques to become more resilient to an unsettling world have contributed to popularizing the philosophy. The techniques in question require viewing the world according to the Stoic division between (i) our internal, mental, rational functions that are within our control or up to us individually, and (ii) the external, social, physical, and circumstantial environments around us that are beyond our control or not up to us individually. As we will review, the orthodox interpretation is that for the Stoics, an individual's well-being is aided by focusing on what we can control (our internal, mental life), and being indifferent to the world we cannot control. The Stoic instruction to be indifferent to what we have no personal mental authority over presents as a tool that can facilitate better mental health because the practitioner relinquishes the anxieties associated with trying to control what they cannot. The abundance of attention on this technique means that it has become Stoicism's most famed and widely discussed feature. Given how this can appear to orient Stoicism's focus toward an *individual's* internal properties and priorities, we must begin this book's work by studying this Stoic principle of what is, versus what is not, up to our individual minds. We can do this via the lectures of a fierce advocate of this principle, the slave turned philosopher Epictetus.

When Epictetus is discussed, one of the first novel features of his life that receives attention is that he was born into slavery. It is noteworthy that one of the most prominent thinkers to have emerged from the ancient eras originally held a social status of relative subservience. As a slave he even for a period served the wealthy secretary of the fifth emperor of ancient Rome, Nero.[12] It is likely therefore that Epictetus' earliest experiences would have emphasized to him that many luxuries and freedoms were out of reach depending on the life or world into which you were born. When this idea is expanded to reflect on the ways in which everyone's lives are restricted, these would have been formative experiences for Epictetus in learning that much about our lives is outside our personal control.

Inversely what was in Epictetus' control was being able to think philosophically. This was further aided, although not entirely dependent on, the permission that his "owner" at the time, Epaphroditus, granted Epictetus to study philosophy.[13] While it is possible that Epaphroditus was a benevolent slave owner, it is also conceivable that Epictetus was allowed to study in order that he become a better slave. In a later chapter we will consider a range of topics related to ancient conceptions that link a philosophical education to private and public service. Whatever Epaphroditus' motivation might have been, we do know that Epictetus' studies led him to the tutelage of the philosopher Musonius Rufus (himself regularly categorized as a Stoic).[14] Musonius' philosophical positions share similarities with those of Epictetus, and in the context of themes around access to study and training we will consider some of them in the aforementioned chapter on education.

12. Epictetus mentions in his lectures, compiled in *Discourses*, that he was born a slave and that he worked for Epaphroditus, the secretary to Nero. For commentaries on this see Dobbin (in Epictetus, *Discourses* [2008], viii–ix), as well as Weaver ("Epaphroditus," 468–79).

13. See Weaver ("Epaphroditus," 475–76) for considerations of whether Epictetus studies with his master's "permission or encouragement."

14. Epictetus (*Discourses* [2014], 1.9.29) reflects on how Musonius would test him regularly to see how he handled adversity. For contemporary reflections on the teacher-student relationship between Musonius and Epictetus, see Dillon, *Musonius Rufus and Education*; Long, *Epictetus*, 13–17; Snyder, *Teachers and Texts*, 18–19.

After Nero's eventual death, a newly freed Epictetus would become a teacher and producer of philosophy. His own philosophy provides somewhat of a connecting hinge between the Greek Stoic world into which he was born, and the Roman Stoic world in which he eventually thrived. Despite having superseded his life as slave, that history shapes his merciless philosophical views regarding how to endure suffering. The most important source of Epictetus' work, a collection of his lectures transcribed by his student Arrian of Nicomedia called *Discourses*,[15] contains numerous examples of Epictetus' brutally straightforward manner. In one such instance, we see Epictetus address students who ask to leave school because of ill health:

> "I'm ill here," someone says, "and I want to go home."
> "What, were you never ill at home? Don't you want to examine whether you're doing anything that may contribute to the improvement of your choice? For if you're not accomplishing anything, it was pointless for you even to come here. Go away."[16]

If you are ill at school in Epictetus' estimation, you will also be ill at home. Being ill is, at least to a certain degree, not up to you. Otherwise, you would choose not to feel ill! Once you feel ill, however, what is up to you is what you decide to do during the illness. Choosing to stay in philosophy class to improve your "will," an improvement that requires studying philosophy rather than lying in bed at home, is one such decision, or mental judgement, over which you have control for Epictetus. The illness with which Epictetus is more concerned in such cases therefore is not the fleeting fever, nausea, or other adverse physical state with which you might temporarily be afflicted. The greater illness is an investment in aspects of life over which you have no control, and the inverse lack of attention and care given to one's philosophical development that would provide the ability to recognize what is in your control. We see this when Epictetus follows with the advice that in his class:

> If you understand that you are getting rid of bad judgements and gaining others in their place, that you have transferred your attention from things outside the will's control to things within ... then why should you take account of illness any more?[17]

---

15. Arrian wanted to convey Epictetus' lectures as closely to their original forms as possible. This explains the convention of referring to the author of *Discourses* as Epictetus. Long (*Epictetus*, 38–43) provides a comprehensive discussion on the relationship between Epictetus and Arrian, as well as an explanation of how we can know the work to "be authentic to Epictetus' own style and language."

16. Epictetus, *Discourses* (2014), 3.5.1–3.

17. Epictetus, *Discourses* (2008), 3.5.4.

While Epictetus' works target several features of our relationships with each other and the entire universe, this theme of how we control our will or mind is the aspect of his philosophy that has received by far the greatest contemporary attention. As indicated by the various terminologies that I have already employed, translations of this directive from Epictetus differ, some replacing the term "control" with "power," "up to us," or "dependent on us." Regardless of the specific wording used, what Epictetus is discussing when we encounter these kinds of passages concerns how we mentally decide on, judge, and appreciate the world. The issue is not whether we can or cannot control the external world (the world outside our mind). It is self-evident for the Stoics that we cannot. What is instead at stake in this Stoic consideration is our internal psychological management of what is dependent on us, that being how we mentally respond to the world.

The Stoic assertion is that there is much that we cannot control about our day-to-day lives. We cannot control the people around us for example, their behaviors and thoughts are not up to us. We might try to influence them and their actions, we might also try to influence their impressions of us. We cannot however ever dictate how they will think and behave. Environmental factors are similarly beyond our personal authority. We do not have the power to control whether there will be a crowd of people in the shops on a day when we need to buy our groceries quickly. Neither can we control whether it will be a warm or cold day when we wake in the morning. We can take steps to try to avoid what we believe are adverse social or physical conditions. In doing this though we will still in Epictetus' view always encounter a world that exceeds what is up to us.

Contrary to the lack of authority we have over the world, Epictetus maintains that we can preside over how we think and feel about the circumstances and people in the world that we encounter. These controllable features of ourselves, our thoughts, judgements, and associated emotions, Epictetus defines in the *Enchiridion* as being "internal" to each of us. Conversely, social factors like our reputation and social class, as well as physical things such as our body, our possessions, or the day's weather, are "external" to us:

> Some things are within our control, and some things are not. Things in our control are opinion, pursuit, desire, aversion, and, in a word, whatever are our own actions. Things not in our control are body, property, reputation, command, and whatever are not our own actions.[18]

18. Epictetus, *Enchiridion*, 1.

We need to be clear regarding what Epictetus means by "within our control," or what is alternatively prominently translated as internal to our "power."[19] Epictetus does not define what is within our control or power as absolutely *all* our thoughts or mental processes. Our minds and thoughts often respond uncontrollably to the contingencies of our social and physical worlds, after all. It is indeed the Stoics' appreciation of this human tendency that partly impels them to develop reflections like Epictetus' on how to mentally manage ourselves.

What *is* internal to, or within, each of us for Epictetus however, is a capacity to regulate our mental responses to life. Even when our instinctive, initial mental responses are unruly and unsettling, for the Stoics we can develop by remembering that we have within us the power to think whatever we want about our lives, despite lacking the power to control everything that happens in our lives. This self-reflective capacity is a key element of what the Stoics refer to as our rationality. While this reflective rationality here presents with apparent individualized investments, as we engage Stoicism's sense of rationality further, we will consider whether it is a condition of how we think and live collectively rather than individually.

For now the understanding I present of rationality is simply of avoiding mental and emotional investments in a world that is outside our control, those external things that are not up to us. As I have indicated, it is probable that Epictetus developed an affection for the conception that we should be indifferent to what is not in our control during his early life as a slave. Epictetus the slave would have lacked authority over his environment, his schedule, his bodily pain, and other daily experiences, but not over his mental judgements and other thoughts. His physical movements would have been determined by his master. The poverty of being a slave would have prevented him accessing the kinds of comforts that the upper classes enjoyed. Any possessions he had could have been taken against his will. The restraints of being a slave might even have extended to actual, material chains at times. Epictetus nevertheless would have been free to hold whichever beliefs and opinions his reasoning capacities decided about his life and the world around him.

It is not only Epictetus of the ancient Stoics who proposes these dichotomous conditions of control. The later Roman Stoic and eventual teacher of Epictetus, Musonius Rufus, partly inspires[20] Epictetus' positions.

19. Epictetus, *Discourses* (2014); taken from *Handbook*, 1.1.

20. The relationship between Epictetus and Musonius comes under greater attention in this book in chapter 5. We can still appreciate now, though, that Epictetus began studying philosophy through Musonius, which informs Epictetus' own philosophies. Inwood ("Legacy of Musonius," 254–76) provides more extensive reflections on what

In a fragment entitled "By Rufus, from Epictetus' Remarks," Musonius is attributed (according to the ancient compiler Stobaeus) with likewise dividing our existence according to what is, versus what is not, within our control:

> Of the things that exist, Zeus has put some in our control and some not in our control. In our control is the most beautiful and important thing, the thing because of which even the god himself is happy—namely, the proper use of our impressions. Such use brings freedom, prosperity, serenity, and stability; it also brings justice, law, self-control, and complete virtue. All other things he did not put in our control. Therefore, we must agree with the god: after we have divided matters in this way, we must concern ourselves absolutely with the things that are under our control and entrust the things not in our control to the universe. And whether it be our children, our fatherland, our body, or anything else that the universe demands, we must yield them readily.[21]

Another Roman Stoic who we will engage in this book is the already mentioned Seneca (the Younger). In his own way, Seneca recognizes a distinction between what we can and cannot control when instructing that we should appreciate what we have (rationality) and not want what we do not have (externals):

> It is in no man's power to have whatever he wants; but he has it in his power not to wish for what he hasn't got, and cheerfully make the most of the things that do come his way.[22]

The later Stoic voice Marcus Aurelius contributes to ensuring the legacy of this general Stoic mandate by referring to it in various forms throughout his *Meditations*. This is not surprising given the influence of Epictetus on Marcus' philosophy.[23] In advising that when being distressed by an "external cause, it is not the thing itself that troubles you but your judgement about it, and it is within your power to cancel that judgement at any moment,"[24] we see in Marcus all the hallmarks of the control distinction. The consistency

---

we can learn about Musonius' philosophy through Epictetus. See also where Starr ("Epictetus and Tyrant," 22) explains how Epictetus follows Musonius' beliefs on the division of things into goods, evils, and indifferents.

21. Stobaeus in Musonius Rufus, *Lectures & Sayings*, sayings 38.

22. Seneca, *Letters from a Stoic*, 123.3.

23. For an analysis of Epictetus' influence on Marcus, see Stephens (*Marcus Aurelius*, 59–70). Gill ("How Stoic and How Platonic?," 189–208) extends such considerations to ask whether Marcus' philosophy was more Stoic or Platonic.

24. Marcus Aurelius, *Meditations* (2011), 8.47.

in Epictetus' and Marcus' respective conceptions of what constitutes an "external" thing or cause also emerges in Marcus' Epictetus-like definition of how "everything that others do or say and . . . everything affecting the body . . . is outside your own control," as is "everything that swirls about you in . . . outward circumstance."[25]

Epictetus' attention on what we internally can versus externally cannot control bears the influences of Socratic distinctions of what is internal versus external to the self. Socrates seems to have been important for Epictetus' philosophical development, given the number of references the Stoic makes to him.[26] In the *Republic*, Plato describes how for Socrates living in "just" ways does not really involve what occurs "on the outside"[27] through "external actions,"[28] but rather is "concerned with what is inside"[29] and what occupies our "inward self."[30] Plato here is specifically discussing how our inner selves are harmoniously structured, a topic that we will engage in a later chapter more thoroughly. While this is not Epictetus' particular concern, the Stoic's distinction of internal versus external nevertheless bears characteristics of the preceding Socratic distinction.

Modern Stoicism's adoption of the dichotomy of control has not been without attempted revisions or corrections. A notable example comes from philosopher William Irvine's *A Guide to the Good Life: The Ancient Art of Stoic Joy*. In this influential work, Irvine reconstructs the dichotomy of control according to a three-part model. Irvine's intention here is to be sensitive to the possibility that the world is not merely divided up into things we can or cannot *entirely* control. It also features things over which we have *some* influence or power:

---

25. Marcus Aurelius, *Meditations* (1964), 12.3. See also the translation by Hard (in Marcus Aurelius, *Meditations* [2011], 12.3): "All that others do or say, and all that you yourself have done or said, and all that troubles you with regard to the future, and all that belongs to the body which envelops you, and to the breath conjoined with it, or is attached to you independently of your will, and all that the vortex whirling around outside you sweeps in its wake."

26. See Epictetus (*Enchiridion*, fragment 50) for one example. Epictetus advises us to compare ourselves to Socrates as we develop philosophically, stating that although we might not yet be "a Socrates," we should live in a way that attempts to become a Socrates. Also relevant is where Long ("Socratic Imprint," 10) observes that Epictetus cites "no other philosopher, not even Zeno or Diogenes" more often in *Discourses* than Socrates.

27. Plato, *Republic* (2004), 443c.

28. Plato, *Republic* (2007), 443c.

29. Plato, *Republic* (2004), 443d.

30. Plato, *Republic* (2007), 443d.

Consider again Epictetus's "dichotomy of control": He says that some things are up to us and some things aren't up to us. The problem with this statement of the dichotomy is that the phrase "some things aren't up to us" is ambiguous: It can be understood to mean either: "There are things over which we have no control at all" or to mean: "There are things over which we don't have complete control." If we understand it in the first way, we can restate Epictetus's dichotomy as follows: There are things over which we have complete control and things over which we have no control at all. But stated in this way, the dichotomy is a false dichotomy, since it ignores the existence of things over which we have some but not complete control.[31]

Irvine's work has contributed much to the modern Stoic community. In this passage however, it embarks on a different project to that of the ancient Stoics. I say this because the question for the Stoics is not literally of controlling, versus of not controlling, aspects of the world. The question is not whether we can partially control some circumstances that we encounter, versus other circumstances not at all. The control principle in Stoicism rather concerns recognizing the control we have, or can develop, over our internal mental and emotional responses to the world. There are conversely no degrees of control regarding our relationship with the external world. It is simply that that world is not up to us.

We will live more practical and functional lives according to Epictetus if we keep this in mind. Epictetus' emphasis on the practical benefits of avoiding personal investments in what is beyond our control is evidence of another influence of the teachings of Musonius. Philosophy means nothing if it is not practiced for Musonius. He argues that it is incumbent on the philosopher to practice their craft in the way that we expect practitioners in other fields to exercise their abilities.[32] It is from this emphasis on the practice that philosophy requires that Epictetus encourages new practitioners to firstly and deliberately "practice philosophy for yourself alone."[33] Once a familiarity with what theoretically constitutes a rational existence has been developed however, for Epictetus living rationally means testing and activating such principles practically and interactively in the world.[34]

Modern commentaries in this regard acknowledge that Epictetus intends his philosophy to not simply formulate abstract reflections about life.

---

31. Irvine, *Good Life*, 87–88.

32. Stobaeus in Musonius Rufus, *Lectures & Sayings*, lecture 5.

33. Epictetus, *Discourses* (2014), 4.8.36.

34. Epictetus, *Discourses* (2014), 1.20.7–10.

It must instead serve our everyday existence.[35] Philosophy should provide real outcomes, and directly inform the way that we live daily, rather than comprise a collection of intellectual thoughts that we conceptually analyze, re-arrange, and re-analyze. Epictetus interprets that much of Stoic philosophy is in this practical mode an order or a system that enacts or activates what we learn while we are learning it. He nevertheless laments that his fellow citizens do not live the philosophy in this manner, because they do not put what they learn into practice.[36]

Part of the concern for Epictetus regards how he regularly perceives people to be thinking and acting in turbulent ways, an indication that a world of uncontrollable external phenomena dictates their internal mental and emotional states. Epictetus is one of the strongest voices of the Stoic view that in living rationally, we must remember that only our internal mental appraisals of the world can harm us. Another person's view of us for example cannot do us damage, only how we judge and emotionally respond to their views can be detrimental to ourselves.[37] How we think about, and feel about, ourselves is an internal experience. While external events might prompt internal responses, we are only ever negatively affected by how we then mentally and emotionally manage, or mismanage, such responses.

Later in this book we will consider how external events and relations can in fact be useful according to the Stoics, if through them we learn how to live in accordance with what is up to us.[38] By invoking his earlier life as a slave, Epictetus posits that whenever we are mentally or emotionally regulated by externalities, they become our "masters" and we their "slaves."[39] Such external masters could be things, circumstances, or other people. While Epictetus was a literal slave for a certain number of years, some people in his estimation live in this general kind of slavery for their entire lives.

35. Long, *Epictetus*, 181; Long, *From Epicurus to Epictetus*, 377–94; Seddon, *Epictetus' Handbook*, 9; Sharpe, "Chrisippus," 279–80; Stephens, *Stoic Ethics*, xiv.

36. Epictetus, *Discourses* (2014), 2.16.

37. Epictetus, *Discourses* (2014), 4.13.8.

38. One example is where Epictetus (*Discourses* [2014], 3.20) discusses how having a bad parent, neighbor, or coach, is something from which we can "draw advantage." We are said to be able to do this if such situations provide us with occasions to develop our indifference to what is outside our control. All adverse circumstances represent opportunities in this sense. Marcus adopts and develops this concept in *Meditations*, various translations describing "obstacles" as useful for our mind's "own purposes" (*Meditations* [2002], 5.20), "objectives" (*Meditations* [1964], 5.20), or "own advantage" (*Meditations* [2011], 5.20). The purpose or objective here is to live rationally. This strategy of mentally turning obstacles into opportunities has been imparted by Holiday's *The Obstacle Is the Way* to public acclaim and commercial success.

39. Epictetus, *Discourses* (2014), 1.29.61.

The directive to only mentally and emotionally invest in what is up to us or within our internal authority seems to be sensible and reasonable. If there are circumstances or people that are not to our liking and that we cannot change, let alone control, what good will it do to allow our minds and feelings to be upended by them? This would be for Epictetus not simply a waste of our time and mental and emotional energy, but also a process via which we distance ourselves from our true rational selves. The appeal of this idea to modern self-help literature and practitioners is clear. There is a real sense of individual self-control and personal stability imparted by such a mentality. Despite this impression of individualized self-determination, we must be careful though not to interpret a simple and absolute division between our individual selves and the rest of the world in this Stoic view.

The Stoic Understanding of "Social"

In demanding that we remain indifferent to what occurs externally to us, Epictetus is not prescribing that we live passively in relation to our surrounding social or physical worlds. We should avoid interpreting Epictetus as recommending for us to be lazily apathetic toward anything that is not ourselves. Stoicism in this mode is not saying that we should ignore everything and everyone else and focus only on our self-centered interests. Epictetus instead emphatically asserts that we are bound by social roles as a guide to conduct. It is by exploring the intricate Stoic understanding of our social existence that we will now begin in this book to unravel how our personal priorities must be social and communal for the Stoics.

This point regarding the importance of social rules might initially appear to be contradictory, given that we have just introduced the Stoic advice to avoid mentally and emotionally investing in a society's arrangements around class, reputation, and numerous aspects of our interpersonal relationships. The Stoics here distinguish between what they call our internal rational nature and the adverse effects of external social influences. When we are prone to becoming irrationally mentally and emotionally dictated by social contingencies such as trends, fads, or groups of the ignorant as Seneca describes them,[40] Stoicism demands that we reflect on and identify what is conversely mentally rationally up to each of us. On this point Anthony Long describes how for the Stoics, we must differentiate our rationally oriented mental judgements, from our socially constructed selves that tend to

---

40. See, for example, where Seneca (*Letters on Ethics*, 7) warns against associating with crowds.

be temporarily shaped and re-shaped by whatever happen to be a period's "dominant social values."[41]

We can acknowledge this Stoic distinction between our rational mental selves and our socially shaped selves, while also recognizing that Stoicism invites a complex discussion about what our rational nature and mind "share" with the rational natures and minds of other people. To live as a Stoic, to practice Stoicism, to undertake Stoic scholarship, is to be conscious of these dual modes of being social for the Stoics.

This consciousness demands that a key to reading this book, and indeed of living as a Stoic, will be to appreciate what being social or communal for the Stoics means. A Stoically social or communal existence is not reducible to the conventional, modern understanding, of people simply contingently or accidently living in the same town, sharing the same interest, spending time together, being swept along by crowds or trends, participating in conversation, and so on. As we will explore in this book, the fundamental feature of a social or communal nature for the Stoics instead refers to how, when you think and act, you do so with an awareness that you are part of and constituted by a greater whole. This requires an appreciation that everything about us that appears to be "individual" or "personal," instead borrows from and shares in something that is dispersed beyond ourselves and is common to all.

We will see that with such kindred qualities indeed come significant and omnipresent responsibilities for the Stoics. In terms of all our thoughts and actions, Epictetus believes a Stoic "never acts in their own interest or thinks of themselves alone, but . . . all its actions and desires aim at nothing except contributing to the common good."[42] That does not sound like a self-insulated, worldly resilient, anti-social, selfish creature, does it!? We will soon explore in detail how what we are said to share specifically in terms of our rational minds signifies that we are fundamentally communally oriented according to the Stoics.

The message embedded in this brief indication of where we will head in this book is this; a Stoic can be engaged with the world around them, particularly where circumstances require their contribution to a common benefit, while not being irrationally destabilized by the world during their contribution to it. The world might require various forms of participation from us. We can practically assist for example in reconfiguring what we

41. Long, *From Epicurus to Epictetus*, 13.

42. Epictetus, *Discourses* (2008), 2.10.4. See also how the translation by Hard (in Epictetus, *Discourses* [2014], 2.10.4) emphatically conveys the communal or collective tone of Epictetus' instruction as: "Never to approach anything with a view to personal advantage, never to deliberate about anything as though detached from the whole."

perceive to be wrong or unjust around us. The key during such participation for the Stoics though, is to not allow the wrong or unjust circumstances to dominate our beliefs about the world by steering us toward irrational, externally dictated, psychological states. Our judgements should instead always follow our internal reason or rationality. I will again remind us that when an "internal rationality" is mentioned, this might sound like an individualizing mentality that contradicts the promised purpose of this book. As we will see however, our rationalities and associated mental processes are not really for the Stoics individually conditioned or personally oriented functions, even when they are described as "internal."

This point returns us to my concern with the view that Stoic philosophy is a tool primarily designed for individualized or personalized outcomes. Where Stoicism is conceptually individualized, the impression of what we control or is up to us becomes disproportionately emphasized. The appeal of the Stoic dichotomy of control is obvious in terms of self-help or personal development content. The powerful message is that what is affecting you adversely is not actually the world around you. Your internal mental reactions to the world are the problem rather, and you can learn to control those internal mental judgements.

This speaks not only to our mental lives. It also refers to our emotional experiences. Where Stoicism is deployed to alleviate personal anguish or anxiety, how you feel can be supposedly better regulated if you know that such feelings are the results of your mental reactions to a world. These mental reactions are not imposed by a world, and you have the power and authority to change and manage those reactions. Stoic commentaries of recent times regularly advertise that through a rational reflection on this internal control, a life of mental and emotional stability is more likely. All that is required is a sense of Stoicism that identifies an individualized territory of the self, distinguished from an external world beyond the self's borders, and the dedication to train the former to be resiliently indifferent to the latter.

It is not difficult to imagine that a contemporary reader of Stoicism, when encountering descriptions of this distinction regarding control and dependency, would feel the promise of a greater power over their personal life. I have earlier qualified my concern about the overemphasis on individualized and personalized outcomes that people associate with Stoicism, with the reminder that we should not discount or doubt the positive results that people are experiencing from this orientation. The anecdotal evidence is that in this format, Stoicism is providing genuine mental health benefits. The presentation of Stoicism as a philosophy for self-determination seems to be instilling people with genuine confidences that they are not finding elsewhere.

I have detailed though that such a recognition does not preclude the need for the kind of study that this book will contribute. In focusing on Stoicism's fundamental commitments to our interconnected rather than individualized constitutions, we will consider whether prosperities and benefits do manifest for individuals according to the Stoics, but only as by-products or expressions of our relationships with each other and with the universe as a whole. I repeat that the Stoics do not deny that positive outcomes or benefits result for individuals who practice the philosophy. It will be our responsibility in this book however to determine whether there are always communal and universal preconditions for our own prosperities and personal developments. Our examination will concern whether targeting our own individualized or personalized ends and outcomes, before recognizing our other-oriented or world-oriented commitments, is not only inconsistent with living Stoically but also impedes the full gamut of benefits that an individual can experience from practicing the philosophy.[43]

It might even be speculated that where people are newly exposed to Stoicism in a way that glosses over the communal and universal commitments of the philosophy, and instead impels them to demarcate their individual minds and selves from an externally uncontrollable world, there is the danger that the mental health benefits of the philosophy become hindered. If the first Stoic instruction you receive is to emphatically distinguish your own mind's "turf" from everything else, a tense border could easily be mentally constructed between yourself and the rest of the world. When this world is the very uncontrollable entity and anxiety-inducing threat that has brought someone to Stoic philosophy in the first place, it is possible that such an approach would increase rather than alleviate their anxiety by amplifying feelings of alienation. By instead engaging Stoicism as a philosophy that is firstly and primarily teaching us about how we are inherently bound to each other and to an entire world, so we will differently appraise the intersection between Stoic philosophy and our psychologies.

It is because of this necessarily nuanced engagement with Stoic principles that I disagree with the kind of sentiment expressed by Ryan Holiday that "Stoicism is a philosophy designed for the masses, and if it has to be *simplified* a bit to reach the masses, so be it."[44] The point of raising a citation like this is not to denounce its author. Holiday's entrepreneurial and marketing careers pair with written works that incorporate rigorous forays

---

43. This kind of recognition is why Sherman (*Stoic Wisdom*, 158) posits that through the Socratic and Stoic ancient eras we see that "virtue was never just about me and my temperance, but about others and my generous and just treatment of them."

44. Alter, "Ryan Holiday," para. 5; emphasis added.

into Stoicism's classical texts,[45] and his knowledge of Stoic theories should be respected. Musonius' and Epictetus' earlier-reviewed directive regarding Stoic philosophy's practical priorities furthermore radiates through Holiday's production of an active Stoicism, whereby he has made the philosophy speak usefully to people who otherwise might not have encountered it.

I cannot however endorse Holiday's specific assertions about simplifying Stoic philosophy. When Stoicism is simplified, it is regularly misrepresented as a school preoccupied with personal development. The point of my book's differentiation from this conceptual reduction is not, as should be clear by now, to entirely discount such approaches to Stoic philosophy. I have recognized in this opening chapter that the Stoics are attentive to themes around an individual's well-being. The issue though is that the apparent communal and universal preconditions in Stoicism for personal well-being do not receive the same attention. In dedicating ourselves now to a study of these preconditions, this book will highlight how all Stoic positions, including that of the dichotomy of control, rely on and reflect our immersed relationships with, and our responsibilities to, all other humans and the physical world.

Such a study is timely, given the collective responsibilities required of populations in response to the COVID-19 pandemic. The era of this pandemic explicitly exemplifies how we have each been asked to consider or prioritize not only our own, individual welfares. We instead also have a duty to the welfares of our fellow community members, almost all of whom we will never actually meet. Without attending to the mechanics of, or arguments about, the pandemic specifically, we will review why this kind of dispersed understanding of responsibility and prosperity is much closer to the Stoic understanding of self-development, than is exploring the philosophy in order to predominantly service one's own psychological needs and well-being.

This notion of sharing social relations with, and having responsibility for, people we not only do not know but will also never directly interact with, proves to be a foundation of Stoic philosophy. We will study this fascinating impression of the grandness of community for the Stoics in coming chapters, particularly in chapter 4 when contextualizing the drives for our own self-preservation within what the Stoics suggest are our primary concerns for communal and universal health and well-being. If it is not already clear, in this book we will be engaging Stoic philosophy on how everything about an individual reverberates with what seems to be situated beyond the individual. We can now begin to review the Stoics' distributed sense of

45. See, for example, Holiday and Hanselman, *Lives of the Stoics*.

ourselves, by considering what it is exactly that we share in when we each think and reason.

2

Shared Minds

You Are Rational Because You Are Human

WHEN CONSIDERING WHICH FEATURES of our individual selves might be counterintuitively shared and dispersed according to the Stoics, there is no more significant topic than that of our mental functions. In Stoicism we find that our mind, as well as our rationality, what we might typically define as individualized and personalized, instead has more complex communal conditions, constitutions, and interconnections.

As indicated in the opening chapter, Epictetus' Stoicism mandates that your mental functions, including your decisions and judgements, occur internally to you. Living rationally furthermore for Epictetus concerns living in accordance with what is in your control, what is up to you, or what is dependent on you. Because your mental life occurs internally, you should be able to control its operations. This is not how the mind *always* works of course. The Stoics appreciate that the "external world" around us regularly affects our thoughts. When we live though with the Stoic awareness that our mind, thoughts, and associated mental processes can be within our control and internally up to us, we approach what it means to live rationally.

Living rationally is the nature of all humans in the Stoic view. Epictetus indeed defines us as the "rational animal"[1] or "rational creature,"[2] because of the belief that we are predisposed to live in rational ways. This categorization of humans as rational animals makes more sense when we compare the different degrees of rationality that the Stoics attribute to human versus

1. Epictetus, *Discourses* (2008), 1.2.1.
2. Epictetus, *Discourses* (1916), 1.2.

nonhuman creatures. Epictetus perpetuates a preceding classical tradition that runs through the works of Plato and Aristotle in positing distinctions in the relative amounts of rationality that things in the world embody.[3] We cannot, demands Epictetus, reduce humans to the mental and rational status of other creatures for example. Nonhuman animals generally "begin and end" at the level of irrational, physical impulses, whereas humans are more mentally complicated according to the orthodox Stoic view.[4]

What then is the justification for this conceptual hierarchization of the rationality that humans supposedly possess over other creatures and entities? On which grounds does Epictetus argue that the "beasts,"[5] as he is fond of referring to nonhuman animals, do not have the same kinds of mental and rational functions as humans?

To explain this, we firstly must contrarily recognize the Stoic view that we and other animals share common impulses or orientations. Epictetus' Stoic perspective is that all animals, human or otherwise, live with the same base functions that often revolve around physical survival. These functions serve necessarily material features of our being, as they do for nonhuman animals. Such a correlation simply reflects that all earthly creatures are physically bodied.[6] As philosopher William Stephens clarifies, the functions in question concern the basic modes of "eating, drinking", reproducing, and moving around the world by "using sense-impressions and the like."[7]

Having established these material or physical consistencies between human and nonhuman creatures, the overwhelming motivation in Epictetus'

3. Plato (*Republic* [2007], 514a–21d) distinguishes a divine realm of Transcendent Forms, which represents full or true knowledge, from the varying lesser worldly expressions of those Forms. Subsequent positions from other thinkers on the different physical, mental, and rational statuses of what exists in the world often owe much to this basic distinction. The concept of a ladder of degrees of the organismic complexity and rationality of worldly entities is extensively outlined in Aristotle's *History of Animals*. Here Aristotle ranks animals over plants due to the respective capacities of each for sense and motion. See Aristotle (*Nicomachean Ethics*, 1.13) for the extension of this theory, in which Aristotle attributes rationality only to humans. Humans are said to also have a non-rational "vegetative" component, which refers to our material bodily constitutions that we share with plants and other animals.

4. Epictetus, *Discourses* (2014), 1.6.14–20. This position is supported by the ancient accounts of the Stoics from Diogenes Laërtius (*Lives and Opinions*, 7.52), who reports that the "Stoics" differentiate humans as "rational animals" from other, irrational animals. Striker (*Essays*, 227–29) reflects on this distinction in terms of reason (humans) versus impulse (plants and nonhuman animals). See also Becker ("Stoic Emotion," 41–44) for a discussion on the earliest Stoic definitions of humans as rational animals.

5. Epictetus, *Discourses* (1916), 1.3.

6. Epictetus, *Discourses* (2014), 1.1.9.

7. Stephens, "Epictetus," 214.

thesis regarding this comparison is then to clarify how humans nevertheless transcend the status of other creatures. Our hierarchized position is attributed to our capacities to reflect on our existence in ways that other creatures cannot. Epictetus posits, for instance, that only humans, not other animals, understand their sense impressions. Humans use sense impressions as other animals do, but we are additionally capable of mentally considering what our senses tell us about our broader nature or existence.[8]

This capacity for mental reflection is why Epictetus demands that it is unacceptable and even "shameful"[9] for any human to live and operate at the same levels as nonhuman animals. Our basic states of being begin where those of nonhuman animals do, in terms of having a material body, eating, drinking, and sexual impulses. Our upper states of being though occur at degrees of rationality that exceed the capacities of other animals.

It is for this reason that Epictetus describes our "ends"—a reference to our purposes, drives, and reasons for being or existing at all—as rational. The point of human existence is to live rationally. Establishing this rationally transcendent level of existence for humans does not quell Epictetus' discomfort however regarding our similarities with irrational forms of life. The bodily consistency between human and nonhuman animals particularly bothers Epictetus because he believes that despite our default higher rational state, we regularly overly "incline" toward or identify with our bodies and other physically external features of the world. An over-identification with our bodies involves, for example, unregulated indulgences in sensory pleasures. Epictetus laments that in this mode we descend to the levels of "noxious creatures like . . . wolves," of "wild, savage, and untamed creatures . . . like lions" and of other "base" animals.[10]

The human divergence from this entirely animalistic mode is, as already indicated, conditioned by our mental capacities of reflection, reason, and comprehension. Not incidentally, these mental functions underpin Epictetus' definition of human freedom.[11] With a rationally functioning

8. Epictetus, *Discourses* (2014), 1.6, 2.10–14. I point us here specifically to Hard's translation given that its terminology concerns the different purposes of different animals, with the human animal's purpose being distinctly of a rational nature.

9. Epictetus, *Discourses* (2014), 1.6.20. Dobbin (in Epictetus, *Discourses* [2008], 1.6.20) translates this as "inexcusable."

10. Epictetus, *Discourses* (2014), 1.3.7.

11. See Epictetus (*Enchiridion*, 1) for the basis of his conception of freedom, in which humans are "by nature free, unrestrained, unhindered," due to what "depends on" or is "up to" us. We can consider what Epictetus means by differentiating his idea of freedom from a preceding Stoic position. As we find in Cicero (*De Fato*, 42–43), what "depends on us" according to the early Stoic, Chrysippus, is what we are responsible for bringing into a particular state. Chrysippus uses examples such as us having

mind we are free to think about and judge the external world in ways that are up to us. A fundamental feature of this liberation from an irrationally physically relegated existence concerns the aforementioned capacity of humans to understand their position in the world. Anthony Long, who we engaged in the first chapter, describes what this "understanding" means for Epictetus as a "reflexive capacity."[12] Epictetus is demanding that humans can reflect on who we are and what our point or purpose is, rather than simply satisfy one physical or sensory craving after another.[13]

Rationality and mind operate together intimately, however they are not the same thing in Stoic philosophy. The distinction between the two will become clearer as we progressively unpack the Stoic definition of rationality. In our brief considerations of mind and rationality to this point though,

---

caused a cylinder to roll, to argue that its rolling state has depended on us causing it to be that way. Bobzien (*Determinism and Freedom*, 330), and Eliasson (*Notion*, 84–95), provide extended discussions on how in Chrysippus' view we are free because we must rationally agree to be these kinds of causes. Such causation is not part of Epictetus' sense of freedom though. Freedom for Epictetus simply equates to what we have already reviewed, regarding being rationally aware of what internally depends on or is up to us. Our capacity to think and judge despite whatever is occurring causally and externally is the necessary and sufficient condition of freedom for Epictetus. Does this mean that we can choose to think whatever we like? Not necessarily, given the physically deterministic aspects of our rationality that Stoicism proposes and that we will explore in the next chapter. Long and Sedley (*Hellenistic Philosophers*, 392–93) observe regarding Stoic considerations of our freedom to think whatever we want in a deterministic universe, that Chrysippus avoids "abandoning altogether" the "could have done otherwise" aspect of our rationalities and decision-making processes. Having said that, we never think or act in isolation outside that determined universe for the Hellenistic Stoics. One example of this interpretation is where the ancient scholar Eusebius (in Long and Sedley, *Hellenistic Philosophers*, 62F; taken from *SVF*, 2.998) conveys the Chrysippean position that "many things originate from us, but that these too are none the less co-fated along with the government of the world." This presents an impression of freedom that occurs in tandem with something bigger than our individually centered whims or desires. The ancient commentator Alexander (in Long and Sedley, *Hellenistic Philosophers*, 62G; taken from *SVF*, 2.979) emphasizes this in describing how the Stoics refute the possibility that we can simply personally choose between opposing options in any given circumstance. All that is instead "in our power" is to mentally recognize how the world manifests through us. What is in our power, as we have already seen, is our internal capacity to think, judge, and accept. We will soon consider the extent to which this internal capacity is linked to the physical structures of a deterministic world for the Stoics.

12. Long, *Epictetus*, 131.

13. Epictetus (*Discourses* [2014], 4.7.7) posits that it is an exclusively human quality to know not only that we are each a "part" of a "whole" world, but also to acknowledge our role and responsibilities as part of that whole. Such responsibilities can include those which appear at times to be self-sacrificing, as we will consider in the later chapter on self-preservation.

both have appeared for the Stoics to be entirely individualistic modes. As we have encountered through Epictetus, the standard reading of our relationship to our mind is that its functions are within our control and dependent on no one else. To recognize this, and to live with a consciousness of this, is to live rationally. Sometimes our mind will be affected by what occurs to us in an uncontrollable external world. This indeed is to be expected, given that our mental perspectives on the world are informed by different kinds of sensory data and impressions,[14] some of which will lead us to deceive, unsettle, and coerce ourselves into irrational responses.[15] If we are conscious though that we have rational control over our mind and how we think and decide about the impressions of the world that we produce, our mental existences will appear to be individually regulated and authorized. We each have our own minds. We can each make our own decisions and determine what we each think about the world around us. Epictetus describes accordingly how we are free from "hindrance or restraint"[16] when we choose to rationally interpret our relationship with the world in this way. By living in accordance with this internal mental control, we live rationally for the Stoics.

Just how *individualized* is this internal rational existence though? For the Stoics, our internal selves constitute our minds, our rationalities, the very aspects of our subjectivities that Epictetus posits depend on, or are up to, each of us. Despite this apparently individualized jurisdiction, Epictetus also portrays how this internal feature of ourselves is connected with a world that is beyond our individual selves. Understanding this bond requires expanding our sense of human rationality. We have seen that part of the reason we occupy a hierarchized rational status in comparison to other creatures and entities for the Stoics concerns our capacity to reflect on who and what we are. As we will now consider, Epictetus claims that an integral feature of this distinctly human, rationally reflective capacity, is to appreciate that we are each a part of a "whole" world system. From this reflection comes an insight into the Stoic belief that a part-to-whole relation governs the connection between individual rational minds, and the entire universe.

14. Epictetus, *Discourses* (2014), 1.27.1.

15. Seneca (*Letters on Ethics*, 58.26–27) likewise recognizes that our senses will sometimes lead us to unstable or unreliable impressions of and experiences with the world.

16. Epictetus, *Discourses* (2014), 4.1.69.

Humans Are Rational Because the World Makes Us Rational

In an everyday sense, when evaluating whether someone is thinking and acting rationally, we typically scrutinize the individual themselves. The assumption is that rationality is tied to the mind, and that each of us has our own. The existence of secrets exemplifies this notion of a plurality of personal minds. You can hold a thought in your mind that is inaccessible to others, that is in your mind but not in others' minds. Whether your mind is occupied with keeping secrets, or with thinking rationally, a common interpretation of it therefore is that human minds have individualized or personalized qualities.

While rationality is in Stoicism a general human characteristic, for Epictetus we each differently enact this rationality because we each have our own mind. He repeatedly uses the basic phrase "your own"[17] when discussing the mental capacities via which we think about and adjudicate on the world.

In a less straightforward regard though, Epictetus actively contributes to a position forwarded by the ancient Stoics that the rationality and associated mental functions that we exercise individually are traces of something grander than any of us individually. That grander something, for the Stoics, is not simply our species. While there is a particular rationality that the human species embodies and that we each, as individual humans, express, our rationality does not originate for the Stoics with the advent of humans. It is undeniable that most of the ancient Stoics assert that we are far more rational than other animals and entities, and that this reflects a human nature. The exclusively human nature of this capacity does not mean though, that our rationality originates from human neurology, biology, or genetics.

The greater source of our rationality to which the Stoics instead refer is the entire universe itself. For the Stoics, the universe is a thinking, rational being. We should repeat this statement because it sounds so odd. The universe itself is rational and indeed functions rationally.

Repeating this point does not make it sound less odd, so we will need to analyze it further. Conventionally we understand that humans can each think rationally. Our thoughts and decisions when rational direct our behaviors that are likewise evaluated as rational or not. These are all unsurprising ideas around what being human means that we can readily digest. We regularly interpret whether our fellow humans are thinking and acting rationally.

---

17. Epictetus, *Discourses* (2008), 1.6.41; 1.25.3–4; 2.6.4; 2.6.21; 2.16.45; 2.19.14; 4.1.82.

Additionally for the Stoics though, this rationality that humans have is attributable to the rationality of a universe. It is accordingly said in Stoicism that we have rational capacities only because we are parts of a structure or system, the universe, which itself is wholly rational and has "assigned"[18] or "granted"[19] us our rationality as a "portion" of its rationality. From this explanation we can comprehend the Stoic theory that we, as parts of something greater, the universe, have inherited our rationality from that greater entity. What requires clarification though is how the Stoics can describe this feature that we have inherited as "rationality." What does it mean that the universe itself is rational? How does Stoicism understand rationality?

A way that we can make this idea more accessible is to think of how we use the word "rational" when describing people's minds. Rational in a human regard implies someone's ordered and systematic thinking. A rational thinker's mental functions, their interpretations, decisions, and judgements, reliably associate effects with causes, and contextualize present events within past patterns of events in order to anticipate future events. A rational mind does not pluck its interpretations of what happens in the world, or decisions about how to respond to the world, from just anywhere. Rational thinking processes instead occur logically, orderly, repeatedly, and in sync with the world around the thinker. There is here a methodical regularity and reliability about the arrangement of a rational person's thought processes, and those who know the rational thinker will come to depend on that orderliness of thought for insights.

The interpretation of human rationality as *ordered* is useful when considering that this is also what the Stoics mean when they describe the world as rational. A rational world is an ordered world. Such order infers that certain causes lead to certain effects, and these causal chains are predictable, repeatable, and reliable. As I have briefly indicated, if the world is rational for the Stoics, and we as parts of that world are also rational, then the source of our rationality is the world's rationality. We think and reason in ordered ways because the world is structured in an ordered way, whereby our rationality is structured in the world's likeness.

How is it that we and the world are rationally ordered in this way? The Stoics explain these processes and relations by directing our attention to the source of the world's rationally ordered nature. The Stoics describe this source as God. The Stoic sense of God, however, is not straightforward. God

18. Epictetus, *Discourses* (2008), 1.1.4. See also where Epictetus (*Discourses* [2008], 1.20.5) similarly asks why "did nature arm us with reason?" Epictetus (*Discourses* [2008], 1.9.5) responds that we are "connected" with the universe's nature "through reason."

19. Epictetus, *Discourses* (2014), 1.1.4.

for the Stoics operates in and as the world, rather than as a transcendent overseer of the world. The Roman statesperson, philosopher, and invaluable commentator of the Stoics, Cicero, tells us in *The Nature of the Gods* that the third head of the Stoic school, Chrysippus, expresses the early Stoic belief that "god is the world itself."[20] The justification for the interpretation that the world is God, is for the Stoics evidenced in the reliable ordering that we see in it. The world is an organized, planned, and controlled system of interconnecting causes and effects, apparent in the "uniform movement and undeviating rotation of the heavens," and the "usefulness, beauty and order of the sun and moon and stars, the very sight of which is sufficient proof that they are not the outcome of chance."[21] If the universe is not the product of chance or randomness, then it must instead be ordered, and such ordering can only be enacted according to the Stoics by what is intelligent and reasoned. God for the Stoics is this unsurpassable intelligence of the world, present in and as the world as the "reason, mind and intellect" of its "universal nature."[22]

The Pyrrhonist skeptic Sextus Empiricus, who we will engage comprehensively in a later chapter on the topic of what we can know about the world, extends our understanding of the logic that conditions this interpretation. Sextus reports that in the original Stoic principles conceived by Zeno, the founder of the Stoic school, "the rational is superior to the nonrational." Given that Zeno's beliefs also cohere with the conventional ancient impression that "nothing is superior to the world," it must duly follow that the "world is rational . . . and intelligent."[23] Another angle from which to look at this logic for Zeno, as Cicero describes it, is that humans are rational beings, with minds and mental functions. Furthermore, we rational humans have been born from the world around us. Because our rational status and minds could only have been born from a rational source, the world which is the source of us must also be the source of our rationality, and therefore be rational itself:

> Nothing without a share in mind and reason can give birth to one who is animate and rational. But the world gives birth to those who are animate and rational. Therefore the world is animate and rational.[24]

20. Cicero, *Nature of Gods*, 1.39.

21. Cicero, *Nature of Gods*, 2.14–15.

22. Cicero, *Nature of Gods*, 1.39.

23. Sextus Empiricus, *Against the Physicists*, 3.104.

24. Cicero in Long and Sedley, *Hellenistic Philosophers*, 54G; taken from *Nature of Gods*, 2.22. Sextus Empiricus (*Against the Physicists*, 3.101) likewise conveys how "Zeno of Citium . . . argues like this: 'What puts forth seed of a rational thing is itself rational; but the world puts forth seed of a rational thing; therefore the world is a rational thing.'"

Where God fits into this discussion concerns the just-observed correlation of rationality with superiority for the Stoics. If (i) the world is rational, and (ii) nothing is superior to the world, then it follows that the rational world must also be God, because just as nothing is superior to the world, likewise nothing is superior to God. The world duly embodies God's rationality, and we are rational because we embody the world's rationality, whereby our rationality is a trace of God's rationality. As Epictetus states, what is "your own," your ordered mind and rationality, is what the God Zeus has "granted you."[25] God's rationality permeates the world or universe, a world or universe of which we and our minds are each a part. This all-ordering rationality conditions a togetherness between humans and the world-as-God for the Stoics. Interestingly in terms of the social and communal themes on which this book will focus, Epictetus describes this togetherness as an "all-embracing . . . society in which human beings and God are associated together."[26] This social togetherness nevertheless has a hierarchical rather than an egalitarian structure, given that the universe's greater rational ordering is the preconditioning and overseeing "generative force"[27] and "source of the seeds"[28] of our own derivative rational being. We will later discuss in more detail the Stoic belief in social hierarchies, based on the already considered notion of relative degrees of rationality.

As a later Stoic, Epictetus arrives on an already established Stoic path. Stoic beliefs regarding how the universe comprises God's rationality do not originate with Epictetus. Diogenes Laërtius' ancient philosophical commentaries and biographies report Chrysippus, for example, discussing these kinds of principles that Epictetus eventually redeploys. Diogenes brings our attention to how, for Chrysippus, not only are we each a part of a universal structure, but that the universal structure which connects everything is rationality (reason), in that "our individual natures are all parts of universal nature," and that nature is a "right reason which pervades everything." As this all-pervasive rationality divinely permeates everything it also *orders* everything, a generative and connective thread that is the "manager of all things."[29]

The idea of a single orderer of the world does not originate with the Stoics. The early Stoic positions are possibly inspired by Plato's exploration of "organicist" themes in his later era works such as the *Timaeus*, which

---

25. Epictetus, *Discourses* (2014), 1.25.3.

26. Epictetus, *Discourses* (2014), 1.9.4.

27. Epictetus, *Discourses* (2008), 1.9.4.

28. Epictetus, *Discourses* (2014), 1.9.4.

29. Diogenes Laërtius, *Lives and Opinions*, 7.53.

conceive of a singularly and rationally ordered universe.[30] An Aristotelian position also resembles the later Stoic belief in a singular source and structurer of an ordered world. "On the Cosmos" provides one example of this, in which Aristotle describes the universe as deriving from a "single power" via which everything in the world is

> well-arranged; for it is called "well ordered" after this "universal order." What particular detail could be compared to the arrangement of the heavens and the movement of the stars and the sun and moon.[31]

I earlier described how the rationality of the world for the Stoics is evocative of how we conceive of the rationality of a human mind that functions in ordered and causally consistent ways. This correlation between human rationality and a world's rationality is more than a metaphor for the Stoics, the former is literally a trace of the latter in their worldview. We find this sense in the accounts that we have appraised from Zeno and Chrysippus. Epictetus follows these early Stoics, as well as Plato and Aristotle, in emphasizing the ordering omnipresence of this rationality that is present in everything about the world. Here Epictetus refers to the regular and predictable physical and ecological arrangements that a rational God activates:

> For how else could it come about with such regularity, as though at God's express command, that when he tells the plants to flower, they flower, when he tells them to bud, they bud, and to bear their fruit, they bear it, and to bring it to ripeness, they bring it to ripeness, and when again he tells them to strip themselves and shed their leaves, and drawn in on themselves, remain inactive, and take their rest, they remain so and take their rest?[32]

Epictetus argues that these regular physical, ecological, rhythms and connections of the universe are overtly apparent between celestial bodies and our planet. Celestial relations reveal the universality of order, which is an indication that the entire world must be rational. This systematic order that is conditioned by God's rationality links the phenomena that we see and experience on Earth, with what we observe that occurs beyond Earth, in that

---

30. In Plato's *Timaeus*, we encounter the consideration that the world is a created, living being, produced according to reason by the "Demiurge." Before such creation, the matter/material of the universe is ordered but not rationally ordered. With the Demiurge's production of the world in the image of the eternal realm, the world is alive, intelligent, and rational. Also relevant is how Striker (*Essays*, 217–18) discusses the links between Socratic and Stoic conceptions of a rationally ordered universe.

31. Aristotle, "On the Cosmos," 5.397a.10.

32. Epictetus, *Discourses* (2014), 1.14.3.

"the waxing and the waning of the moon, and the coming and going of the sun, coincide with such obvious changes and fluctuations here on earth."[33]

The reliability and predictability of the universe's rationalized physical patterns correlates with our everyday sense of human rationality as dependable and predictable. In the preceding chapter I have introduced the Stoic correlation of rationality with control. What we now encounter therefore is another illustration of the Stoic equation of rationality with control. Such control though is dispersed beyond an individual rational agent, to define a universally regulated mode of interconnected things, from which a human agent's personal rationality derives. An insight from this interpretation duly concerns how important features of the self, namely our mind and rationality, are situated in a system beyond the self. Individual self-control is attributable to a universal order of control. Through this rationalized unison of all things, including humans, we witness for Epictetus the universe's controlled state, an ongoing regularity that explains how such a "vast and beautiful structure could be kept so well ordered" and could not operate "by mere chance and good luck."[34]

In the next chapter we will comprehensively review how this universal rationality, that the Stoics also call God's rationality, infuses the actual material, physical substance of plants, fruits, planets, and even humans. In that phase of the discussion, we will therefore attend to how the physical stuff of ourselves, our bodies, and the world around us is rational for the Stoics. For now though, it suffices that we have understood that for the Stoics, God's rationality is everywhere, in everything, it is simply the universe. Rationality orders everything in the world and is the world itself. As we have discussed, in Stoicism some creatures, the earlier raised "beasts," do not embody rationality in the same way that human creatures do. Nonhumans cannot reflect on what it means to be what they are, nor on their position in the universe in relation to all other things. Nevertheless, for the Stoics, nonhuman creatures, and indeed inanimate entities, will still be permeated by and directed according to the unified orderings of a rational universe. This is consistent with the impression we have encountered that the world is a singular entity of collectively ordered parts. Cicero reports on this that for the Stoics, every single thing is "made for the sake of other things," and that "there is nothing which is not included" in this universal system of interconnection.[35]

The Stoic belief as we have seen is that humans have the capacity to reflect on our rational existences. Human rationality for the Stoics is second

---

33. Epictetus, *Discourses* (2008), 1.14.4.

34. Epictetus, *Discourses* (2014), 2.14.26.

35. Cicero, *Nature of Gods*, 2.37–9.

only to God's rationality,[36] whereby each of us is aware of being rational and of how to live rationally. As the universe's common rationality becomes identifiable in each of us, so the relationship between the universal order and our individual minds emerges. Rationality, the universal phenomenon that disperses throughout the world, becomes apparent as a specifically human phenomenon due to its presence in what Epictetus defines as the "wonderful fruit in the human mind."[37] In nonrational nonhuman creatures, plants, and other entities, the universal rationality's presence is only apparent in how their physical behaviors are ordered and interconnected with other creatures, plants, and entities. With humans however, this universal rationality also emerges in our mental control of our decisions, as well as in our awareness of how that control and those decisions serve our well-being and our integrated relationship with a broader world.

If the rationality and associated mental functions that we each have are traces of a universal or worldly rationality, what we must now tackle are the ramifications for our understanding of "individual minds." We have reviewed that Epictetus perpetuates ancient observations of interconnected celestial, ecological, and generally physical, rhythms and orderings. It is from this impetus that Epictetus wonders why human mental processes would not also be implicated in this unified system:

> If plants and our bodies are so intimately linked to the world
> and its rhythms, won't the same be true of our minds—only
> more so?[38]

Epictetus is proposing that because a singular rationality permeates everything in the world, this rationality must not just condition interconnected physical rhythms and things. What we therefore now need to ask is if rationality orders everything, and our rationality is our internality, does this mean that our internal minds are interconnected with a rationally ordered universe? Is what we consider to be emphatically individualized or personalized about ourselves, our rational mind, actually an expression of an impersonal universal order? These are the kinds of questions at stake in the rest of this chapter.

---

36. There are many examples of this hierarchy being observed by the Stoics. See where Cicero (*Nature of Gods*, 2.16) recounts the distinctions Chrysippus makes between humans, God, and other entities. See Epictetus (*Discourses* [2014], 1.3.1–3; 1.9) for more on such distinctions.

37. Epictetus, *Discourses* (2014), 1.4.32.

38. Epictetus, *Discourses* (2008), 1.14.5. Hard (in Epictetus, *Discourses* [2014], 1.14.5) translates "mind" instead with the word "soul."

We should recall that Epictetus' belief is that what happens on Earth physically is rationally ordered and unified with what happens in the rest of the universe. Our bodies are of course such physical things. What he is opening now though is the consideration that if in a rational universe our bodies are physical things that are interconnected and ordered with that universe and its rhythms, similarly our minds and rationalities must be interconnected and ordered with it too. Our minds, after all, are inherently linked with our physical behaviors that form parts of that ordered universe.

The Stoics of course also refer to this universal rationality as God. Given the contentious nature of ascribing the source of human individuality to God, the nature or constitution of this Stoic God requires immediate attention. We must not misinterpret that in linking humans with God, a Stoic such as Epictetus is proposing a spiritual and mental relationship with a transcendent deity. I have already presented the Stoic position that God is internal to the physical order of the world, rather than presiding over the world as an external creator of it. The recent discussion has provided a strong indication of this for Epictetus, in that he has just compared our mental links with the rational world, which is God, as akin to the relations shared between all physical aspects of the world.

Your Mind Is a Fragment

When the Stoics refer to God, what they are describing is the world or universe in which we exist. The Stoics use other terms besides God to define the world or universe, all of which have the same meaning. Some of these terms sound theological, like Zeus, or the Divine. Other terms with which "God" is interchangeable however appear to be more naturalistic or less theological in a modern regard. This is closer to what the Stoics are really intending, when they describe God either as Nature, the Universe, the Whole, and of course, Rationality or Reason.

With the impression of God as Nature, as the Whole Universe, we build on our understanding of God's rationality as that which orders the physical world's chains of causes and effects. In the next chapter we will consider whether this means that what the Stoics refer to as rationality, or as nature, is in fact a singular web of physical interactions that in the current day we might explain via scientific principles and call the laws of nature. Of more immediate concern though is the point that because the Stoics call this singular reason for everything "God," we must think of the Stoics as *pantheists*.

Conventional definitions of pantheism refer to the interpretation that God is present in all parts of the world or consists of the whole world. We have just seen that the Stoics use this term "Whole" as a reference to the world itself, a world that is equally understood to be God. A pantheistic world is therefore one in which everything in that world either is God, is identical to God, or is an expression of God.[39]

A pantheistic outlook is apparent in the earliest incarnations of the Stoic school. In *The Fragments of Zeno and Cleanthes*, translator Alfred Pearson observes how from the second head of the school (Cleanthes) onwards, the Stoics express a belief in a pantheistic universe in which "God and the world are identical."[40] This is an interpretation supported by the commentaries of Cicero, who is quoted in this collection of fragments describing Cleanthes as "a pantheist" who wholly "identified God with matter."[41] We have already determined the equation of God with the world for the Stoics. Where the early Stoic Cleanthes now specifically associates God with and as "matter," and where matter is the material/physical substance of the world, we find that the Stoics are saying God is our material/physical world.

We need to nuance our understanding here with the reminder that Stoic pantheism is not simply a case of the physical substance of the world *being* God. More specifically, we have seen that God is what intelligently and rationally *orders* and animates the physical world.[42] The Stoics here describe a singular energy or animative force according to which plants and minds and all things function in unison. I have speculated that in the current day we might explain these interconnected rhythms and orderings according to scientific evaluations of natural/physical laws. For the Stoics though, as Diogenes Laërtius reports, this singular system was explained in pantheistic, rational terms:

> They [the Stoics] also teach that God is unity, and that he is called Mind . . . and by many other names besides. And that . . . as the seed is contained in the produce, so too, he being the seminal principle of the world, remained making matter fit to be employed by himself in the production of those things . . . And Zeno speaks of these in his treatise on the Universe, and so does Chrysippus in the first book of his Physics.[43]

39. Owen (*Concepts of Deity*, 8) provides one of the most cited and well-known definitions of pantheism that includes these parameters.

40. Pearson, *Fragments*, 22.

41. Pearson, *Fragments*, 17.

42. Baltzly ("Stoic Pantheism," 8) describes this as how the Stoics' God "enacts the cosmos."

43. Diogenes Laërtius, *Lives and Opinions*, 7.68.

The immanence of God within the world has been well documented by Stoic scholars of past and present eras.[44] Two of the more prominent and recent voices on this topic have been Kai Whiting and Leonidas Konstantakos.[45] Their ongoing project asserts that because the Stoic God is just the world in which we live, we should view what is described as divine in Stoicism simply as our tangible, touchable, material reality. When engaging Stoicism, the requirement here is to relinquish any preconception of God as that which transcends the world, to instead appreciate God as immanent to it.[46]

What we can take from much of this preceding discussion is that our minds, when functioning in accordance with our internal nature, operate as a rationality that is present not only internally to us but also in the world around us. The world presents one unified arena of a generalized internality in this regard. This insight might present a slight confusion, given that our opening engagements in this book have conversely presented the Stoic idea that the external world is outside our rational control. However, just because the external world is outside *our* rational authority, does not mean that this world is without rational systematization in Stoicism. As we have just covered, the world is ordered and structured, as are humans, by and as a universally ubiquitous rationality.

A world in which a rational order pervades does not mean that every aspect of it will always function rationally though. Our fellow humans' behaviors for instance will often not orient toward what we rationally have in common. This concerns how our freedom functions for Epictetus. As he instructs in the *Enchiridion*, to live as a Stoic you must assent or agree to live in accordance with a rational and universally pervasive nature.[47] Such assent or agreement does not always occur. Epictetus laments in the lecture "About the Art of Argument" in *Discourses* that we should expect to interact with people who do not think or act in accordance with a universal nature, and thus are "lost." It is important that we are mentally prepared for such irrationally adverse encounters, so that when they occur, rather than "abuse or make fun of" the people concerned because we are angered or surprised by their behaviors, we will instead be able to guide them.[48] Marcus Aurelius famously expresses the same idea in terms of the lack of shock we should feel about people behaving irrationally toward us, in the same way that it

44. Bénatouïl, "Divine Activity in Stoicism"; Bobzien, *Determinism and Freedom*; Lapidge, "Stoic Cosmology"; Levine, "Pantheism, Ethics, and Ecology"; Sambursky, *Physics of the Stoics*; Todd, "Monism and Immanence."

45. See, for example, Whiting and Konstantakos, "Stoic Theology."

46. Whiting et al., "Sustainable Development," 15.

47. Epictetus, *Enchiridion*, 1.

48. Epictetus, *Discourses* (2014), 2.12.1–4.

is not unexpected that a fig tree bears figs.[49] This should further remind us of Seneca's warning, raised briefly in the previous chapter, regarding the irrational mob mentalities of crowds about which we must be careful.[50] Epictetus indeed addresses similar themes in the lecture in *Discourses* titled "That We Should Enter into Social Intercourse with Caution."[51] The point from all such discussions is that the world might be rationally ordered, but the human capacity of rational reflection incorporates the possibility that we will not always think or reflect absolutely rationally in accordance with that order.

The purpose of highlighting this string of Stoic advisories regarding the irrational behaviors of our fellow humans is to remind us of the Stoics' concerns about our everyday social existence. While Stoic first principles instruct us that the world is wholly rationally ordered or systematized, the Stoics also stress that our experiences with other people regularly expose us to irrational and therefore harmful behavior. As seen in the first chapter, the instruction accordingly when it comes to social phenomena is to engage much of it with indifference. Where social class, reputation, or other contingent or temporary elements about ourselves are concerned, not to mention when we fraternize with people who gossip about others,[52] we should be careful about the effect it has on our thoughts and judgements. If such experiences start to shape how we view ourselves or others, perhaps coercing us into thinking and adjudicating in ways that disconnect us from our investment in our common rationality, then we begin for Epictetus to be harmed by what is not up to us.[53] We cannot control how people will behave interpersonally, we can only control our mental reflections on our relationships with other people. Epictetus accordingly criticizes our enthusiasm for what he believes are the trivial aspects of social life.[54]

While people have a certain freedom to avoid mentally assenting to the requirements of a universally rational nature, equally in Epictetus' view we are inversely always internally free to be rationally common and interconnected beings. Rational freedom is a liberation from a mental and emotional dependency on the uncontrollable phenomena that presents every day via contingent social trends. Philosophy, for Epictetus, provides the method through which we can reflect on the fundamental mode of being

49. Marcus Aurelius, *Meditations* (2011), 8.14–15.

50. Seneca, *Letters on Ethics*, 7.

51. Epictetus, *Discourses* (2014), 3.16.

52. Epictetus, *Discourses* (2014), 3.16.4.

53. Epictetus, *Discourses* (2014), 3.16.4.

54. Epictetus, *Discourses* (2014), 2.16.11.

for all humans, and complementarily defy investments in transient social classifications, divisions, fads, and events.[55] If we cannot develop this self-control and resilience to what is external about social life, Epictetus typically extremely suggests that we should change our surroundings. Epictetus here imparts the severe instruction that we might have to "leave our homeland, because old habits distract us," meaning that in a new environment we will not encounter temptations such as gossiping with old acquaintances about trivial matters.[56] We will see in a later chapter that Seneca refutes the suggestion that we must physically or geographically move in order to cohere better with our rational natures, instead advising that we are better to direct our attention to what is internal about us no matter where we live.

Despite this apparent emphatic negation of our social existence from Epictetus, we must engage his lectures on this topic with a certain nuance. His point is not that our relations with other people are *always* external to us simply *because* they are social relations. There are rather numerous features of social existence, that we have listed, to which we should remain indifferent. Without this indifference, such features divert our attention from a life in accordance with our shared rational nature.

How then can we begin to establish the aspect or aspects of our interpersonal existences that conversely, and more positively, *are* in accordance with our rational nature? What are the conditions for a rational, communal way of life for the Stoics? We can begin to answer these kinds of questions by reinviting our earlier considerations of the universality of rationality. I state that we will in this chapter only "begin" to answer these questions, as this project will occupy us for the remainder of this book.

We have seen that an element of being rational is the ability to reflect on our position in, and relationships with, the world. Being human means appreciating the kind of creature that we humans are, what our purposes are, and even what our responsibilities are. Nonhuman animals do not have these capacities for the Stoics as they lack the rationality. Once we reflect on our relationships with and responsibilities toward the world, we begin to become aware of ourselves as parts of an interconnected order or system. This rational awareness that we are parts of a greater whole is the crucial first step to understanding what "social" really and positively means for the Stoics.

The comings and goings in the town square or other public spaces for example, while presenting important arenas for the practice of philosophical activity and intercourse, are not in themselves reliant on rational modes of interconnection and therefore are not rationally social in the Stoic view.

55. Epictetus, *Discourses* (2014), 1.15.

56. Epictetus, *Discourses* (2014), 3.16.11.

Such socialization in the places we together frequent might indeed occur without any concern for our grander, rationally shared, conditions. We can instead begin to understand our shared, and therefore our social, rational constitutions if we return to Epictetus' insight that all our minds are bonded to the same universal reason. There we have reviewed his logic that if our bodies are linked to the world and its rhythms, then why would our minds not also be.[57] It is according to these mental rational links, and in particular to how Epictetus attributes these links to what he calls our "daimons," that we can more comprehensively explain our mutual, kindred, and inherently communal or social existences for the Stoics.

What then is a daimon? Furthermore, in what way can a theory of this daimon convince us that in Stoic philosophy, what is internal to the self—rationality—is something shared with a world beyond the self? To understand what Epictetus means by the daimon, we firstly must appreciate the context from which his sense of the daimon derives.

We can here commence with a preceding position from Plato. In his work *Apology*, Plato reports that Socrates speaks of a "divine sign" that guides him when he thinks, decides, and performs other mental functions. Also called an inner "voice," this is said to be the "daimon" within Socrates that prevents him from making irrational decisions that he otherwise would be "about to do."[58] The grander point is that this kind of internal guide is not exclusive to Socrates but rather inhabits all rational beings.

Given the Socratic influences in Stoicism, it is not surprising that this interpretation of a daimon that is our divine voice and caretaker is taken up by Epictetus. Diogenes Laërtius reports in fact that across the Stoic eras the daimon is understood to have this kind of guardian role, according to the belief that "there are some Daemones, who have a sympathy with human-kind, being surveyors of all human affairs."[59] Before the time of Epictetus, possibly the most important surviving Stoic impression of the overseeing function of our daimon comes from the middle era Stoic, Posidonius. Cicero's *On Divination* informs us that for Posidonius, this caretaking and even ruling daimon that we embody steers each of us toward what is true.[60]

As we move through Posidonius' Stoicism, we encounter the sense that the daimon provides genuine guidance for each of us, and that this guidance derives from a rational source that is beyond ourselves. Our decision-making rationalizations lean upon this element of ourselves that is not reducible

57. Epictetus, *Discourses* (2008), 1.14.5.

58. Plato, *Apology*, 31d.

59. Diogenes Laërtius, *Lives and Opinions*, 7.79.

60. Cicero, *On Divination*, 1.64.

to any of us individually, and even circumvents our own adverse emotional impulses.[61] The internal part of each of us that is our daimon, which is also a part of the world that operates beyond our strict personal borders, duly contributes to how we steer ourselves toward rational lives, even seemingly during the most basic decisions we make every day. How though does this feature of the self that is called the daimon perform this role?

In the translations of Posidonius' fragments, we encounter a standard classical era definition of daimons as "immortal" and "divine go-betweens."[62] While the term "go-betweens" can present some confusion, it just refers to how daimons operate between each of us and God. In raising the topic of God, we must of course take into consideration our earlier qualification regarding our comprehension of what is divine. If the Stoic God is the rational order and rhythm that permeates the universe, then our daimon as our go-between is part of our access to that order and rhythm. This coheres with our ongoing definition of our rationality also as an expression of that universal order and rhythm, meaning now that our daimon is our access to our own rationality. The same applies for all other rational humans. We are all accessing the same rationality. We are all integrated with the same worldly order.

Our daimon does not simply from within us "access" a universal rationality though. More interestingly it represents the aspect of ourselves that is simultaneously beyond ourselves. Our daimon is internal to each of us, we each have our own "fragment of God"[63] as Epictetus describes it, whereby our rationality is composed by "a particle of God; there is a bit of God within you."[64] The daimon therefore is our own rational function, however what is our own is never really ours alone. For Epictetus our internal self is a trace of something that is also common to everyone else. The source of what is fundamental about you, your rational functions, is also the source of what is fundamental to someone else's rational functions, and indeed of what is fundamental to the ordering and functioning of everything, and everyone, together. In this way, each of our internal selves, our minds and rationalities, are for Epictetus the shared traces of what is not exclusively internal to any of us.

What is up to you, what is internal to your rational nature, conventionally infers something housed within you locally, in your brain or mind, as a capacity that moves around with you solely. With this Stoic conception

61. Posidonius, *Fragments*, fragment 187.
62. Posidonius, *Fragments*, 166.
63. Epictetus, *Discourses* (2014), 2.8.11.
64. Epictetus, *Discourses* (1916), 2.8.11.

though, it becomes apparent that what is internal to your rational nature is a reference to a nature that functions beyond your individualized self. This means that what is internal to you is never absolutely localized to your specific brain, mind, or the particular spot in the world where you are. Your internality is out there in a world, where the word "out" does not designate what is external or peripheral to you but rather is an indication of how dispersed we each are. Our internal self is the rational universe and order. Marcus Aurelius reiterates this kind of definition in which our rationality and our mind are that of God as the universe, in that when living rationally we are

> obedient to the will of the guardian-spirit which Zeus has granted to each of us as a portion of his own being to serve as our overseer and guide; and this guardian-spirit is the mind and reason of each one of us.[65]

Where Marcus here describes our personal rational existences as "portions" of a greater will that we "obey," we get the sense that what we might believe that we control individually and rationally, actually occurs in concert with the overall source of that rationality. We can each think because we think through and with a rationalized world and condition. We do not think, we do not control our thoughts, separately from that world and condition. The shared territory between our individually internal self, and what might otherwise have appeared to be outside the individual self, is further emphasized in Epictetus' description of what is omnipresent and internal to us about the universal: "when you close your doors and create darkness within, remember never to say that you're on your own, for in fact, you're not alone, because God is within you, and your guardian spirit too."[66] When we each think individually, when we each act individually, we do so in accordance with a universal rationality that involves and implicates all of us. Regarding a point that we will expand thoroughly in the coming chapters concerning our inherent Stoic responsibilities to a world of people and things beyond

65. Marcus Aurelius, *Meditations* (2011), 5.27. See also where Staniforth (in Marcus Aurelius, *Meditations* [1964], 5.27) translates that for Marcus our mind and rationality are each a "fragment" of God and follow God's "commands." This is what Long (in *Meditations* [1900], 5.27) similarly translates as our "portion" of God that does what is wished of it. Beyond Marcus, Epictetus (*Discourses* [2014], 1.14.11–17) instructs that we should swear an oath to God. This oath is defined by Dyson ("God Within," 237) as both a self-oriented and a universe-oriented impetus: "In Stoic theology, each person's reason (*logos*) is literally a portion of Zeus' divine mind (*koinos logos*). Epictetus is pointing out that in swearing allegiance to Zeus, one is pledging to honor one's own rationality and vice versa."

66. Epictetus, *Discourses* (2014), 1.13–14.

ourselves, what this means for Marcus is that our rational thoughts and actions are never reducible to motivations of individualized or personalized prosperities or benefits. In thinking and acting rationally rather, we think and act on behalf of, and in service of, the source of that rationality, the world itself. Rational acts are those which function in accordance with this universal order, Marcus instructing that if "you live and act as it dictates, then everything in you is intelligently [rationally] ordered."[67] This belief from Marcus is evidently informed by the preceding position of Epictetus:

> Don't you want to keep in mind, when you eat, who it is that is doing the eating, and whom it is that you're feeding? And when you engage in sexual intercourse, who it is that is doing so? In your social relationships, in your physical exercises, in your conversations, aren't you aware that it's a god whom you're feeding, a god whom you're exercising? You carry God around with you . . . Do you suppose that I mean some external god . . . ? . . . It is within yourself that you carry him.[68]

The God that you service in this sense is the interconnecting ordering thread among all things in the universe. If acting rationally is acting in accordance with the divine fragment that constitutes us mentally, we do not serve a transcendent creator but instead all rationally interconnected things. Where such things are humans, because our rationalities and associated mental processes share in these kindred, rationalized conditions, the Stoic view follows that when we think and act rationally, we do so communally.

Common Interests, Common Benefits

Because the rationality or reason that you embody is this universal structure, in that your reason for anything and everything is a unified reason, Epictetus posits that everything you rationally do orients toward a common interest. When you view yourself as a rational "human being," you must simultaneously view yourself "as part of some whole."[69] If the source of, and condition for, our own rational impulses is the same as that of our fellow humans, how could our decisions and actions be separated from other people or be oriented toward anything but people collectively? In thinking beyond

67. Marcus Aurelius, *Meditations* (2002), 6.40.

68. Epictetus, *Discourses* (2014), 2.8.12. See also where Epictetus (*Discourses* [2008], 1.14.6) states of how our actions occur within a world nature: "And if our minds are so intimately connected with God as to be divine sparks of his being, is he not going to perceive their every movement, since the parts in motion participate in his nature?"

69. Epictetus, *Discourses* (2014), 2.5.25.

the localized domain of individualized or personalized ends, Epictetus duly reminds us that we should never approach any thought or undertaking with any "motive other than by reference to the whole."[70]

When thinking, making decisions, and acting on those decisions, you might nevertheless have the impression that sometimes such processes do result in your own individual benefit and well-being. Epictetus observes how in being conditioned to always think of the whole, a Stoic might from time to time feel "selfish" if what "we do is done for our own ends."[71] Such ends are able to be accommodated, however, if they are always situated within grander concerns. If we think and act as what the Stoics call a "rational animal," any decision or task that requires a consciousness of ourselves as individuals will always involve a preconditioning orientation toward the world from which our individuality has been ordered. This does not negate the fulfilment of personally preferred outcomes or ends. It instead contextualizes them within the priorities of an entire world structure. Being this rational animal involves having, what we have seen Epictetus describe as, the capacity to reflect on ourselves and other humans as fellow rational beings with mutually embedded prosperities. This implicates what appear to be purely individualized purposes and outcomes within communal and universal conditions. Developing the habit of perpetually situating the personal within an impersonal fabric will engender the appreciation that our own individual prosperity is not possible unless it is understood within a greater good. Epictetus posits that the rational individual is a collectively oriented and constituted individual accordingly, meaning that we are "incapable of attaining any . . . private ends without at the same time providing for the community"[72] or "contributing to the common benefit."[73]

Epictetus here reconceives the site of our self-interest, where to be rational requires appreciating what is non-local about being rational. This does not discount concerns about our own well-being. As we will study in a later chapter occupied with the topic of self-preservation, and as Epictetus can be shown now to describe, because being rational is the ultimate form of personal well-being the Stoics do not expect anyone to be "aloof" from their "own interest"[74] or to "show no concern for oneself."[75] We must understand though that our welfare or well-being only manifests in accordance

70. Epictetus, *Discourses* (2014), 2.10.4.

71. Epictetus, *Discourses* (2008), 1.19.11.

72. Epictetus, *Discourses* (2008), 1.19.12–13.

73. Epictetus, *Discourses* (2014), 1.19.13.

74. Epictetus, *Discourses* (1916), 1.19.

75. Epictetus, *Discourses* (2014), 1.19.15.

with a shared rationality and correlatively kindred ends. This determines that it is not "antisocial" to act in ways that appear to be self-interested or from which you individually benefit.[76] The condition though, is that you think and act with an appreciation of the inescapable kinship of your own rationalized benefits with the benefits of others.[77] Or in more simple terms, what is required are perpetual reflections on whether what benefits you also benefits other people, whole groups or populations, and the world in general.

The Stoic position is that whenever we think and act rationally, we think and act with universal and collective processes and outcomes in mind. As I have repeatedly indicated, this is not to say that prosperities that benefit us personally will not arise through such grander perspectives. We will continually be attentive in this book to how our universal and collective orientations incorporate and manifest positive outcomes for individuals. No matter how individually directed or motivated our internal functions might appear to be to us though, for Epictetus if we are living rationally by being conscious of the shared rational conditions of which we are each just one trace, our internal functions will always default toward an entity not restricted to the self. As a Stoic individual, if you are thinking rationally you are not primarily thinking of how you personally benefit from actions and outcomes that are associated with such thoughts, but instead according to Epictetus you are occupied with "reflect[ing] on the social roles you play." This socially oriented consciousness requires appreciating the various part-to-whole relations in which we are involved. Because the universe's rationalized whole is greater than each of us as a part of it, and indeed is the precondition for any of us being rational, Epictetus demands we must be conscious that "the universe has precedence over a constituent." When we act rationally as universal constituents, we are likewise conscious that our rational nature is interconnected and shared with our fellow humans, which requires incorporating the associated view that "the whole is more important than the part, and the city than the citizen."[78] In terms of this theme of citizenship, we will soon consider how for certain Stoics, this rational kinship means that the entire universe can be described as one singular city.

---

76. Epictetus, *Discourses* (2014), 1.19.14.

77. The localized nature of being just one part of the overall universe determines that we are each not able to describe, appreciate, or know *everything* about our connections with the universe according to Epictetus. Reydams-Schils (*Roman Stoics*, 38) notes however that for Epictetus, recognizing our rationally conditioned fellowship does "help us realize that Nature also made humans intrinsically social beings."

78. Epictetus, *Discourses* (2014), 2.10.5.

Being rational for Epictetus hence means participating in common prosperities, because each of our rationalities already has a universally common composition. This Stoic sense of the daimon is neither straightforwardly representative of an external protector or an internally active self. It rather treads both roles. Our appreciation of this duality is served as effectively by an early twentieth century translation of the daimon as our "genius,"[79] as it is by the more recent translations of the daimon that we have reviewed as a "guardian spirit."[80] The use of the word "genius" to describe a common rationality in which we each partake is particularly striking though in terms of its contrariness to how it is typically used. We might usually attribute the title of "genius" to individuals. The notion of the genius as a brilliant or innovative individual is romanticized and mythologized. We admire and even worship individuals whom we identify as geniuses, we conceptually separate them from the ordinariness of the masses, and we revere them for this distinguishability.

The Stoic use of the term genius shifts here though. Our genius, our rationality and its connection to our minds and thoughts, describes our internality that is not separable from that of our fellow humans. Genius instead is an aspect of the self that we all share. The daimon as genius is our trace, our fragment, of a universally common mode of being, as it is for all other rational beings. The notion of a separate individual, of an autonomous genius, is destabilized via this sense of the daimon within us. This does not negate the possibility of particularly interesting, individualized narratives. We each still orient ourselves in different ways. What the insight of the shared source of our rational minds does though, is situate the internal spark of the rational self within the collective context of all humans, rather than within the subjective context of a singularized intellect. What you control or will about yourself, and how you control or will it, is conditioned by something that is not exclusive to you individually but is common to all rational beings. From such a discussion, what is subjectively mental to each of us might now look less than purely subjective. Epictetus affirms this when he states that "if you will, you are free,"[81] however your subjective will acts "in accordance with what is not merely your own will, but at the same time the will of God."[82]

The will of God here is a reference to the rhythms and orders of the universe from which humans have emerged. That Epictetus recognizes the

---

79. Epictetus, *Discourses* (1916), 243.

80. Epictetus, *Discourses* (2014), 1.14.12.

81. See n11 in this chapter for a discussion on the meaning that freedom has for Epictetus.

82. Epictetus, *Discourses* (1961), 1.17.28.

daimon as a universal or shared orientation that concurrently manifests as an individual's orientation motivates a useful appraisal from philosopher and psychoanalyst Donna Orange, regarding what she describes as unexclusive about our rational and mental selves. Where Orange states that our internal constitutions mark a "selfhood" that is "neither subjective nor objective,"[83] I interpret a definition that captures the ambiguity of the self for the Stoics.

Once we interpret that the internally rational and controllable features of the self (as introduced in the preceding chapter) are not entirely subjective, we concurrently develop an impression that what defines each of us is not solely, locally internal. All our mental internalities are common to the world in which we exist, they are not reducible to us alone or restricted to our apparent personal borders. Kindred mental conditions manifest, even if we all manifest those kindred conditions in slightly unique ways.

This dispersed sense of individual subjectivity lurks in what Anthony Long describes as the "normative" constitution of our rationality. Normative in terms of human characteristics refers to what is present in a significant proportion of the members of a population. It invokes what has perpetuated over generations as the normal ways of being, or as the normal properties of people. The daimon, the source of our rationality for the Stoics, perpetuates the criteria via which understandings of how to live normally in a rational regard are universally standardized. Additionally for Long, our individual minds do not just indicate how we fit in with a rational universe by being normally rational. Our minds instead also exhibit how we are always already to a degree "equivalent" to the rational features of that universe, for such features *are us*.[84]

Our work in this chapter has already illustrated that "equivalent" in this context means living in accordance with a rationally ordered world system. The Stoics are not proposing that our individual rationalities, and the rationality of God that we know to be the world's orderings, are identical.[85] We have reviewed the Stoic belief in a hierarchy of rationalities that ranks us below God, but above nonhuman animals, in terms of the degree of rationality embodied.[86] "Equivalent" as Long describes it instead refers to

83. Orange, "Pre-Cartesian Self," 492.

84. Long, *Epictetus*, 166.

85. See, for example, where Epictetus (*Discourses* [2014], 2.5.13–14) instructs that it is incumbent on the rational individual to distinguish themselves as a "part of the whole" that is "not everlasting."

86. Clay (in Marcus Aurelius, *Meditations* [1964], xxvi) describes this hierarchy as "the great ladder that reached from the inanimate to the animate, from the animal to the human and rational, and, finally, from the human to the supreme rationality of the

a qualitative comparison. Our rationality is the same *kind* of rationality as that which permeates the entire universe. How indeed could this relationship be anything but that, given that our rationality is a trace/fragment of that universal rationality.

Marcus Aurelius takes inspiration from Epictetus' characterization of this relationship. Following Epictetus, Marcus perpetuates the idea that living rationally requires being indifferent to what is beyond our internal mental control.[87] Fundamentally though, being rational requires living with a "cosmic" awareness that one's own mind and the entire universe share a kindred bond. It is only by firstly reflecting on our inherent connections with the world that we can appreciate how tiny our role is within it, and just how external to our personal control the world's whole ordering of everything (including us) is. These allied conditions extend interpersonally between humans, and universally between humans and the world. As a trace, a fragment, a part of the whole, this form of mind that Epictetus and Marcus describe marks our internal self as a "universally" collective phenomenon. Marcus expresses this when discussing our mind as a kinship:

> Hurry to your own directing mind, to the mind of the Whole, and to the mind of this particular human. To your own mind, to make its understanding just; to the mind of the Whole, to recall what you are part of; to this human's mind . . . and at the same time to reflect that each is a kindred mind.[88]

In the preceding discussion we have examined how for Epictetus and other Stoics, our individual rationalities and associated mental functions are parts of a common order. The next chapter will see us focus our examination of this union on its physical conditions. We have in this chapter though established how the Stoics propose interconnections between individuals and the universe, and considered why in Stoicism this indicates that we have inherently social or communal orientations. While we have only briefly detailed this position—that we think and act with collectively social rather than with individually personal ends in mind—there is much to come regarding our study of the pivotal communal features of Stoicism. The ideas through which we have here worked have opened the possibility for that kind of study. By engaging Epictetus, this chapter has served the purpose of directing us toward Stoicism's social priorities. In a way this is akin to the tone of Gretchen Reydams-Schils' scholarship on the Stoics, which highlights that

divine."

87. Marcus Aurelius, *Meditations* (2011), 12.3.
88. Marcus Aurelius, *Meditations* (2006), 9.22.

Epictetus' reflections "help us realize" that the world "made humans intrinsically social beings."[89]

Our most recent considerations have concerned the Stoic idea that what is internal to us—our mind, our rationality—is *not* housed away from the rest of the universe. We have been reviewing perspectives that instead portray each of our minds and rationalities as traces of a universe's rational order. There is something shared between our mind and an entire universe, and therefore between our mind and other humans' minds. This unsettles straightforward oppositional distinctions between what is supposedly internal versus external to the self. Such considerations might duly spark discussions that unsettle the branding of Stoicism as a tool that individuals can use to mentally defy an anxiety-inducing "out there" world. There is a voracious appetite in the self-help market for reductions of Stoic philosophy to assertions around mental self-definition and personal control. Such adaptations must be complemented though with the kind of reading presented in this chapter, which appreciates that for the Stoics, your rational mind is dispersed in and among other people's minds. If what is mental has shared roots and operations, then mental control is a collaborative exercise.

I believe that an appreciation of the mutual, kindred, and common conditions regarding what is internally rational about each of us, more genuinely and faithfully adheres to original Stoic principles. Perhaps even more importantly though, in my view this approach also provides the foundations for better mental well-being for new practitioners of Stoicism. What I mean by this is that there is the potential for improved mental health benefits from Stoic engagements, if discourses around Stoicism prioritize the points raised in this chapter from Epictetus and others concerning how bonded we are with each other because our mental functions share the same source and orientations. This would require a shift in the emphasis of Stoic commentaries, where the primary instruction would not concern what we each individually mentally control but rather what we collectively mentally share. Where Stoicism is presented as an insight into what is common and structurally ordered about the way we each personally think, so it can alleviate at least some of the anxieties and alienations that people feel in relation to each other and the world. With this portrayal of the Stoic mind, the rhetoric shifts from an emphasis on controlling our own identity in defiance of the rest of the world, to instead identifying ourselves in and with our fellow humans.

This perspective of the shared conditions and territories between our mental selves provides the basis for the coming chapters' analyses of various

89. Reydams-Schils, *Roman Stoics*, 38.

Stoic commitments to our social or communal selves. Through a series of themes, we will explore that far from being resilient to the people and world around us, Stoic philosophy wants us to understand that we are inherently socially natured and made for each other. We will explicitly address how our internal decision-making processes are firstly designed for collective rather than for personal benefits. We have indeed already seen Epictetus introduce this feature of Stoic virtue.

How we understand the control that we have over the rational mind changes accordingly. The mind is not an autonomously self-controlled mechanism. It instead represents something bigger than each of us alone. Our rational mental functions are orderings of the Stoic world in which we participate instead of individually possess. The ramifications for this insight regarding our subjectivity or sense of ourselves are considerable. If our mind is a feature of the universe, then likewise it is in being part of the universe that we exercise our own internality. Through our discussions on the daimon we already get a sense that our internality, our rationality, is a trace, a fragment, an aspect, of a universe of which we are each a part. It is now time to take this discussion of Stoic part-to-whole relations into an entirely physical realm.

3

Common Bodies

Only Bodies Exist

IN THE PREVIOUS CHAPTER we encountered the Stoic understanding that our internality, our mind, our rationality, shares kindred relations with the minds and rationalities of other people. This is because all rational minds are traces of a universe's rationality. We have further seen that this rationality for the Stoics is responsible for ordering and binding the universe, interconnecting all its ecological patterns, linking our planet to other celestial movements, and embedding us within the world around us. Given the momentous material or physical aspects of this claim, what requires our attention now is how for the Stoics the entire physical universe, including our embodied selves, is rationally ordered. How does rationality function as a system of physical substance?

We will in this chapter be studying the physical, tangible, material features of the universally rationalized or ordered world of the Stoics. This will examine how connected humans are to each other, and to the world, through our physical, material substance. In examining these physical conditions, our bodies will become significant. This dimension of Stoicism will sit interestingly with the Stoic positions that we have reviewed in which the body is conceptually situated outside a human's internal rationality.

While considering the physical, material conditions of our bonds with a rationally ordered universe, we will also review which entities the Stoics believe are included in the societies and communities to which humans belong. If the entire universe is rationalized, or in other words, if a single causal order permeates everything, could our rationally kindred connections incorporate *all* physical and material things, beyond simply humans? To begin this discussion of physicality and bodies, we turn to Stoicism's formal beginnings via Zeno.

Zeno emerges after a period of thinkers, now categorized as the Presocratics, for whom the physical universe occupied some of the most important philosophical questions.[1] The Presocratic influence is apparent in Zeno's reflections on the causal, or "cause-effect," relationships that comprise a physical universe. In studying the physical associations between things, Zeno asserts that only one type of thing can act or cause action; bodies.

This might be surprising given the Stoic views on the body that we have reviewed. In previous chapters the Stoics have linked our mind and rationality, not our body, to our thoughts, decisions, and actions. The body indeed has been described as outside our internal, rational capacities that cause ourselves to act. Now however, we will be studying how Zeno believes not only that bodies *can* be causes, but that *only* bodies can be causes. Will this contradict the Stoic principles we have learned so far?

To comprehend Zeno's position—that only physical, material bodies can act—it is necessary to firstly situate this belief in relation to Plato's preceding and opposing position.[2] Contrary to Zeno, Plato attacks materialist theories in his work, *Sophist*. Written just before Zeno is born, for Plato we cannot accept materialism's reduction of what exists to bodies exclusively. Plato here criticizes how materialists hold that the only things which have "being" are touchable things, the things that have bodies.[3]

A major concern that Plato has with the materialist perspective is that it negates the existence of unbodied things like souls, not to mention virtue and justice.[4] Plato instead maintains that souls, virtue, and justice do exist but are not physically bodied.[5] He proposes a less extreme set of beliefs accordingly in which souls exist separate from bodies. The apparent purpose

1. I here concur with Guthrie (*History Greek Philosophy*, 3–4) that Presocratic philosophy from its outset was "endowed with an indefatigable curiosity about the nature of the external world . . . and its physical composition."

2. There are many facets to the relationship between these two philosophical heavyweights. Zeno reportedly writes a book for instance called *Republic*, in response to Plato's identically titled work. See Long ("Plato and the Stoics," 118) for how Zeno's intention in this work seems to have been to distinguish his ideas from those of Plato. Such "debates" extended to Zeno's and Plato's respective philosophies of the city-state, as detailed in Annas (*Platonic Ethics*, 92–93), Erskine (*Hellenistic Stoa*, 27–33), and Schofield (*Stoic Idea of City*, 22–56).

3. Plato, *Sophist*, 245.

4. Plato, *Sophist*, 246–47.

5. Plato, *Sophist*, 247.

of this assertion is that if those holding materialist views accept that souls are not bodied, then this will lead to a more general concession from the materialist that not everything that exists is bodied. Such a position coheres with Plato's broader definition of what exists as anything that is involved in action. Plato here defines what exists as what can act or be acted upon, including what can "affect or be affected."[6] This reflects a belief in the capacities of an immaterial soul and mind to act, and their receptivity to be acted upon.

Zeno will disagree with Plato on most aspects of these positions, mainly because for Zeno "only bodies exist."[7] This presents a fundamental contradiction between Platonic philosophy and Stoicism's first principles. Zeno *does* agree with Plato's condition that what exists can act and be acted upon. These dual features indeed come to define the universe for the Stoics. The Stoic universe is comprised of what acts and is enacted. As Cicero tells us though in *On Academic Skepticism*, for Zeno these dual capacities are only attributable to bodies, and not to immaterial souls and minds as Plato supposes.[8]

With this position, Zeno avoids conceding to Plato that either souls do *not* exist, or that they exist but are not bodied. Zeno instead maintains that souls *do* exist, and that this existence is due to souls (and minds) being bodied.[9] The soul is a body that acts and is acted upon, countering Plato's

---

6. Plato, *Sophist*, 247.

7. Aristocles in Long and Sedley, *Hellenistic Philosophers*, 45G; taken from *SVF*, 1.98. Frede ("Stoic Epistemology," 302–3) notes that where Zeno posits only bodies exist, we get an insight regarding "what is" for the Stoics. Related to this topic is how Johnson (*Deleuze*, 26–36) discusses the respective Stoic and Platonic impressions of the roles of what is corporeal versus incorporeal. While only what is corporeally bodied can act and be acted upon for the Stoics, incorporeal properties of bodies still manifest in their view. The catch is that incorporealities are dependent on bodies, meaning that bodies not only cause other bodies (to be the bodies/states that they are) but also cause incorporealities. See where Sextus Empiricus (*Against the Physicists*, 1.211) presents Zeno's discussion about this in terms of how a knife, as a body, causes another body to be a cut body, as well as causes the incorporeal predicate of being cut. As correlatively conveyed by Stobaeus (in Long and Sedley, *Hellenistic Philosophers*, 55A; taken from *SVF*, 1.89 and 2.336), a Stoic view is that the body is "that because of which" of other bodies and their incorporeal predicates. Inwood (*Ethics and Human Action*, 97) discusses this point that incorporealities are caused by the material bodies from which they are otherwise separate.

8. Cicero, *On Academic Skepticism*, 1.39.

9. Cicero, *On Academic Skepticism*, 1.39. While the earliest Stoics do not all share identical views on the relations between what is bodied or corporeal and what is incorporeal, ancient scholars suggest that the subsequent heads of the Stoic school agree with Zeno that our soul and mind are bodied. Nemesius (in Long and Sedley, *Hellenistic Philosophers*, 45C; taken from *SVF*, 1.518) reports that for Cleanthes, because "no

belief in the soul's distinction from the body. Other features of the universe about which Plato was concerned, such as virtue, justice, and intelligence, for Zeno also only exist because they are bodied. This worldview leads to the ultimate point that if only bodies can act and be acted upon, then even God must be bodied.[10]

While we can comprehend that God would be able to act, how might we accommodate the notion that God is also "acted upon"? This counters usual portrayals of God's all-commanding relationship with the world. Our answer to this question concerns the Stoic principle that we have already encountered; the entire universe is God in its orderings. If the ordered universe is God, then any causal act is both an act of God and that which acts upon God as a physical effect. Evidence of this conception of God's materiality exists before the Stoic eras. The Stoics evidently draw inspiration from the Presocratic Heraclitus, in holding that God is embodied and universally ordered. Fragments from Heraclitus reveal a correlation of God with and as physical change, rather than as externally overseeing such change:

> God (is) day (and) night, winter (and) summer, war (and) peace, satiety (and) famine, and undergoes change in the way that (fire?), whenever it is mixed with spices, gets called by the name that accords with (the) bouquet of each (spice).[11]

From earlier discussions we have become familiar with the Stoic belief that God is just the world in which we live. God is not a transcendent deity, outside the world. The Stoics are pantheists, believing that God is present throughout the world. We have also seen that Stoicism describes God's pantheistic omnipresence as the world's rationality. God, as rationality, interconnects and orders everything that we see occurring ecologically and physically in the world. We are now going to discuss how the Stoics explain that God/rationality is present in the physical substance of everything ecological and physical. To do this in a way that coheres with the Stoic principle that all that exists are acting and acted upon bodies, we need to comprehend the underpinning Stoic belief in active and passive principles.

---

incorporeal interacts with a body, and no body with an incorporeal," this must mean that "the soul is a body." Chrysippus (in Long and Sedley, *Hellenistic Philosophers*, 45D; taken from *SVF*, 2.790) is likewise reported to hold that because "an incorporeal does not make contact with a body," and that in death the "soul both makes contact with and is separated from the body," it must be that "the soul is a body."

10. Aristocles in Long and Sedley, *Hellenistic Philosophers*, 45G; taken from *SVF*, 1.98.

11. Heraclitus, *Fragments*, fragment 67.

Everything Is Made of the Same Substance

Zeno believes that what exists in the world is comprised of a common substance.[12] According to this first Stoic principle, everything that exists, you, trees, oceans, buildings, is made up in varying ways of the same physical stuff, the same substance, the same material.[13] This common substance is physical and includes active and passive "aspects" or what the ancients refer to as "principles." We can situate these dual aspects or principles within Zeno's conception that all that exists are bodies that can act or be acted upon.

The active aspect or principle is the feature of bodies that acts. Complementarily, the passive aspect or principle is the feature of bodies that is acted upon. This passive aspect or principle of worldly substance, of bodies, of material physical stuff, cannot on its own take forms or cause motion. Diogenes Laërtius points us to the Stoic definition of the passive aspect as "unqualified substance, i.e. matter."[14] The skeptic, Sextus Empiricus, further details the Stoic definition of this passive principle or aspect, as that which has no shape or motion of its own accord and must be shaped or moved by something that is not it.[15]

Sextus here indicates the Stoic belief that the passive aspect of the world's common substance needs a cause to activate, move, and shape it into forms and things. This activation, the active principle, is the rational ordering otherwise referred to as God that pervades and causes the entire universe. Given that God in Stoicism is internal to the world rather than transcendently overseeing it, God's role as a rational causal agent is not

12. Calcidius in Long and Sedley, *Hellenistic Philosophers*, 44D; taken from *SVF*, 1.88.

13. "Everything that exists" does not equal absolutely everything associated with the Stoic universe however. Stobaeus (in Long and Sedley, *Hellenistic Philosophers*, 49A; taken from *SVF*, 2.503) reports that Stoics such as Chrysippus additionally identify a "void" that is infinite, not bodied, and encircles the universe outside it. As Cleomedes (in Long and Sedley, *Hellenistic Philosophers*, 49C; taken from *SVF*, 2.541) further elaborates, because the void is not bodied, it neither acts on, nor is acted upon by, bodies. The void is acausal. While the Stoic belief that the universe does not *contain* a void or vacuum coheres with Aristotle's worldview, the interpretation that a void exists *outside* the universe diverges significantly from the Aristotelian understanding that Book IV of his *Physics* presents. The role of the void for the Stoics concerns the everchanging conflagrative cycles of the world's perpetual destructions and reconstructions. Even though the void is acausal, it can receive the world's bodily conflagration, inspiring Sambursky (*Physics of Stoics*, 109) to characterize it as a "receptacle." We will briefly consider what conflagration means for the Stoics later in this chapter.

14. Diogenes Laërtius, *Lives and Opinions*, 7.68.

15. Sextus Empiricus, *Against the Physicists*, 1.75. The duplication of content resulting from how Sextus Empiricus' works have been compiled means that Bury's translation of Sextus Empiricus, *Against the Professors*, also features a similar passage.

external to the worldly material that it activates. Activation does not come from outside to the world's otherwise passive materiality. God, rather, is always already internal to the world's material or physical substance, as the ordering aspect of it that causes it to take shape and to interact with other material and physical things. As Diogenes informs, the Stoics therefore believe

> that there are two general principles in the universe, the active and the passive . . . [T]he passive is matter, an existence without any distinctive quality . . . [T]he active is the reason which exists in the passive, that is to say, God. For that he . . . existing throughout all matter, makes everything.[16]

Because this active principle is singular, it causes and shapes the world's material forms in a systematically ordered way. This explains for the Stoics how the world physically occurs or manifests in reliably repeatable versions of plants, humans, and revolving planets. Reiterations of the same types of things and rhythms over generations become indications of a structurally explainable and empirically verifiable physical world. We have encountered this characterization of universal order for the Stoics in the previous chapter via Cicero[17] and Epictetus.[18] It is also why Diogenes Laërtius communicates that rationality, or reason, is for the Stoics the universal condition that is responsible for all physical causation:

> They think that there are two general principles in the universe, the active and the passive. That the passive is matter, an existence without any distinctive quality. That the active is the reason which exists in the passive, that is to say, God. For that he, being eternal, and existing throughout all matter, makes everything. And Zeno, the Cittiaean, lays down this doctrine in his treatise on Essence, and so does Cleanthes in his essay on Atoms, Chrysippus in the first book of his Investigations in Natural Philosophy, towards the end, Archedemus in his work on Elements, and Posidonius in the second book of his treatise on Natural Philosophy.[19]

The Stoic conception of an active principle shaping a passive material borrows some inspiration from Socrates. In both *The Symposium* and *The Republic*, Plato distinguishes Forms, which are the templates that structure

---

16. Diogenes Laërtius, *Lives and Opinions*, 7.68.
17. Cicero, *Nature of Gods*, 2.14–15.
18. Epictetus, *Discourses* (2014), 1.14.3.
19. Diogenes Laërtius, *Lives and Opinions*, 7.68.

what exists, from material or bodied objects in the world that manifest in accordance with those templates.[20] Whilst the notion of shaping and shaped aspects of the world is not entirely Stoic in origin therefore, what we have established from this discussion is that for the Stoics, the shaper and causal agent of matter is internal to, rather than transcendent from, matter:

> They [the Stoics] also teach that God is unity, and that he is called Mind, and Fate, and Jupiter, and by many other names besides. And that . . . he turned into water the whole substance which pervaded the air; and as the seed is contained in the produce, so too, he being the seminal principle of the world, remained behind in moisture, making matter fit to be employed by himself in the production of those things which were to come after; and then, first of all, he made the four elements, fire, water, air, and earth. And Zeno speaks of these in his treatise on the Universe, and so does Chrysippus in the first book of his Physics.[21]

If, as the Stoics believe, every individual thing is materially/physically bodied, then every one of these physical/material bodies contains its own internal cause (God, as rationality). This means that every individual thing contains its own cause for being. This does not individualize causation or activation, given that every individual thing/body contains the same cause. Anthony Long duly finds a certain similarity in human and nonhuman bodily causation. If the Stoic material world has a singular source of production, this means that "stones are like men in being 'unified' bodies, and their unity is due to the same cause . . . which pervades all the rest of matter."[22]

There are no causes that are external to the world of physical/material bodies. As we have seen regarding the daimon, the universe's ordering impulse is within each of us. Seneca advises here that any reference to the divinely infused matter of objects in the world necessarily includes the divinely infused bodies of humans. The universe as God not only represents an arena in which human bodies exist. It also constitutes the very substance of human bodies by internally rationally ordering them:

> Things in the universe are made up of matter and God. God controls them, and they are his followers, ranged about him as

20. Plato (*Symposium*, 211a–b) presents one version of this theory. See Plato (*Republic* [2007], Book IV) for another. Three active agents are cited: the "Forms," "Demiurge," and "World Soul." There is one complementary but distinct passive materiality known as the "Receptacle."

21. Diogenes Laërtius, *Lives and Opinions*, 7.68.

22. Long, "Soul and Body," 38.

their ruler and guide . . . in a human being . . . what matter is in the world is in us the body.[23]

Consistent with these refrains around God and our internal functions, Cicero in *On the Nature of the Gods* likewise defines the Stoic position that God is a natural cause and director that is "immanent" to our nature.[24] Humans do not simply share the source of our minds, as we have learned in the previous chapter. Our physicalities are also linked, together ordered as are all bodies by a universally singular system.

When talking of causation, of bodies being what causes and are caused by, of bodies being what acts and are acted upon, we are attending both to an internal aspect of bodies and to an apparent *interactive* feature of bodily existence. Regarding this apparent interactive feature, for Zeno the body must therefore regularly actually be a "site" of something greater than simply an individual body. This might be confusing, given that we have just defined causation as activating *internally* to bodies. If the argument though is that rationalized bodies not only cause/act, but are also caused by/acted upon by other bodies, does this latter function of being acted upon suggest that bodies can be *externally* caused?

The answer is no, a rationalized body cannot be externally caused. All interaction between rationalized bodies, in a rationalized (ordered), bodied world, instead occurs internally. The advent of a rationalized, bodied world posits not just that everything that exists in it is rationally bodied. The world itself must also be a rationally ordered body. All bodies belong to, or are parts of, its system. We have reviewed how Zeno argues that the source of rational and animate beings, the world, cannot itself not also be rational and animate.[25]

Sextus Empiricus reports how for the Stoics not only is the "world a body," but more importantly that it is a "unified body . . . held together . . . by nature."[26] For the Stoics the universe is indeed the most perfect body,[27] given that it contains all individual bodily parts, and it is "not possible for

---

23. Seneca, *Letters from a Stoic*, 65.23–24.

24. Cicero, *Nature of Gods*, 1.10. Later in this work, Cicero (*Nature of Gods*, 1.36) further details how Zeno's books describe a "reason which pervades the whole of nature and is endowed with divine power."

25. Cicero in Long and Sedley, *Hellenistic Philosophers*, 54G; taken from *Nature of Gods*, 2.22. Also see Sextus Empiricus (*Against the Physicists*, 3.101) for this discussion on Zeno.

26. Sextus Empiricus, *Against the Physicists*, 79–84.

27. Plutarch (*Moralia*, 8:1054) portrays how the Stoics describe the universe as "a perfect body, whereas the parts of the universe are not perfect."

the whole to be worse than the part."[28] This evaluation of the world's bodily being is later reiterated by Seneca, for whom "our school" (the Stoics) holds that the universe must be body, because "what is good is a body" and there is nothing that is more good than the world itself.[29] What unifies this body, and what unifies this body with all individual body parts (such as our bodies), is its singular rational ordering. Every individual, every one of us, is for Sextus "held together by the best nature," which for the Stoics is our "rational nature."[30] Universal nature, our nature, is the rational thread in and through all things. It permeates even the things that lack the rational minds of humans, given that as we have seen, it orders such things to be what they are. The result of this universally shared order is that things are rationally *internally* rather than *externally* related. Rationalized bodies share internal or kindred causal relations with other rationalized bodies.

Because each body contains its own active principle, its cause for being, taking shape, and moving, and because the world itself is a body, the world in Stoicism is self-moving. The world is both an arena of rationally internally activated bodies, and a rationally internally activated body itself. There is no external cause for any body to be the body it is.[31] Just as we have discussed that for the Stoics all rational minds share in the same internal

28. Sextus Empiricus, *Against the Physicists*, 85.

29. Seneca, *Letters on Ethics*, 117.2.

30. Sextus Empiricus, *Against the Physicists*, 85.

31. Sextus Empiricus (*Against the Physicists*, 76) observes the Stoic belief that the active principle is an agent internal to each body, meaning that the body "is self-moving." The quality of self-moving must furthermore be eternal for each body, for without an external cause, a body must never have been activated by what preceded it. The active principle is "in motion for ever" through both universal and particular bodies, whereby bodily "change is eternal." We can note how this Stoic view counters theories of an external origin or agent, as forwarded by Aristotle's position in *Metaphysics* that the origin of being and things is the "unmoved mover" that is God. Galen, the Greek surgeon, philosopher, and physician to Marcus Aurelius, strongly contests this Stoic interpretation. See Hankinson ("Explanation and Causation," 482) for the translation of Galen's concern that the Stoic belief around internal causation involves not only causes of perpetual becoming and of being moved from here to there, but also assumes causes of being or existing. If only bodies exist, and bodies are what causes and are caused and house their own activation, then within each body is the reason for its own existence. Galen refuses to accept this view because such a cause would have to contain its own cause for being, and that cause would have to contain a preceding cause for its being, and so on down a never-ending line of causes requiring preceding causes, that could not end with the body concerned. Galen posits that there must always be another aspect to bodies that causes an act, an activation, a movement, and being. Gill (*Naturalistic Psychology*, 51–55) is also relevant when discussing Galen's sense of causation for the Stoics, as is the commentary from Bénatouïl ("Divine Activity in Stoicism," 30) on the Stoics' characterization of God as nature's cause of its self-moving.

rational function, likewise we now see that all bodies share the same internal rational function. Where the Stoics describe kindred minds as traces or fragments of a universal mind, we now similarly can interpret that all kindred bodies, including us/ours, are parts of the same universal body.

Is the Stoic God Scientifically Explainable?

We will discuss this notion of kindred rationalized bodies more extensively soon given its importance in appreciating Stoic conceptions of a global community. For now we can recognize though that a communion exists for the Stoics among all bodies, and therefore between all existing things, due to their shared rational *and* material constitution. Because of this rational unity, the ancient commentator Stobaeus illustrates how for Zeno, bodies that act and bodies that are acted upon share a mutual "belonging." It is not possible that an individual body exists and "not belong,"[32] for as we have covered, to exist is to be a body that acts and is acted upon and is therefore embedded within a collectively and causally ordered world.

This shared, rationally ordered, materiality, refers to the Stoics' pantheistic impression of the universe. Pantheism is the belief that everything in the universe follows a singular divine order because everything in the world is that divine order. Given the physicalism or materialism of the Stoic worldview, what are we to make however of the fact that the Stoics call this singular order or system "God"? This question has never been more pertinent than now. Considering our current era's increasingly secular and scientific outlook regarding our ecological surroundings, how can we accommodate the Stoic characterization that something called God is what causes, interconnects, and arranges the physical world?

We have reviewed that God for the Stoics is not an external overseer of a created universe. The Stoic God instead exists in and as the universe's physical patterns and from a current day perspective seems more akin to the natural world's scientifically explainable processes. The pantheistic element of the Stoic material, physical world, has as a result been the source of much debate. In *A New Stoicism*, Lawrence Becker's celebrated reconceiving of the Stoics argues that Stoicism's "quasi-theological"[33] foundations are not something we can casually dismiss, so entrenched are they in the philosophy's tradition. Because the Stoic God is a "naturalistic" rather than an ethereal force though, Becker constructs an approach via which we replace

32. Stobaeus in Long and Sedley, *Hellenistic Philosophers*, 55A; taken from *SVF*, 1.89 and 2.336.

33. Becker, *New Stoicism*, 46.

the features of Stoicism's vernacular that refer to living in accordance with a divine nature, with more scientifically consistent terminology.[34]

Philosopher Massimo Pigliucci's more recent commentaries are even more explicit on this topic. Pigliucci asserts that how we now conceive of God has very little to do with what God meant for the Stoics.[35] This is the kind of point that I have raised in addressing how God is not a creative deity outside the world in Stoicism. God instead permeates and binds the physical world internally to it. Pigliucci consequently believes that the modern sciences offer better descriptions than "universal reason" to explain the Stoic world, a perspective consistent with his previous academic career in the sciences. In *A Handbook for New Stoics*, Pigliucci and Gregory Lopez further posit that most people currently identifying as Stoics do not subscribe to pantheistic beliefs but conversely agree with "contemporary scientific" appraisals of the physical world.[36] In response to such directions, Kai Whiting and Leonidas Konstantakos express a concern about the anti-pantheistic trend that they identify in aspects of modern Stoicism. Just because Stoicism's inherently theological symbols are often misinterpreted as referencing a transcendent, spiritual, supernatural deity, that does not justify removing them.[37]

Such debates should impel all of us as modern readers of Stoicism to remember that the ancient Stoics would *not* have sharply distinguished religion from science in the way that we might do in the current day. Stoicism instead posits that God always already is the scientifically or empirically investigable world, an environment of ordered, structured cycles of physical causes and changes.[38]

One interpretation I have of this debate is that aspects of it appear to be as concerned with how Stoicism will present to a secularly oriented public, as they are with accessing the essence of the ancient theory. I am not critical of the first concern, given how notions of God and pantheism might hinder Stoicism's appeal to contemporary learners that are not inclined to lean on theistic traditions when using philosophy to reflect on themselves or the

34. Becker, *New Stoicism*, 8–32; 46–86.

35. Pigliucci, "Becker's *A New Stoicism*"; Pigliucci, "Growing Pains"; Pigliucci, *How to Be a Stoic*; Pigliucci, "Disagree."

36. Pigliucci and Lopez, *Handbook New Stoics*, 59.

37. See where Whiting and Konstantakos ("Stoic Theology," 8) assert that the pushback against Stoicism's divine themes reflects a modern monotheistic interpretation of God that carries much "supernatural baggage."

38. A related and long-established comparison of Christian and Stoic conceptions of God is provided by Rendall ("Immanence," 3), who explains that the notable characteristic of Stoicism's God is that it "is not transcendent, imposing orders from without, but inherent, immanent, acting from within, and therefore circumscribed by the organism in and through which [God] acts."

world. Becker relatedly suggests that we replace Stoicism's demand to live according to a pantheistic rational nature, with the more concrete advice of living in accordance with, or following, the facts. This is a reference to how we investigate and learn about the world currently, by scientifically or otherwise "getting the facts about the physical and social world we inhabit."[39]

Whiting and Konstantakos' intervention though is to provide a reasoned response to modern Stoic calls to replace its pantheistic heritage. While supporting Becker's project in reinvigorating Stoicism for modern readers, in their view the ancient Stoics were already demanding that we live in accordance with facts. Whiting and Konstantakos refer to the Stoic world as a "natural theological" realm of facts, whereby when engaging the ancient Stoics we do not need to remove references to God because God simply designates that scientifically or empirically knowable world.[40] Theological study is in this sense scientific study.

Numerous other commentators also consider that the concept, God, is essential to Stoicism and does not contradict scientific studies of the natural world.[41] Philosopher Dirk Baltzly provides one such voice in recognizing Stoicism's accommodation of both theological parameters and natural science. Baltzly's assertion is that Stoicism's pantheistic beliefs only arose due to their already existing scientific beliefs. That is, the Stoics empirically observed and recorded the universe's physical orders and patterns, and from those scientific observations then conceived of God as the cause of such a wonderfully organized system.[42] This means that to study the material universe is to study the universe's divine conditions, because in Stoicism what is physically material and what is God are "one and the same body."[43]

We have seen how Epictetus and other Stoics witnessed and described flowers blooming in regular patterns, day and night recurring in objectively reliable cycles, and celestial bodies appearing and revolving uniformly. From such observations they interpreted a connecting thread permeating all such physical patterns. This interconnection they called rationality, God, the Whole world. Secularly minded modern Stoics might instead call this thread the world's physical laws. Either way, the reference is to the same phenomenal process.

---

39. Becker, *New Stoicism*, 46.

40. Whiting and Konstantakos, "Stoic Theology," 8.

41. Boeri, "Cosmic Nature"; Glassborow, "Without the Divine"; Jedan, *Stoic Virtues*; Long, *Stoic Studies*; Striker, *Essays*.

42. Baltzly, "Stoic Pantheism," 3.

43. Baltzly, "Stoic Pantheism," 10.

Everything Is Interconnected Change

I have deliberately ended the previous sentence's and section's description of this rationality, this God, these physical laws, the universe, with the term *process*. The importance of describing the rational world as a process for the Stoics becomes apparent when considering the emphasis that they place on change.

The Stoic conception of the world as change is one of the hallmarks of the philosophy. In Plato's worldview, the divine realm of God is eternal, unchanging, perfect, separate, and distinguished from the transient, changing nature of the physical, material world in which we live.[44] By conversely implicating the rationally perfect God in and as the physical, material world, the Stoics might represent quite a diversion from orthodox impressions of the time. In discussing this Stoic perspective, we will be considering not only the world's material changes in general. Also under examination will be the interconnections between all of us as bodily parts of this material change. This will lead us to considerations of the explicitly social and communal aspects of our embodied being for the Stoics.

There is no Stoic work that is more interested in the topic of change than Marcus Aurelius' *Meditations*. Its series of aphorisms repeatedly defines change as unavoidable, as an inherent part of our and the world's existences, and therefore as something to which we should be indifferent. Change will occur whether we want it to or not. The world's physical substance is subject to constant transition, as is our own physical aspect, our bodies. Often these changes are uncontrollable. Examples include when the weather is uncomfortably cold one day, or we physically age despite a preference that we did not. The way in which physical change relentlessly defines us and our existence means for Marcus that we are causally and materially changing entities.[45]

It is worth remembering that Stoic materialist views which precede and overlap with Marcus' era continue themes from the Presocratic, Heraclitus. Diogenes Laërtius reports that the Stoics knew Heraclitus to have "written an influential book on Natural Philosophy."[46] We have of course already considered the correlation between Heraclitus' sense that God is in the natural world, and the similarly oriented Stoic view. The shared perspective on which we will now focus concerns Heraclitus' interpretation that the world's constant process of change or transition comprises a materially

44. As just one example, see Book 2 of Plato's *Republic*, in which Plato argues that God cannot change in order to improve, nor to worsen.

45. Marcus Aurelius, *Meditations* (2011), 5.13.

46. Diogenes Laërtius, *Lives and Opinions*, 9.9.

regenerative process of fiery deconstruction and reconstruction. Heraclitus specifically posits that all things are consumed by fire before resolving back into distinguishable forms: "All things change to fire, and fire exhausted, falls back into things."[47] Elements of this interpretation are adopted by various Stoic understandings of *conflagration* as the process via which the entire material universe cyclically destructs and resurrects. The Platonist philosopher Plutarch for instance conveys Chrysippus' sense that the conflagration involves stages that are "fiery" as well as those where the world "condenses" and turns into "water and earth and what is corporeal."[48] If the unavoidable condition of universal being and becoming is this perpetual transition and transformation, we too as bodily parts of that universe are bound by the same condition.

Within this sense that the entire universe constantly materially changes, Marcus posits that our own physical changes simply reflect the conditions of the universe. On this theme he constantly refers to the universe as the "Whole," and to each individual entity as one part of this Whole. We are each a bodily physical limb-like aspect of a universal physical body, where the nature of the whole is also our personal nature. This shared nature between part and whole applies for Marcus whether one adopts the non-Stoic interpretation that the world is a collection of separate atoms, or the Stoic impression of a universally common substance.[49]

Our own physical changes thus never occur in isolation. What appear to be localized and/or individualized changes, for Marcus are instead symbolic of the world's inescapable condition. Marcus declares that any changes to our individual selves should not alarm us, for they can only be understood within an entire world of change. He dismisses as "absurd" people's limited perspectives that are unable to appreciate that the particular changes

47. Heraclitus, *Fragments*, fragment 22. Diogenes Laërtius (*Lives and Opinions*, 9.6) alternatively terms this materializing conflagrative change for Heraclitus as the creation and dissolution of everything from fire.

48. Plutarch, *Moralia*, 8:1053b.

49. Marcus Aurelius, *Meditations* (2011), 10.6. Marcus refers throughout *Meditations* to the question of whether the world is made of "atoms." One effect of this is to distinguish the non-atomistic, monistic Stoic view regarding the world's physicality, from the Epicurean belief in a world of atomistic particles. This position from Epicurus (*Epicurus Reader*, 5–8) is itself adapted from the theory of the Presocratic Democritus. For a comparative commentary on the atomistic views of each, see Cicero (in Epicurus, *Epicurus Reader*, 47–51). While Marcus might appear to be setting up a distinction between atomistic and non-atomistic beliefs, as Harriman ("Disjunctions," 858) clarifies, the actual ideological difference is between the "providential ordering of the Stoic universe and the chaotic chance-ridden Epicurean model" that comes from a world of atoms. Marcus Aurelius (*Meditations* [2011], 4.3) directly addresses this point.

they experience or undergo are entirely natural and necessary, because they are "parts of the whole" whose nature is also to change.[50]

In Marcus' view, accepting that change is the "originary condition" of the world will induce mental well-being for the Stoic. When our bodies and lives change unexpectedly or unpleasingly, or when the world around us with which we are familiar and comfortable transitions disconcertingly, we should in Marcus' philosophy remember that all such things of which we were fond were only ever themselves brought about by change. Every single thing and every single person represent a link in an ongoing chain of the universe's ever-transitioning material. This is a process that Marcus demands requires our acceptance and indifference, because we as bodies and the world as a body share a "substance" that "is like a river in perpetual flow . . . its activities are ever changing" and succeeding through "causes infinite."[51] As we physically change, decay, and ultimately die, so the substance that comprises us, in turn manifests something new:

> Every part of me will be appointed by change to a new position
> as some part of the universe, and that again will be changed to
> form another part of the universe, and so on to infinity.[52]

This is evocatively described as the dependence of all things on a prior something. Our bodily existence is reliant on, and composed of, already existing rationalized substance. Our bodily substance then becomes the substance of further rationally ordered things:

> Constantly observe everything coming into being through
> change, and accustom yourself to the thought that universal na-
> ture loves nothing so much as to change the things that are and
> to create new things in their likeness. For everything that exists
> is, in a sense, the seed of what will arise from it.[53]

With this kind of language throughout *Meditations*, Marcus emphasizes that the material substance that makes up humans, our bodies, our rationalities, is the same material substance of the rest of the world. Humans are rationally ordered to a unique degree that affords us minds, unlike nonhuman animals and other entities. For the Stoics nevertheless, all parts of the world are still composed of the same systematized substance. In describing this common constitution as a "universal substance," Marcus begins to emphasize the collegial ramifications of our unified physical conditions.

50. Marcus Aurelius, *Meditations* (2011), 10.7.

51. Marcus Aurelius, *Meditations* (2011), 5.23.

52. Marcus Aurelius, *Meditations* (2011), 5.13.

53. Marcus Aurelius, *Meditations* (2011), 4.36.

Our kindred material constitutions mean that we are "meshed together"[54] or "implicated with one another."[55] We are all together effects of the conflagrative cycles of continuous, physical transition. The ancient historian Eusebius reports that straightforwardly Hellenistic Stoicism believed that the conflagration's deconstructing and reconstructing of the physical world is the "inescapable law of what exists." More interestingly for our considerations of Stoicism's emphasis on our communal states though, it is what bonds all cyclical physical change, as a singular force through unified entities determining that "everything in the world is excellently organized as in a perfectly ordered society."[56]

These organized and inescapable attributes of universal substance's transitions motivate Marcus' Stoicism to even posit that the material change marking our death should not be a fear-inducing change. Marcus explains in *Meditations* that he is inspired by Epictetus' instruction not to be concerned about our own death or anyone else's, because death exhibits a "natural event" or process.[57] We are each a part of a universally changing nature, and so it is to be expected that we all come into and leave being, not to mention change irrevocably during our being as readily as every other part of the universe. The death of one's child is accordingly for Marcus not something that should shock nor destabilize the Stoic mind.[58] Given that only six of Marcus' fourteen children lived to be adults, this view on death possibly contributed to his insistence on accepting the material change of absolutely everything. He demands of anyone who is fearful of their death to recognize that just as during your life you have lived as one part of a greater Whole, similarly during death you will continue to serve part-to-whole relations through a "process of change" via which you physically re-integrate into a "world . . . which brought you to birth," and into which you "entered . . . as a part."[59]

54. Marcus Aurelius, *Meditations* (2006), 7.9.

55. Marcus Aurelius, *Meditations* (1900), 7.9.

56. Eusebius in Long and Sedley, *Hellenistic Philosophers*, 46G; taken from *SVF*, 1.98.

57. Marcus Aurelius, *Meditations* (2002), 11.34.

58. Marcus Aurelius, *Meditations* (2011), 1.8; 10.34; 10.35; 12.26. Marcus Aurelius (*Meditations* [2011], 11.34) also declares that this position is indebted to the philosophy of Epictetus, who advises that when we kiss our children, we should remind ourselves that they could be dead the next day.

59. Marcus Aurelius, *Meditations* (2011), 4.14. See also the translation by Hays (in Marcus Aurelius, *Meditations* [2002], 4.14): "You have functioned as a part of something; you will vanish into what produced you. Or be restored, rather. . . . By being changed."

Death is far from a material finality according to *Meditations*. Marcus instead states that upon dying the rational material substance that comprises you is "scattered"[60] or "dispersed"[61] around a rational, physical universe. This scattering or dispersing operates within and among a worldly material substance from which you, every other human, and every other thing, has originally been made. After death, the substance that was you (as the universe) during your life, and which before your life was the universe as some other thing, simply becomes another part of the universe.[62] Understandings of death as negation are here reconceived. We and all other "parts of the Whole" must "necessarily perish" as Marcus notes. Perish, though, does not mean destruction or annihilation. It rather indicates where the reconfiguration of the substance that makes us up redefines us as bodies that "undergo change."[63]

The Stoic representation of death as less dramatic than it appears is not exclusive to Marcus. We have indicated Epictetus' influence on Marcus' position in this regard. In a later chapter we will also review Seneca's argument that we often carry an irrationally emotional fear of death.[64] Marcus tempers anxieties around death most straightforwardly of the three Stoics though, when arguing that the idea of our mortality should not unsettle us because it is just another instance of universal, rationalized, systematized change. If death is just change, then death cannot be unnaturally harmful, because change is the universe's nature. In responding to this logic, we must now ask whether this means that no change is harmful in Stoicism. Is *all* change the universe's rational, harmless, systematic processes in motion?

Our Purpose Is to Serve the Whole

To begin answering this question we must firstly work through Marcus' assertion that as parts of the whole universe, our actions are inherently tied to its welfare. As we have reviewed, Marcus believes that all bodies are internally interconnected or "enmeshed" because they are parts of a singular universal body. All bodies are unified given that the same universe, the same

---

60. Marcus Aurelius, *Meditations* (2006), 10.7.

61. Marcus Aurelius, *Meditations* (2002), 10.7; Marcus Aurelius, *Meditations* (2011), 10.7.

62. Marcus Aurelius, *Meditations* (2011), 9.3.

63. Marcus Aurelius, *Meditations* (1900), 10.7. See also where Hays (in Marcus Aurelius, *Meditations* [2002], 10.7) translates this not as "destruction" but as "meaning transformation."

64. Seneca, *Letters on Ethics*, 104.6–12.

order, the same system, is "present within them."[65] What we can now add to this definition of the kindred relationship between the bodily parts of the bodily Whole, is Marcus' view that the ordered changes of such parts cannot be harmful to the Whole, because the Whole as a perfectly rational order has no reason to do wrong to itself through its parts.[66] Externally caused harms are not possible for the whole universe, given that as we have reviewed, the Stoic universal body has "no cause outside itself" that could "compel it to generate anything that is harmful to itself."[67] Neither though are internally caused harms seemingly possible, given that for Marcus the universe's perfect rational order could not accommodate such an impetus. Since change is this universe's internal nature, dictating both the composition of the whole and its parts, does this therefore mean that all change must be rational and harmless?

The notion that there is no reason that is internal to the universal whole for it to do itself harm, does not infer that every human will always act in accordance with the whole though. There is an overwhelming number of assertions in *Meditations* which indicate that a singularity and unification to our existences does not signify that such unity *always* pervades. Our individual connection with this harmony is broken for example when we act irrationally and "cut ourselves off" from "our common nature" and "society."[68] Marcus describes how being overly upset by how our lives seemingly unfavorably change makes us an outcast from the rational unity of humanity and the universe.[69] When we do not appreciate that the changes that occur to us individually are parts of a whole changing universe, we irrationally ignore that such changes are not harmful to us because "nothing which benefits the Whole can be harmful to the part, and the Whole contains nothing which is not to its benefit."[70]

Marcus' associated point is that the changes themselves cannot harm us. What does harm us is having an individualized sense of our outcomes or ends and reacting adversely when different changes and outcomes eventuate. This evokes Epictetus' instruction from chapter 1, concerning how adverse circumstances cannot hurt us, only our reactions to them can. In

---

65. Marcus Aurelius, *Meditations* (2002), 6.40.

66. Marcus Aurelius, *Meditations* (2011), 6.1.

67. Marcus Aurelius, *Meditations* (2011), 10.6.

68. Marcus Aurelius, *Meditations* (2011), 4.29.

69. Marcus Aurelius, *Meditations* (2011), 8.34.

70. Marcus Aurelius, *Meditations* (2006), 10.6. Hays (in Marcus Aurelius, *Meditations* [2002], 10), and Hard (in Marcus Aurelius, *Meditations* [2011], 10.6), both translate that the universe "does" nothing that can harm itself, rather than use Hammond's translation here of "contains."

such a mode we will still experience changes that are not up to us. Such changes will be in accordance with a universal order or system of change. Our mental and emotional responses to change, if unable to recognize that we and they interconnect with a changing universe, will mentally dislocate us from that order or system.

This capacity for self-ostracization concerns the nature of freedom in Marcus' philosophy, again evoking a similar theme that we have discussed in Epictetus. Our internal rational nature is a trace of an ever-changing universe. We are enmeshed with each other because of that shared state, we are all traces of the same order, the same source. We must mentally accept that we are interconnected in this way however if we are to live in accordance with it. We are free to not accept this, and to experience the consequent detachment from our nature. It is however also in our rational freedom for Marcus to live with the consciousness that each of our lives occurs as a "brief and fleeting moment" in a great physical chain, and to accept the perpetual changes that come with being such a "tiny share" and playing a "small role" in this sequence.[71] If we are not willing or able to live with this awareness, our lives will be harmfully oriented. This is because we will be fighting a pointless mental battle against our inescapably changing and universally enmeshed existence. We will be denying our rational nature, "our common nature," if we individually "flee from the reason that governs our social life." Marcus' mention of our "social" life here refers to our interconnected constitutions, which we earlier defined as the Stoic understanding of sociality. Conditioned by our shared reason, an appreciation that everything about ourselves is systematically entangled with others requires us to be indifferent to what is not up to us individually, and to not be "dissatisfied with what comes to pass" for each of us personally.[72] To directly respond then to our original question in this section, while change is a rationally natural condition of the universe, change is seemingly not harmless when we conversely interpret it to be harmful. We must be careful though regarding where we attribute the cause of harm. For the Stoics, changes in the world, or changes that occur to ourselves, are not what cause harm. It is rather our judgements and other mental responses that refuse to accept such changes that are the cause of harm to ourselves. Epictetus emphasizes this when observing that change is the universal condition which dictates that everything follows a common order, including us, and we would be wise to align ourselves mentally with it:

71. Marcus Aurelius, *Meditations* (2002), 5.24.
72. Marcus Aurelius, *Meditations* (2002), 4.29.

All things obey and serve the universe, both earth, and sea, and sun, and all the other stars, and the plants and animals of the earth; and our body, too, obeys it, both in sickness and in health, as the universe wills, and both in our younger years and in old age, and as it passes through every other change. It is thus reasonable, too, that what lies within our own power, namely, the decision of our will, shouldn't be the only thing that sets itself in opposition to it; for the universe is mighty and superior to us, and has taken better counsel on our behalf than we can, by embracing us, too, in its governing order in conjunction with the whole. And besides, to act against it is to align ourselves with unreason, and while bringing nothing but a futile struggle, it involves us in pains and miseries.[73]

Marcus follows Epictetus' lead in similarly observing that it is only our faulty and fearful judgements of change that damage us. One example of this in *Meditations* is where he warns that "what is bad for yourself lies neither in . . . another, nor yet in any change and alteration in the things that surround you," but only in "that part of you which judges" harm in change.[74] We can avoid such harm by viewing particular changes, concerning ourselves or otherwise, as integrated parts of the whole universe changing.

Change is only harmless when it is rationalized. Rationalized change requires a consciousness of the interconnectedness of all parts, including ourselves, with the whole. Change could therefore be harmful if someone who is enacting, causing, or participating in change, does not appreciate their integration with a whole of which we are each a part. Marcus is not asking us to know exactly how our every thought and action radiates around and relates to a rationally ordered system or world. We just need to be aware that when we think and act, we do so in harmony with a universal order that is grander than our individual existences.

Marcus emphasizes this by asking us to live with the view "from above,"[75] sometimes referred to as the "cosmic perspective." This view or perspective demands that when thinking, acting, or observing change, we direct ourselves not in a way that focuses on individualized outcomes or personal well-being, but instead are conscious of the "substance and time" of the world "in its entirety."[76] If we do this, if we remember our communion with an entire universe by knowing that we are tiny component parts of its gigantic scale, then when we think, act, or experience unpleasant change,

73. Epictetus, *Discourses* (2014), fragment 3.
74. Marcus Aurelius, *Meditations* (2002), 4.39.
75. Marcus Aurelius, *Meditations* (2002), 9.30.
76. Marcus Aurelius, *Meditations* (2011), 5.24.

we will know that "all that happens to the individual is for the benefit of the Whole."[77] Thinking and acting rationally, and therefore avoiding harm, involves appreciating that the origin and the end for everything about our individual lives (even the most "trivial actions") is the "reason and law" of the universe, *not* merely of the individual.[78]

Another translation of this passage makes the Stoic emphasis on our default social status overt, in describing the universe to which our thoughts and actions orient as "the most ancient of communities."[79] With all such interpretations, Marcus emphasizes that well-being requires a conscious acceptance of how our existence serves an entity well beyond the individual alone. The primary mode of living as a Stoic does not comprise erecting resilient borders between our own minds and the rest of the world. The Stoic consciousness instead fundamentally requires an awareness that each of us as an individual is an expression of a world system. What happens to us is what a whole worldly web of happenings systematizes, inspiring Marcus to demand that we "passively accept" whatever fate "universal nature brings."[80]

Other translations describe this passivity instead with the terms "bear,"[81] "accept,"[82] and "endure."[83] The action that is inherent to the definitions of such terms indicates that we should be careful with any interpretation of straightforward passivity. It is true that Marcus is insisting with "passivity" that we humbly accept that our life and the changes in it, however unsatisfactory they might seem at times, are each a link in the interconnected physical chain of the universe. This passivity is not an apathy though. Marcus demands that we actively take responsibility for cohering our lives with a universal rational nature, by acknowledging and living according to our unity with our fellow humans and the world. If we do not accept this communion, we are said to grow away from the universe, as what Marcus describes as an "abscess."[84] Such outgrowth does not literally remove us from our immersion in the world's causal and material chain. Every individual is embedded in the Whole physical system after all. Such separation rather occurs through a harmful internal mental existence that lacks agreement with

77. Marcus Aurelius, *Meditations* (2011), 6.45.

78. Marcus Aurelius, *Meditations* (2011), 2.16.

79. Marcus Aurelius, *Meditations* (2002), 2.16.

80. Marcus Aurelius, *Meditations* (2006), 12.32.

81. Marcus Aurelius, *Meditations* (1964), 12.32.

82. Marcus Aurelius, *Meditations* (2002), 12.32.

83. Marcus Aurelius, *Meditations* (2011), 12.32.

84. Marcus Aurelius, *Meditations* (1900), 2.16; Marcus Aurelius, *Meditations* (2002), 2.16; Marcus Aurelius, *Meditations* (2011), 2.16.

our unavoidable nature and the associated rational well-being. To avoid this self-harm, Marcus demands that we always be conscious that the world is

> a single harmony that embraces all things, and just as all bodies combine together to make up this single great body, the universe, so likewise, all individual causes combine together to make up the single great cause known as destiny.[85]

Living rationally does not mean focusing on what we can personally gain from distinguishing what is in our control. Its emphasis is instead on recognizing the limits of our control, and accepting our role in a grander harmony of causes and relations. This highlights the universal and communal priorities of Stoicism. Marcus duly lists our primary responsibilities as being to everything but the individual:

> First, to your environment; second, to the divine cause which is the source of all that happens . . . third, to your fellows and contemporaries.[86]

We have such responsibilities because we are rationally bonded with the world body that is our "environment," which implies our association with the cause or "source" of this rationality, and with our "fellow" rationalized humans. If we neglect these responsibilities, if we forget about our entangled state of being, we irrationally and therefore harmfully estrange ourselves from our fellow humans, our communities, and the universe. Marcus' key contribution to this kind of discussion is a recognition of how we and our physical aspects are integrated parts of a perpetually changing physical whole. Where we can now apply this sense of our rationalized physical kinship is to questions concerning our social and communal existences.

We have thoroughly established that for the Stoicisms of Epictetus and Marcus, the entire universe is unified. This unification is what Marcus has called an "harmonious Whole." Marcus here expresses a position that we

---

85. Marcus Aurelius, *Meditations* (2011), 5.8. See also how Hays (in Marcus Aurelius, *Meditations* [2002], 5.8) translates this as "a single harmony . . . comprising all purposes . . . in a harmonious pattern."

86. Marcus Aurelius, *Meditations* (2006), 8.27. The translation from Hays (in Marcus Aurelius, *Meditations* [2002], 8.27) adds an apparent extra nuance to this structure by describing our first responsibility as being to our "body." See also the Long (in Marcus Aurelius, *Meditations* [1900], 8.27) translation which does likewise, however with the qualification that "body" means "form" for Marcus. Given that the principal form of body that we inhabit is the world environment itself, I find the Hammond definition that I originally engaged to be the closest to Marcus' intended meaning. In a related way, Hard (in Marcus Aurelius, *Meditations* [2011], 8.27) translates our world environment, or body, as the "vessel that encloses us."

can not only trace to Epictetus but also to the earliest fragments of Stoic thought. Plutarch informs us that Chrysippus identifies a cosmological singularity and unity in positing that the "universe, being one and finite, is held together by a single power."[87] Marcus will elsewhere involve in this unified Whole even things that exist distantly from us, such as "the stars."[88] This denotes a "union" between everything, even between what appears to be absolutely physically separated.[89] Such unification of course is attributable to the common substance of the world, a substance from which we are constituted and by which we are ordered. This omnipresent substance, remember, is responsible for the patterns and interconnections between all things, including planets revolving, plants growing, and entire environments changing:

> All things are interwoven, and the bond that unites them is sacred, and hardly anything is alien to any other thing, for they have been ranged together and are jointly ordered to form a common universe. For there is one universe made up of all that is . . . and one substance and one law, and one reason common.[90]

Marcus' belief in a singular bond among things extends from considerations of the physical universe, to a series of associated assertions about our social and collective existences. Things in the universe might seem "distinct," as he describes. Even with significant spatial separation though, distinct things are nevertheless involved in each other. All things as bodies "permeate each other"[91] and are "bound together"[92] because of their common substance. Where we are such things, our distinctness means that we are each individually distinguishable, apparently with our own particular motivations and orientations. Our individual psychological and physical ways of being though, our motivations and orientations, are all inherited or borrowed from a world source, or as Marcus puts it, "the nature of the Whole" world, is exactly "what my own nature is."[93] It is by implicating our own personal natures within what otherwise seems to be distinct from us, that we can articulate a Stoic sense of being social and communal.

---

87. Plutarch, *Moralia*, 8:1035b.

88. Marcus Aurelius, *Meditations* (1900), 9.9. This terminology is used across most translations.

89. Marcus Aurelius, *Meditations* (2011), 9.9.

90. Marcus Aurelius, *Meditations* (2011), 7.9.

91. Marcus Aurelius, *Meditations* (2006), 4.27.

92. Marcus Aurelius, *Meditations* (2011), 4.27.

93. Marcus Aurelius, *Meditations* (2011), 2.6.

The World Is One Social Body

To understand what being communal means in Stoicism, Marcus wants us to always keep in mind his characterization of the universe as a unified body, a "single living being,"[94] of which we individual bodies are parts. Remembering this ensures that when we direct ourselves to do anything, we know that we are directing ourselves in tandem with a whole system of other parts. We are each firstly not an individual entity but are a part of a bigger entity. This is why Marcus demands that every day we should "reflect again and again on how all things in the universe are bound up together and interrelated."[95] We function together as parts of an all-encompassing universal body or organism, where

> as with the limbs of the body in individual organisms, rational beings likewise in their separate bodies are constituted to work together in concert.[96]

Marcus here speaks to the understanding of the universe as a *unified* body, and wants us to view ourselves as collectively functioning components of it, for we "have been constituted for one co-operation."[97] Our individual bodily integrity seems separate from other bodies, however it is actually a part of a collective material "system."[98] This mandates that we are primarily cooperative physical beings, reflecting how limbs on a human body do not operate autonomously but act in harmony with the body's other parts. At the scale of the universe, each of us as an individual body is likewise integrated with other bodies, as a collection of limbs and parts in service of the universal body, making "all bodies . . . united with and co-operating with the whole, as with the parts of our body with one another."[99]

We can trace this characterization of the universe as a body, and of us as its limbs or components, to a passage from Epictetus that we earlier reviewed. There Epictetus emphasizes that our actions never primarily orient toward our separate welfares. When we act Stoically rather, we direct ourselves toward the Whole of which we are each a constituent part:

> A person never acts in their own interest or thinks of themselves alone, but, like a hand or foot that had sense and realized its

94. Marcus Aurelius, *Meditations* (2011), 4.40.
95. Marcus Aurelius, *Meditations* (2011), 6.38.
96. Marcus Aurelius, *Meditations* (2011), 7.13.
97. Marcus Aurelius, *Meditations* (2002), 7.13.
98. Marcus Aurelius, *Meditations* (2002), 7.13.
99. Marcus Aurelius, *Meditations* (1900), 7.19.

place in the natural order, all its actions and desires aim at nothing except contributing to the common good.[100]

From this recognition of the cooperative features of physical beings comes insights regarding what is communally ordered about the bodily universe for Marcus. Physicist Samuel Sambursky's study of Stoic physical science interprets that Marcus' sense of organic collegiality defines everything that we undertake not as restricted personal pursuits, but more broadly as "endeavors of society as a whole."[101] We have already likewise encountered how Epictetus' demand that our actions serve a population's common benefit, provides inspiration for Marcus' sense of our innate fellowship.[102] When we think or act rationally, we do so not simply with our own benefits or outcomes in mind according to Marcus. Built into our rational thoughts and actions are instead the ends of our fellow rational beings and the Whole:

> My nature is that of a rational and sociable being . . . [M]y city and fatherland is Rome; as a human being, it is the universe; so what brings benefits to these is the sole good for me.[103]

Do you notice how Marcus stipulates that outcomes which benefit others or the universe are not merely the *most important* benefits for an individual, but rather that they are the *only* or "sole" benefits for an individual? We only prosper through being mentally oriented toward contributing to our social environments, our communities, and our entire world. This is because each of our rationalities, each of our minds, thinks as a trace or part of its world-source, and therefore toward something much grander than individualized or personalized ends. The universe for Marcus is not simply the source of all mind and reason. Such a world is also a site of the unification of all individual expressions of this mind and reason. This unified impression inspires his definitions that "the mind" or "intelligence of the Whole is a social intelligence"[104] that is "concerned for the good of all."[105]

When first coming across this characterization of the Stoic rational universe as a social and communal realm, it is normal to be confused about how this sits with the Stoic concerns that we have already reviewed which

100. Epictetus, *Discourses* (2008), 2.10.4. See also the translation from Hard (in Epictetus, *Discourses* [2014], 2.10.4), which states that our "calling" is "never to approach anything with a view to personal advantage" or as if "detached from the whole."

101. Sambursky, *Physics of Stoics*, 115.

102. Epictetus, *Discourses* (2014), 1.19.13.

103. Marcus Aurelius, *Meditations* (2011), 6.44.

104. Marcus Aurelius, *Meditations* (2006), 5.30.

105. Marcus Aurelius, *Meditations* (2011), 5.30.

position social phenomena outside our rationality. We might recall from our opening chapter Epictetus ordering us to be indifferent to numerous aspects of social being, to not let our social class or reputation affect our sense of self, because these are things not in our control or dependent on us.[106] As I indicated at the time, Marcus presents a similar view, clearly informed by Epictetus, that we should ignore the mundanities of people gathering, gossiping, and diverting their attention together toward frivolous topics.[107] All such socialized developments for the Stoics are separate from our inner rational natures. We now find though with Marcus the correlation of our nature with social or civic life. How do we accommodate these two, seemingly conflicting, positions in Stoicism?

The answer to this question concerns how the Stoics understand "being social." Reviewing this understanding will require us to expand on our earlier considerations that what is social or communal for the Stoics implies a consciousness of our interconnected selves. We might typically think of social existence as a reference to interpersonal activity and behavior, of speaking, mingling, and living with other humans. A "social person" desires, or prospers through, human interaction. Being social conventionally means being around other people.

The Stoics too emphasize the importance of a practical, communal life, where in coming chapters we will see them order us to enact our philosophical and rational natures in public by speaking with others. For the Stoics though, we are social beings not merely because of interpersonal activity or company. Our social status is rather affirmed through what we share with each other and the rest of the universe, as entities systematized by a common, rational substance. When Marcus states that "we are born for community,"[108] "born for fellowship with others,"[109] and "made for society,"[110] this is not a description of how humans straightforwardly *seek* attention and company from others. It is instead a reference to how our rational natures involve a consciousness of ourselves as interconnected parts of a unified body. We should avoid a dependency on the aspects of communal life that are external to this rationality. It is not necessarily harmful to participate in contingent, collective behaviors that result when humans live together and interact daily, provided we do not mentally and emotionally define ourselves by such behaviors. We are truly social for the Stoics though

106. Epictetus, *Enchiridion*, 1.
107. Marcus Aurelius, *Meditations* (2011), 1.5.
108. Marcus Aurelius, *Meditations* (2006), 5.16.
109. Marcus Aurelius, *Meditations* (2011), 5.16.
110. Marcus Aurelius, *Meditations* (1900), 5.16.

when we are conscious of the fellowship that we share with each other and the universe. This is a fellowship that might manifest in collaborative daily practices, or it might follow us as we live "alone." All such practices are Stoically social when undertaken with the awareness that what seems highly individual and personal about each of us, are in fact traces of a collegial and impersonal source.

We have considered how a rational order permeates this universal source, and how this rational order physically bonds all that exists. It is for this reason that Marcus defines living rationally as living communally, whereby "rational directly implies social."[111] Given that the source of this rationality, this sociality, is universal, he likewise posits an unrestricted sense of kinship between rationally ordered things. Or in plainer terms, Marcus' impression of what constitutes this social environment extends beyond humans alone. The entire world shares social relations, because all things are rationally ordered by the same source. This means that the "world" as a whole is a "community."[112] All things, not just human things, exist together, as all things partake in the common substance of the world and are systematically arranged by that substance. Marcus even describes this in terms of a universal familial bond of "mutually intertwined"[113] things that "have a family feeling for each other."[114]

The common substance of everything is not solely responsible though for these interwoven and communal relations between things. While such substance is the condition of the relations, it is the rational, systematic, ordering of these things that is the unifying cause. We see this ordering in the world's physical patterns. We can again here think of the ecological networks that Stoicism describes, such as when Marcus rhetorically asks, do "you not see how the little plants, the little birds, the ants, the spiders, the bees, each do their own work and play their part in the proper running of the universe?"[115] Human labor does not contribute only to human matters in this web accordingly. What Marcus describes as our "work" instead serves a universal community of rationally ordered and activated behaviors.[116]

---

111. Marcus Aurelius, *Meditations* (2006), 10.2. Hays (in Marcus Aurelius, *Meditations* [2002], 10.2) translates this as where rational implies "civic." Long (in Marcus Aurelius, *Meditations* [1900], 10.2) correlatively interprets rational as equating to a "political [social] animal."

112. Marcus Aurelius, *Meditations* (1900), 4.3; Marcus Aurelius, *Meditations* (2006), 4.3.2.

113. Marcus Aurelius, *Meditations* (2011), 6.38.

114. Marcus Aurelius, *Meditations* (2006), 6.38.

115. Marcus Aurelius, *Meditations* (2011), 5.1.

116. Marcus Aurelius, *Meditations* (2011), 5.1; 6.42.

As all things participate in and perpetuate the Whole's order, so their social contribution emerges. Where each thing, whether human, nonhuman animal, or some other entity, plays its part as a link in the casual chains of being, so for Marcus everything "helps produce everything else." This reaffirms the universal kinship of bodies. Comprised of the same substance, and joined by the same causal chains, the mutual dependencies of everything are unavoidable because everything is "spun and woven together."[117]

Marcus' position is one of almost inextricable cooperation. Two ramifications emerge from the sense of a world's ordering in which "all things work together to cause all that comes to be."[118] Firstly, the notion of the self-producing, self-authoring, or self-determining individual being is seriously destabilized. This unsettling of characterizations of a personality type that is independent or self-sufficient occurs because according to this Stoic view every personality and every individual reverberates in conjunction with other things and people. The citations drawn from *Meditations* in these recent paragraphs indicate furthermore for Marcus that given our shared compositions, we are at once in collaboration with, *and* involved in the literal production of, each other. Marcus proposes a universally entangled collective state from which we each continually emerge and re-emerge. This he calls the "web" of all things.[119]

Secondly, as observed, this characterization of the world's omnipresent mode of collective production appears to incorporate nonhuman animals and things as fellow constituents that contribute to a common purpose. This theme is not as simple as that though. While such interconnections and interdependencies are attributable to all things being permeated and ordered by the same system of rationalized materiality, we also must factor in that the Stoics (along with Aristotle and others) believe that there are degrees of this material rationality that things mentally embody. Such rational differences qualify for the Stoics the extent to which "all things" socially cohere. If, as we have seen, what is rational is what is social, then animals and entities that are not as rational as humans will correlatively not be as socially oriented as rational humans will be. This diversified structure is not an accident nor unfair though for the Stoics, for we exist in a systematically rationalized universe. The universe for Marcus has been deliberately ordered like this, as a ladder of differentiated but complementary rational states that has "made the lower for the sake of the higher, and adapted them

---

117. Marcus Aurelius, *Meditations* (2002), 4.40.

118. Marcus Aurelius, *Meditations* (2011), 4.40.

119. Marcus Aurelius, *Meditations* (1900), 4.40; Marcus Aurelius, *Meditations* (2006), 4.40.

to one another."[120] While humans, along with other things, are citizens of a universal community, it is humans that bear the greatest social responsibilities as superior rational citizens. Marcus reminds the less socially energized humans that:

> When you are unhappy about being aroused from your sleep, remind yourself that the fulfilment of your social duties accords with the requirements of your constitution and of human nature, while sleep is something that you have in common with animals devoid of reason.[121]

The Stoics do not recognize an equal existential or ecological status among things in this world.[122] As we have encountered with Epictetus, a Stoic perspective even arrives at the extreme position that nonhuman animals are created to serve humans. This is because for such "beasts" it is interpreted to be enough simply to perform basic biologically related functions. Humans too perform such functions, however we additionally understand and interpret the role of these functions, along with comprehending our relationship with the world. This is attributable for Epictetus to our rational minds, whereas conversely for nonhuman animals:

> It is enough merely to eat, drink, take rest and procreate, and perform such other functions as are appropriate to each, whereas for ourselves, who have been further endowed with the faculty of understanding, that is no longer enough . . . So where a being's constitution is adapted for use alone, mere use suffices; but where a being also has the capacity to understand that use, unless that capacity be properly exercised in addition, he will never attain his end. What of the animals? God has constituted each according to its intended purpose, one to be eaten, another to be used in the fields, another to produce cheese, and another for some comparable use; and to be able to perform these functions, how is it necessary for them to be able to understand impressions?[123]

In perpetuating a philosophy that hierarchizes rational humans over less rational nonhumans,[124] Marcus likewise reiterates the notion of a "natural

120. Marcus Aurelius, *Meditations* (2011), 5.30.

121. Marcus Aurelius, *Meditations* (2011), 8.12.

122. See Stephens ("Stoic Naturalism," 278) for a discussion on whether the Stoics neglect the worth of ecological, nonhuman things, such as flowers and trees, "independent of a human valuer."

123. Epictetus, *Discourses* (2014), 1.6.14–20.

124. This leads Baltzly ("Stoic Pantheism," 15) to describe features of Stoicism as

ladder" of beings in the world. I have considered in the notes of the previous chapter how this idea predates the Stoics, and is perhaps most explicitly described by Aristotle's presentation of the "scala naturae" in his *History of Animals*.[125] Marcus' application of this idea articulates, as we have seen, that less rational "inferior" creatures and entities are "made for the sake of the superior."[126] Marcus' associated argument is that through this discriminated attribution of rationality, differently rationalized creatures are designed to serve the Whole, the universal "community," in different ways. It is through such structures that the ordering of a rationalized world system becomes apparent.

In describing what is particular about the human membership in this world community, Marcus refers to a collective human citizenship in a "universal city." This invokes the Stoic idea of *cosmopolitanism* that we will explore in chapter 4, a reference to all humans in the world belonging to a single community. Conceiving of the universe specifically as a city though can be traced to Stoicism's origins.[127] Perhaps most notably via Cleanthes, we find the conceptual correlation of the universal city with notions of civility and of living in a just manner. For Cleanthes, the city is not only a reference to where people live, but more interestingly is said to be where people "take refuge" in order to access a "civilized" environment that orders its citizens according to principles of "justice."[128] I will return us to this idea of the Stoic city as a "refuge" in a moment.

Rudimentarily the description of the city as the seat of justice exhibits the Stoics' commitments to legal and judicial order. The intensified amount of activity found in the centers of towns and burgeoning metropolises seems to exhibit for Stoic thinkers the need for ordered controls around personal behaviors. The ancient commentator Dio Chrysostom conveys this sense that the Stoic city in one regard is the seat of collective order and the regulation of justice, in that the Stoics believe that the city is where people are grouped together and are "administered by law."[129] What the Stoics mean

---

intensely anthropocentric.

125. Aristotle, *History of Animals*. See also Lovejoy (*Great Chain of Being*) which studies the development of this idea from ancient eras through to recent scientific considerations.

126. Marcus Aurelius, *Meditations* (2011), 5.16.

127. Diogenes Laërtius (*Lives and Opinions*, 7.28–33) reports that a Stoic interest in the city is initially represented by Zeno's *Republic*, as well as by a text from Chrysippus of the same name.

128. Stobaeus in Long and Sedley, *Hellenistic Philosophers*, 67I; taken from *SVF*, 1.587.

129. Dio Chrysostom in Long and Sedley, *Hellenistic Philosophers*, 67J; taken from

by this administrative order cannot be reduced entirely though to human legal affairs.

The universally grander understanding of administration and law indicated here is evident from Stoicism's outset. Plutarch tells us that Chrysippus describes justice as manifesting from God's "universal nature" and "His administration of the world."[130] Cleanthes' *Hymn to Zeus* complementarily tells us of a divine administration responsible for keeping things just, orderly, and unified.[131] The law or order that administers this world is, unsurprisingly, rationality. Because the order is rational, and what is rational is universal, the rationally ordered city in Stoicism is the entire universe. The Stoic city does not stop with a distinct urban environment, or a specific, geographically situated, metropolis.[132]

We consequently need to accommodate two senses or sites of the city for the Stoics. One city community, as just mentioned, is the Whole rational universe. We should not neglect though, that while the Stoic city is not restricted to localized, urban metropolises, this does not mean that such sites are unrecognized at all as cities by the Stoics. This latter, conventional form of city, simply comprises a lower form of the city phenomenon in the Stoic landscape. Marcus is attentive to, and responsible for perpetuating, these dual understandings of citied existence, describing each of us as "citizens of that highest of cities of which all other cities are, as it were, mere households."[133] This terminology reminds us of Stoicism's priority on our relations and interconnections with the Whole, in positing our membership of the universe-as-city as our primary mode of being, in comparison to the somewhat subsidiary nature of our localized town citizenship. To reflect that we are firstly parts of a universal cooperative, each of us permeated by our rationalized allegiance to the world, Marcus implores us to refer to the world as our dearest city, and to call it "Zeus."[134]

With this position established, I can now return as promised to Cleanthes' earlier description of the city as a "refuge." In the immediately preceding discussion, we see how the Stoics across the ancient eras, including that of Cleanthes, infer that the entire universe comprises a singular administration within which we are citizens. We have identified that later ancient

---

SVF, 3.329.

130. Plutarch in Long and Sedley, *Hellenistic Philosophers*, 60A; taken from *SVF*, 3.68.

131. Thom, *Hymn to Zeus*.

132. See Annas (*Morality*, 304) for one analysis on how the city "proper" for the Stoics is the universe.

133. Marcus Aurelius, *Meditations* (2011), 3.11.

134. Marcus Aurelius, *Meditations* (2011), 4.23.

Stoic accounts, such as that of Marcus, similarly describe the universe as a single city. This theme of our citizenship to a single arena which is the world itself raises an interesting question though. If the ordering law of that city/administration of which we are all parts is rationality, or in other words, if the entire universe is a rationalized city and we are members of it, from what is the universe as a city providing us refuge? What else exists apart from the rational universal city, from which we would require being "refuged"? Is not the entire world part of that city, and therefore part of that refuge?

My answer to this question is that for Cleanthes, the city, which is just a rationally systematized world, provides us refuge from a life that could otherwise lack as many rationally just ways of being. This universal city, after all for the Stoics, is the setting for our shared rational compositions. The city comprises all rational humans, and so provides the "most perfect" environment for us to enact our inherently rational, socially oriented, natures. We can enact these natures by being conscious of our interconnections with each other and with the world when we think and act, duly marking our thoughts and actions as communal. This is why the city is not exclusively a particular urban environment. The city more broadly is a universally rational order in which our common constitutions are exercised.

We have noted that citizenship of this universal city is not unconditional. When we think and act irrationally we are ostracized from it, and the Stoics are hesitant to extend full inclusion to what they believe are less rational animals and entities. There is nevertheless an overwhelming recognition of a structurally unrestricted collegiality between all things in Marcus' *Meditations*. This is due to the common rationality that permeates, systematizes, and activates all things. While through our minds, humans are more rationally activated than other things, there is an appreciation from Marcus that our substance, our human physicality/materiality, could have alternatively easily manifested in this present as part of a less rationally superior creature or object, and at another time it likely did or will:

> From the substance of the whole, as if from wax, universal nature moulds first a little horse, and then, melting it down again, uses its material to make a little tree, and then a human being, and then something else again.[135]

Marcus posits hierarchies of social existence according to interpreted levels of a thing's or creature's rationality. The Stoics also identify associated degrees of social roles and responsibilities based on these differentiated rationalities. There is nevertheless a Stoic belief in an internally conditioned

135. Marcus Aurelius, *Meditations* (2011), 7.23.

collegiality pulsing through all things, evidenced in the above description of our systematically ordered and shared substance. Marcus' *Meditations* is repeatedly an ode to the universe as a community. Having placed much emphasis in this chapter on the Stoic prioritization of serving others and the common good, we will now consider what the legacies are of this inherent collegiality for our primary impulses to care for ourselves.

4

Caring for the Self
Is Caring for Others

We Share the Same Primary Purpose

To this point we have characterized our minds, our rationalities, and our bodies, as fragments, parts, or traces of a shared phenomenon. The developing portrayal is that according to Stoicism, what appears to be individualized about each of us in fact has kindred origins and common ongoing conditions.

From this we have learned that the fundamental mode of our existence and the primary outlook on life required by the Stoics goes well beyond concerns about our personal benefits and outcomes. Stoic philosophy's attention on our authority over how we think and act is not predominantly concerned with how we individually feel about our own lives. We find in Stoic philosophy a set of concerns far grander than those occupied with individual well-being. As has been well documented, the Stoic priority is to live with a consciousness of what we inextricably share with a communally interconnected universe.

The notion of well-being will nevertheless be the topic of this chapter. When considering our default orientations toward community and universe for the Stoics, what also becomes apparent is how interrelated individual well-being is with the welfare of the whole of which we are each a part. This is not surprising given that as we fulfil our social roles and responsibilities in our daily lives, be they related to work, family, or personal relationships, our own well-being is never far from our minds. The company we keep, the practices we undertake, the paths we choose, all to some extent factor in what we believe is good for us personally.

Perhaps the ultimate expression of this regard for ourselves concerns considerations of our survival. Like many creatures, we are predisposed to care about staying alive. This orientation possibly does not have the prolongation of our own lives as its priority though. Naturalist Charles Darwin, psychoanalyst Sigmund Freud, and a host of other theorists have associated our instincts regarding survival instead more broadly with the ongoing existence of the entire species.[1] Our sense of avoiding danger is in such characterizations attributed to a genetic or biological code that is designed to serve the perpetuation of our species rather than merely to ensure the survival of any particular instance of it. This raises the question of whether when we care about or for ourselves, and when we exercise ways to serve our own well-being and even self-preservation, to what extent are we enacting a drive that has grander concerns than our individual selves?

Given the default communal and universal orientations for individuals that I have identified in the Stoics, it is appropriate that this will be the question that occupies us now. Attending to this question will involve considering how our inclinations toward our own well-being relate to our commitments for the Stoics to the well-being of the populations and world to which we belong. We have seen Stoicism bond our own individual rationality with the rationalities of our fellow humans. Our examination of this shared sense of rationality will in this chapter ask whether for the Stoics, when we care about ourselves and our ongoing preservation and well-being, are we doing this primarily to benefit ourselves, or are there more dispersed motivations?

Our inclination to preserve our existences, to survive, manifests in our thoughts and associated actions. We avoid obvious and implicit dangers and harms. Inversely we are drawn to self-sustaining sources of food and water. Self-preservation and self-care refer to a lot more than staying alive for the Stoics though. To begin to discuss the different Stoic positions on our self-preserving and self-caring tendencies, we require a basic understanding of the feature of ourselves that the ancients call *hormê*.

Hormê, also spelled hormai, is a Greek term used to refer to impulse, or more specifically, to our impulse to act. Where self-preservation and hormê are linked, self-preservation in Stoicism will therefore have something to do with what impels us to act in ways that account for our well-being.

1. Buck, "Genetics"; Dudley and Fine, "Kin Recognition"; Freud, *Introductory Lectures*; Maclean, "Limbic System"; Pearce, "Ecological Economics."

Self-preservation is understood by modern commentators to be a universal theme for the Stoics, identifiable as it is in all the ancient eras.[2] Marcus Aurelius' discussion on self-preservation provides an example of the later ancient Stoic generation's interest, describing how our "mind can preserve its calm by withdrawing itself" in order that one "comes to no harm."[3] The most comprehensive insights on the Stoic sense of hormê emerge though via an earlier generation's interchange between Cicero and the Stoic (or Stoic follower) Cato.

Cicero has never exactly been viewed as a Stoic philosopher. Roman citizens instead were aware of him as a politician, a lawyer, and an orator of peerless reputation. As a commentator of Stoicism however, Cicero invaluably conveys the relevance of the Stoic school to peoples' lives. An explicit example of this is his *On Duties*, in which he details the advantages for Roman society of a philosophy such as Stoicism, given its commitments to the connections between action and virtue. He states accordingly that it is our "first source of duty"[4] or "appropriate action"[5] to engage thinkers that show us that "all praise of virtue consists in action."[6] This imperative should remind us of Epictetus' later demand that philosophy serve practical action.

In his work *On the Ends of Good and Evil (On Moral Ends)*, Cicero discusses the importance for the early Stoics of practical considerations of how we act, specifically in the context of hormê. The hormê part of ourselves is said to comprise the personal impetus that we each embody, a "natural desire, what they [the Stoics] call hormê."[7] Given that we and other animals each have a unique form of this impetus or hormê, Cicero posits that "every living creature has its own nature."[8] Our initial forays into Cicero's Stoic account therefore present an impression of hormê as a relatively individualized or personalized impulse.

We each in this view live with our own version of hormê. This does not mean for the Stoics however that we can individually do anything we want with our hormê. Cicero clarifies this by stating that Stoic terminology[9]

2. Clay in Marcus Aurelius, *Meditations* (2006), xxvi; Eastman, *Paul*, 37; Jedan, *Stoic Virtues*, 100; Sellars, *Art of Living*, 57–58; Sharples, *Stoics*, 101; Stephens, *Stoic Ethics*, 13.

3. Marcus Aurelius, *Meditations* (2011), 7.33.

4. Cicero, *On Duties* (1991), 1.19.

5. Cicero, *On Duties* (2016), 1.19.

6. Cicero, *On Duties* (2016), 1.19.

7. Cicero, *On Moral Ends*, 4.39.

8. Cicero, *On Moral Ends*, 5.25.

9. Rackham (in Cicero, *De Finibus Bonorum*, 3.24) translates this as "Stoic phraseology."

instead defines that hormê applies to a "particular form of living."[10] What is this particular form? A rational form. We can each have our own hormê, our own impulse to action. Every hormê though serves a common, rational existence, which for each actor includes "sharing the goal of fulfilling their nature."[11] As we each steer our actions in accordance with our hormê therefore, we fulfil not simply personal natures but also universally rationalized outcomes.

It is worthwhile to pause momentarily to remind ourselves what rationality means. The entire universe is rational because it is systematically ordered. Our own rationality is a trace of that universally interconnected system. To be rational is to be aware, and to accept, that our individual selves are really parts of a greater whole. If for the Stoics our impulse that drives us to get up in the morning is rational, an impulse that gives us the appetite to do the things we do during the day and to be who we each are, then this impulse as rational must come from that greater whole. This is consistent with Epictetus' sense of the daimon that we reviewed in chapter 2, in which our individual rationality is a trace of a universally shared rationality. It likewise evokes our communal spark as detailed in chapter 3, in which Marcus demands that the compulsion to rise each day and perform our social duties is attributable to our rational status.[12]

Zeno's impression of hormê, conveyed to us by the Stoic Balbus, inspires Cicero's account of it for the Stoics that we have just reviewed. Zeno, we should recall, is the originator of the Stoic school. Balbus attends to how in Zeno's earliest of formal Stoicisms, each of our rationalities reflects a universally common rationality. It is therefore contentious to suppose that an individual's rationalized impulses are capable of entirely novel thoughts or behaviors. In one translation we see that Cicero describes the Hellenistic Stoic sense of hormai in terms of a "world-nature which experiences" every received form of "individuals' will."[13] This phrasing suggests that each individual hormai or will has some capacity for originality, that the world-nature then "experiences." This implication is negated though in other translations, in which we see the same passage described as where "the nature of the universe itself . . . constrains and contains everything within its embrace."[14] Cicero here informs us that for Zeno, the universe is "not just creative" but more emphatically the absolute "creator" of us, as the condition of all

10. Cicero, *On Moral Ends*, 3.23.

11. Cicero, *On Moral Ends*, 5.25.

12. Marcus Aurelius, *Meditations* (2011), 8.12.

13. Cicero, *De Natura Deorum*, 2.57–58.

14. Cicero, *Nature of Gods*, 2.57–58.

"thought" and "what is useful." In this mode, our impulses and desires, if consistent with the universal rational nature, express the whole "mind of the universe."[15]

This collection of passages provides a further reminder of the dual aspects of hormê in Stoicism. Hormê has an objective quality in being the same presence in all individual creatures. It nevertheless also manifests with subjective qualities, in that hormê occurs slightly differently in each creature's specific expressions of impulses. The connection between our individual rational nature and the ordering of the universe that the Stoics call rationality, is duly emphasized via these tandem modes of our hormê. Any apparent individualized causing of action is a trace of the universe's overall causing of individual action. Because this causing of action derives from the world's rational ordering for the Stoics, Anthony Long defines the impulses produced by hormê as not only prompting action generally, but more importantly as prompting through us the world's systematized actions.[16]

Hormê therefore comprises our drives toward actions that are embedded within an overall causal order. Despite this systematic definition of hormê, the apparently personal or individual nature of such drives re-emerges when we explore what constitutes the most primary mode of our hormê for the Stoics. Cicero does much of our investigative work on this topic when engaging in discussion the Stoic follower, Cato the Younger. We use the Younger title to distinguish Cato from his great-grandfather, the Roman senator and historian, Cato the Elder. Cato the Younger is of interest given that apart from also being a Roman politician, he was also an advocate and commentator of the Stoics.

When considering the purposes or ends of our various impulses, Cato explains that for "Zeno and the Stoics" self-preservation is the most important. Self-preservation is the basis of our rational nature in this Stoic view and is the fundamental feature of existence toward which our hormê impels us to act. An indication that self-preservation is our primary hormê or impulse to act for the early Stoics is apparent according to Cato when we see it in animals, including humans, at birth:

> Every animal, as soon as it is born . . . is concerned with itself, and takes care to preserve itself. It favours its constitution and whatever preserves its constitution.[17]

15. Cicero, *Nature of Gods*, 2.58.
16. Long, "Stoic Concept of Evil," 337.
17. Cicero, *On Moral Ends*, 3.16.

Just as we naturally incline toward preserving ourselves, likewise we tend to avoid apparent harms. Our behaviors and those of other creatures see us "recoil" from what we encounter in the world that we believe could cause our own "destruction." Through the discussion between Cicero and Cato we learn that Zeno justified his belief that self-preservation must be our primary impulse by observing it even in infants. Cato tells us of the Stoic view that infants naturally reject things that suggest danger to their well-being, even when they have never experienced such things. An infant's instinctive preference for things that seem to contribute to their ongoing existence exhibits for Zeno that humans naturally "value their own constitution."[18]

Zeno is not the only early Stoic to hold this perspective. Through Diogenes Laërtius we believe that Chrysippus, the next leader of the school, likewise explained in his work *On Ends* that "the first inclination an animal has is to protect itself, as nature takes an interest in it from the beginning."[19] Later in this chapter we will engage the Roman-era Stoic, Hierocles, who evokes both Zeno's and Chrysippus' assertions in his *Element of Ethics* when stating of our first impulse that

> each animal does what contributes to its own preservation, avoiding every attack even from afar and contriving to remain unharmed by dangers, while it leaps toward whatever brings safety and provides for itself from far and wide whatever tends toward its survival.[20]

Do you notice that in these accounts of self-preservation the Stoics refer to all animals, human and nonhuman? We have of course seen that in the Stoic view, nonhuman animals do not have the rationality that humans do. As we will soon review, while the Stoics believe all creatures embody the impulse to care for themselves and their self-preservation, humans do this in rationally different ways to other animals.[21]

In considering this impulse toward self-preservation, what we are discussing are concepts concerning our relationship with the world that the Stoics use the term *oikeiôsis* to describe. Oikeiôsis involves plural layers of meaning, the most prominent of which attend to how we identify ourselves in each other. While that theme will occupy us more thoroughly soon, one

---

18. Cicero, *On Moral Ends*, 3.16.

19. Diogenes Laërtius, *Lives and Opinions*, 7.52.

20. Hierocles, *Hierocles the Stoic*, 19; taken from Hierocles, *Elements of Ethics*, 1.6.55.

21. Long and Sedley (*Hellenistic Philosophers*, 352) clarify that in Stoicism we do not orient toward self-preservation because we are animals, but that nonhuman animals and human animals each follow their natural and appropriate behavior to self-preserve.

aspect of the meaning of oikeiôsis that is immediately relevant is its reference to how we rationally appraise the world around us. In this evaluation of the world, we are said to ask whether something about the world that we encounter fits who we are, will benefit us, and is worth appropriating or integrating as part of our lives.[22] Where hormê therefore denotes our rationally oriented impulse of action toward the world, our oikeiôsis concerns how when we act, we assess whether the aspect of the world toward which we act is appropriate for our rational nature.

This process or activity, categorized under oikeiôsis, is for the Stoics innate[23] to all animals and further explains why we primarily behave in self-caring or self-preserving ways. For animals that lack the human degree of rationality, their oikeiôsis will extend only to their bodily being.[24] This is consistent with what we have reviewed previously regarding the purely material bases for much of nonhuman existence. For humans though, we evaluate the world around us according to our rational being, whereby as Cicero tells us of the Stoic account, the "task" of rational "wisdom is to be aiding and preserving both body and mind."[25]

Because we are primarily rational beings, our oikeiôsis defaults toward what accords with our rational nature. Where pleasure is conversely occupied with sensation and feelings rather than with reason, it cannot comprise our primary oikeiôsis. Cato's commentary conveys this hierarchical distinction between self-preservation and pleasure in which the former is believed to be much closer to our rational nature than the latter, reflecting that "most Stoics do not believe that pleasure should be ranked among the natural principles" or our "primary objects."[26] Diogenes Laërtius also conveys that for Chrysippus and other Stoics it is "false" to interpret that either a human or nonhuman animal's first impulse concerns pleasure.[27]

22. See where Brennan (*Stoic Life*, 156) describes this as our impulse that is concerned with preserving the thing that we identify as ourselves.

23. Long, "Stoic Psychology," 352.

24. See how Hierocles (*Hierocles the Stoic*, 15–21; taken from Hieocles, *Elements of Ethics* 1.3.10–7.55) presents the different stages of oikeiôsis through which humans and other animals progress.

25. Cicero, *On Moral Ends*, 4.16. Later in this work, Cicero (*On Moral Ends*, 4.34) also tells us that for the Stoics the "ultimate" position is to be inclined toward self-preserving "all parts" of the self, encompassing our bodily *and* mental features.

26. Cicero, *On Moral Ends*, 3.17.

27. Diogenes Laërtius, *Lives and Opinions*, 7.52. Numerous modern commentaries recognize this about the Stoics. See Annas, *Platonic Ethics*, 147; Becker, *New Stoicism*, 124–37; Graver, *Stoicism and Emotion*, 32; Inwood, *Ethics in Early Stoicism*, 192; Reydams-Schils, "Authority and Agency," 318; Schofield, "Stoic Ethics," 247; White, *Stoic Ethics*, 145.

Distinguishing that self-preservation has rational importance over pleasure for the Stoics coheres with the associated impression that hormê, our impulse to act, occurs in accordance with an entire universe's rational nature and ordering.[28] Pleasures on the other hand, by deriving from sensory phenomena, are contrarily occupied with particular or localized bodily states that are not entirely up to us. We might recall in this regard Epictetus' situating of the body when categorizing what is versus is not within our control. Conversely for the Stoics, self-preservation arises from being conscious of what is up to us, what is in our control, which is a mind that by default must be aware of more than simply our individual self or personal experiences. An individual's internal rational function is linked to and results from a source beyond the self, instead finding its origins and orientations in the universe's rationalized order. Our self-preserving hormê is universally directed and distributed.

This subordination of the importance of bodily pleasure does not discount the body entirely from self-preserving inclinations though. While we must evaluate which aspects of the world accord with our rational nature, there is also a bodily element of our rational existence. We are still physical, bodily beings for the Stoics after all. We have additionally seen in our preceding considerations that this physical material of ourselves is systematically or rationally ordered bodily material. Plutarch conveys an all-encompassing Chrysippean sense of self-preservation in *On Stoic Self-Contradictions* that is useful to us here, describing how we have a "natural," and therefore rational, "congeniality to ourselves" in which what is congenial is sensorily physical because it includes a "sensation or perception of what is congenial."[29]

The body with which we live day to day exemplifies the rationally interconnected physical order for the Stoics. If anything about our physicality contradicted this unified order, Zeno's originary principles for Stoicism would deem that the body must be "rejected."[30] All the bodily parts that perpetuate across generations of our species, such as our limbs and organs, must as Cato describes have been attributed to us by rational nature because they were of use.[31] While certain body parts might appear to be purely aesthetically decorative for the Stoics, such parts must actually be pervaded by the interconnecting system of universal rationality—what we might in the current day describe as the universe's physical laws. As we have seen,

28. Cicero, *On Moral Ends*, 4.32–33.
29. Plutarch, *Moralia*, 8:1038.
30. Cicero, *On Moral Ends*, 3.20.
31. Cicero, *On Moral Ends*, 3.18.

the Stoic universe is not random in construction. Every part plays a role in an overall purpose, an all-encompassing function that extends even to our bodies. It is rationally self-preserving to remember that such bodies are not entirely within our control, however this does not dismiss all importance of the body. The point is to always situate how we act with and through our bodies, within a universal system of connections and conditions.

As our hormê directs us toward what about the world serves our self-preservation, so Cato informs us that for the Stoics we undertake "appropriate actions."[32] "Appropriate" is a term said to be used by Chrysippus in his *On Ends*, concerning our predisposition for preserving our "own" well-being and "existence" and reflecting our "consciousness of this" preservation.[33] Pleasure is contingent, circumstantial, compulsive, and therefore external to our control for the Stoics. We simply sensorily *feel* pleasure. Self-preservation inversely is an internal, rational impulse on which we can reflect. We can internally control, as in rationally adjudicate on, our decisions about what in the world is appropriate for our self-preservation. Because of this rational condition of self-preservation, Cato notes that for the Stoics, thoughts and acts that are "appropriate" must have been designed for our nature.[34] If self-preserving thoughts and acts are in accordance with our nature, the conclusion is that they are worthwhile to exercise "in their own right."[35] This coheres with the Stoic observation with which we should by now be familiar, that the purpose of human rational animals, our end in itself, is to live according to our rational nature.

We have considered that the source for our hormê, our oikeiôsis, and our self-preserving inclination, is a universally ordered and shared rationality. Despite this recognition of a common origin for what then becomes our individual, self-preserving natures, the emphasis in these opening sections of this chapter has been on the priority of self-preservation for *individuals*. Kindred themes regarding self-preservation have not been entirely absent. We have of course considered how for the Stoics we derive the self-preserving impulse by each being a part of a rationally ordered, universal system. Our discussions of our activations of that impulse however have focused on how innate it is to us as individuals.

Complementary insights into the communal activations and orientations of our individual self-preserving tendencies nevertheless lurk in everything we have covered to this point. These insights will more prominently

32. Cicero, *On Moral Ends*, 3.23.

33. Diogenes Laërtius, *Lives and Opinions*, 7.52.

34. Cicero, *On Moral Ends*, 3.22.

35. Cicero, *On Moral Ends*, 3.17.

frame our discussions in the next section, as we explore how people's self-preserving motivations expand beyond concerns about their apparent subjective limits or ends.

Self-Preservation Is a Communal Outcome

At the outset of this chapter I briefly considered how an animal's tendencies toward preserving its own existence might be situated within a shared drive or genetic coding that is common to all members of its species. We speculated that the purpose of this shared drive could be to counter the threat of extinction. An individual creature's preference for self-preservation in this regard might point to concerns well beyond the individual themselves.

Cicero will likewise ask whether our self-preserving hormê is not simply concerned with each of us prolonging our own individual, organic, material, bodily, heart-beating existence and well-being. He instead reflects on whether our first impulse of self-preservation and self-care primarily serves broader, less individualized or personalized, outcomes. While this theme is present in his discussion with Cato about the early Stoicisms of Zeno and Chrysippus, in *On Duties* Cicero also presents somewhat of his own argument. I qualify this as "somewhat" Cicero's own argument, given how clearly it is informed by the Stoic principles that we have reviewed. Here Cicero discusses the collective prosperities or outcomes that arise from what otherwise rudimentarily appear to be self-interested, self-preserving actions.

Cicero indicates that because all humans derive the self-preserving tendency from the same source, which is what the Stoics refer to as a universal rationality, then when each of us exercises that self-preserving rationality we are not doing so as self-determining, autonomous individuals. We are enacting something about the world in which we all share, and from which we have together been "sparked." Because our rationalities are common, what concerns us individually concerns everyone else too. His eloquent description of this shared investment is that what is of interest to one individual is "identical" to what is of interest to other people, and therefore is the collective interest of an entire population.[36]

When we are motivated to act in a self-preserving manner, our personal interest is also the impersonal interest of an entire population according to this view. By acting in a self-preserving way, we are acting rationally. By acting rationally, we are living in accordance not just with our own interests

36. Cicero, *De Officiis*, 3.26. See also how the translation by Newton (in Cicero, *On Duties*, 3.26) describes this as how "the utility of each individual and everyone as a whole is the same."

but also with the interests of other rational beings. This mutual coherence emerges because it is in others' interests to live rationally too. Cicero duly posits that because of this inherent kinship, each Stoic individual is "bound to their fellow-citizens"[37] in any particular population, and that these localized bonds are expressions of a universally "common fellowship of the human race."[38] If we ever interpret that we think or act in ways that orient toward individualized or personalized outcomes, benefits, or purposes, we ignore that we are made in the form of a "common good" and a "human fellowship."[39] To think individually is in this regard to think collectively, in that personal advantages can only result from mutually conditioned prosperities to begin with. Cicero here channels what Cato Stoically imparts about benefits being shared, in describing how our general understanding must shift to realize that "the benefit of each individual and the benefit of all together should be the same."[40]

Never is Cicero more explicit on this point than when he situates our self-preservation firmly in the realm of this fellowship. His position, now clearly cohering with what Cato is informing him of regarding Stoic virtues, states that the self-preserving compulsion is where someone's actions are done "for the sake of others beside themselves." Cato in turn is described as conveying that for the Stoics, self-preservation is an impulse generated through communities of the rational who share the same interest, where individuals participate in "bonds of mutual aid" that lead us to "form unions, societies and states."[41] Collaboration is our rational nature, provided that what is of interest to the collaborative entity is rational. What is most rational, as we have covered, is to be aware that we are interconnected parts of a whole. We can protect that rational feature of ourselves by exercising it in wholly shared ways, meaning that the collective or group should always have precedence for us over "any single individual" or "particular person."[42] Given that our primary impulse is toward our rational self-preservation, and our rational self-preservation is conditioned by identifying with our systematically interconnected and communal status, we are said to always

---

37. Cicero, *De Officiis*, 3.28. Cicero's discussion here incorporates a critical response to those who deny the existence or nature of mutual fellowship.

38. Cicero, *On Duties* (1991), 3.28.

39. Cicero, *De Officiis*, 3.26.

40. Cicero, *On Duties* (1991), 3.26.

41. Cicero, *De Finibus Bonorum*, 3.63.

42. Cicero, *On Moral Ends*, 3.64.

"prefer the common advantage to our own,"[43] or "the welfare of all above the welfare of individuals."[44]

We can now appreciate that the theme of self-preservation, beyond relating to personal benefits and stakes, in Stoicism presents with communal and collective commitments. There are examples of modern Stoic scholarship which recognize that when the Stoics discuss self-preservation, the direction of this impulse is not restricted to or preoccupied with the rational individual.[45] The scientific views that I briefly touched on at this chapter's outset already suggest that an individual's well-being relates to the preservation of a group. This Stoic notion, though, that our self-preserving inclinations primarily direct toward something other than the self is still surprising. We might even ask to what extent there is room for the individual self at all in this account, if the conception of the self is of an entity that is always directing themselves toward the well-being of something greater than themselves.

This question of the individualized nature of our self-preserving tendencies is an important one, given that our acquisition of such tendencies is automatic and even robotic. We might typically think that as we become more experienced in life we also educate ourselves about how to look after ourselves. Our tendencies for our own self-preservation develop and mature. As we have reviewed though, there is a naturally innate and assigned quality of the tendency toward self-preservation for the early Stoics. Through Cicero's recounting of his discussion with Cato, we are told the Stoics observe that infants have no experience with destructive things yet nonetheless often exhibit an aversion to such things.[46] While therefore we do each develop in individually different ways, in that we are each exposed to particular environmentally specific, self-preserving habits as we mature, we do not have to actively seek and acquire a self-preserving nature.[47] Our self-preserving hormê or impulse is in-built from birth, it is our primary way of being rational, our primary way of being embedded within an ordered system or universe. We can reflect on it, be conscious of it, and recognize it in the behaviors and actions of other humans, however we have not individually chosen to be self-preserving entities. We will return to the topic of our recognition in others of rationally self-preserving tendencies later in

43. Cicero, *De Finibus Bonorum*, 3.64.

44. Cicero, *On Moral Ends*, 3.64.

45. Annas, *Morality*, 265–66; Byers, "Augustine's Debt," 59–60; Evans, "Stoic Mayor," 89; Irvine, *Good Life*, 129; Long, "Stoic Philosophers," 23; Miller, *Spinoza*, 107.

46. Cicero, *On Moral Ends*, 3.16.

47. Cicero, *On Moral Ends*, 3.16.

this chapter, when expanding on how our rational evaluation of the world around us, our oikeiôsis, reflects our mutual bonds for the Stoics.

Given the emphatic equation of self-preservation with rationality, we must not for the Stoics reduce our conception of self-preservation to the prevention of loss of physical health or life. Stoic self-preservation is not simply about staying alive. A notable example of this presents in Cicero's assertion that in certain circumstances, death serves the Stoic ends of self-preservation better than remaining alive would. How could this be? Would death not be the opposite of self-preservation?

Self-Preservation Means Remaining Rational, not Remaining Alive

The answer to these questions concerns the priority the Stoics give to living with a rational consciousness. As I have furthermore detailed, the most rational consciousness that we can have is one that appreciates that as individuals we are just parts of a whole system. If nothing is more important than living rationally, then nothing could be worse for the Stoics than living irrationally. Dying in a way that is rational is preferable to living in a way that is irrational. Suicide is in this regard even sometimes self-preserving for the ancient Stoics, if through taking their own life a person avoids descending into an irrational existence. Living irrationally might, as just one example, involve perpetually being controlled by emotions, particularly adverse emotions, that an external world of contingent things and events prompts. Consistent with the communal themes embedded within Stoicism's attention on self-preservation, concerns about living emotionally and irrationally are not simply attending to an individual's welfare. Living irrationally would more broadly concern the effect on collective prosperity, because like our fellow creatures, we are supposed to be living in accordance with a collective and communal rational order. It is in their interest that we live rationally, and complementarily in our individual interest that others do likewise. Rationality is mutually shared.

Cicero and Cato's discussion on suicide describes it rather alarmingly at times as somewhat of a duty, provided the context is appropriate.[48] Diogenes Laërtius similarly recognizes aspects of Zeno's thought which posit that if circumstances demand it, an irrationally afflicted individual will exercise a "well-reasoned suicide" in order to serve all their fellow humans, and in particular their closest associates.[49]

48. Cicero, *On Duties* (2016), 1.112.
49. Diogenes Laërtius in Long and Sedley, *Hellenistic Philosophers*, 66H; taken

The topic of Cato's eventual own suicide illustrates this logic for Cicero, who does not characterize Cato's death in terms of the tragic loss of a life.[50] Cicero rather describes his suicide as the Stoic exemplification of self-preservation. At the time of Cato's suicide, he was under extreme pressure to live irrationally. Julius Caesar, his political rival, was reported to have had an inescapable power over both him and aspects of the Roman world. The required subservience to what Cato perceived to be a source of immeasurable irrationality, would have compromised his capacity to live and serve others with a rational mentality:

> Nature had bestowed upon Cato an incredible resoluteness, which he himself had strengthened with ceaseless constancy, and he had always persevered in the counsel he proposed and supported, he had to die rather than look upon the face of a tyrant.[51]

Much context is required when encountering these Stoic assertions around suicide, whereby it is necessary that I qualify their apparent directness. You should not read the preceding characterizations of suicide as instructions or directives to suicide whenever you feel disempowered or emotionally unsettled. This is not the Stoic intention. What instead Stoicism is more productively providing in my view through such voices is a rhetorical device that demands that we each live rationally if we are not already. The Stoics do not want you to suicide at all, they want you to live rationally.

While the Stoics prioritize communal outcomes for our self-preserving tendencies, Cato's suicide provides an example via which the Stoics incorporate an individual's circumstances into evaluations of how we each cohere with a rationally ordered world. Or in other words, general rules do not encompass absolutely everything for the Stoics. As Cicero notes in *On Duties*, it is a moral imperative that each citizen lives according to their specific rational "characteristics."[52] To self-preserve is to each maintain our particular expression of a universal rational nature, to live according to our own hormê, in the context of a kindred, rationally ordered, world.

---

from *SVF*, 3.757.

50. Marcus Aurelius (*Meditations* [2011], 10.8) later also critiques the notion of staying alive just for the sake of it. Self-preservation involves attending to rational rather than simply biological outcomes, where to "suffer the lacerations and defilements of such a way of life, is the part of one who is utterly insensitive and clings to mere existence, like the half-devoured beast-fighters in the arena."

51. Cicero, *On Duties* (2016), 1.112. Seneca (*Letters on Ethics*, 104.32) similarly characterizes Cato's suicide as an action of self-preserving rationality, defying the impositions of unjust rulers by dying "by his own decree."

52. Cicero, *On Duties* (2016), 1.110.

Most definitely accordingly to Cicero's account, our rational nature for the Stoics is more than self-serving because it reflects our role in a community of mutually beneficial interests. We each though have our own unique perspectives and circumstances, and these are not forgotten when we offer ourselves to collective well-being. Yes, our primary rational nature means that we co-exist with a population of identically ordered or oriented people. The individual's view or circumstance is not lost in this sea of communal instincts and intentions though, in that the specific rational decisions and outcomes that are appropriate for one person might not be appropriate for another. Cicero speaks to this point directly in noting that of Cato, while "one person ought to resolve to kill" themselves, other people in their own situations, or even in the "same situation ought not."[53]

As I have indicated, Cicero's reflections on suicide are in this regard not primarily about suicide or even physical death. They instead offer a meditation on how we each commit to living rationally, and the positive effects that has on our own lives. Having a consciousness of our interconnected rational status as an individual is often portrayed as a duty or responsibility. Indeed, much of the dialogue between Cicero and Cato on these points is taken from Cicero's work called *On Duties*. As we have seen with Epictetus, Marcus, and others, Cicero implores us to remember that when thinking and acting as apparent individuals, we remain aware that "the interest of society is the interest of the individual."[54] Being conscious of the identical nature of individual and social interests also means though that we each individually benefit from communal prosperity. Where our impulse is the collective, so we prosper individually from being parts of the collective outcome.

The grander scope of Stoic self-preservation goes beyond maintaining the physical health or function of individual bodies. If having a healthy body and being physically well cohere with living in accordance with our common rationality, then certainly it would be self-preserving to ensure our bodily health. The priority regarding our self-preserving well-being though is our consciousness of our common rational existence. If our self-preserving outlook concerns simply our own physical constitution, or our own health goals, we are not Stoically self-preserving. Self-preservation manifests and is felt communally because self-preservation is rational and being rational requires the consciousness that we are each a part in a greater

---

53. Cicero, *On Duties* (2016), 1.112. See Griffin ("Philosophy," 64–77) for an analysis of Cato's suicide in the context of Roman Stoic conceptions of the self. Sorabji (*Emotion and Peace*, 45) rightly notes that Cato's suicide might not in Cicero's estimation be right for others in the same circumstances.

54. Cicero, *De Officiis*, 3.27. Or as Newton (in Cicero, *On Duties* [2016], 3.27) translates: "there are things that are useful to everyone that everyone shares in common."

whole order. None of us originated, or ever live that imperative, separately or individually.

To this point in the chapter, we have learned that our individual or personal self-preservation is a shared function. This is the Stoic *theory*. By now moving onto the perspectives of the later Roman Stoic, Hierocles, we will consider a set of interrelated techniques and methods via which such theory might be practically enacted. This is an important next step, given that as noted in our initial discussions in this book, Stoic first principles mandate the practical application of philosophy.

Living More Closely with Others

There seemingly could be no more conventionally communal, practical application of Stoic philosophy, than in the guidance it offers for how to interact with each other. Stoic philosophy proposes an order to the world, and correlatively there is in an everyday regard a strict set of orders and rules that seems to govern how we interpersonally behave. Those rules determine that we typically act and interact differently with people we are "closer to" or more familiar with (such as certain family members and friends), than we do with people we have never met.

Such rules relate to the Stoic interpretation of the world as a unified, ordered, system and community. It is via this theme of universal sociality that we are, however, now going to consider how the Stoics destabilize the just indicated rules that exist around interpersonal familiarity. It is these rules, with which we are instilled from an early age, that irrationally restrict and localize our impressions of interpersonal connection according to the Stoics. Consistent with this chapter's theme, it could for the Stoics instead be more self-preserving to expand our interpersonal horizons.

This reflection will concern the different kinds and degrees of affection and openness that we offer to people. Our primary discussant will be the second century Stoic philosopher, Hierocles. Not much is known about Hierocles. We do have near-complete versions of his text *Elements of Ethics* though, as well as the ancient commentator Stobaeus' extracts from Hierocles' *On Appropriate* Acts, and some assorted fragments.

Of specific interest to us is where Hierocles discusses how we act and behave toward members of our family, and how significantly that differs from our behaviors and actions with the rest of the population. Stobaeus conveys how Hierocles' essay, "How Should One Behave toward One's Relatives?" graphically represents this comparison via a series of concentric circles that increase in size. The people we know well are in the smallest circle closest to us, whereas the people we do not know at all are in largest circles furthest away from us.[55]

The scope of this representation is not just to provide an image of our *interpersonal* relations though. The closest relation that we have, indicated by our most inner circle, concerns not our relations with other people but with our own mind. This circle is sometimes represented as two circles, the most inner circle denoting our relationship with our mind, the next encompassing circle representing our mental relationship with our body. Once we get to the third circle we see the integration of our fellow humans, this circle containing our immediate family members, "parents, siblings, spouse, and children." The circles that proceed, increasing in size and distance from the center of the inner circle, respectively include members of our local tribe or community, then people from neighboring towns, then "fellow citizens" from the same country or culture, before finally we reach the circle of all "human beings."[56]

Hierocles is not the only thinker associated with Stoicism who categorizes our interpersonal relations in this way. Cicero, for example, offers a similar model in his work *On Duties*. As I have indicated, Cicero is not a part of the Stoic school. A significant bond with Stoicism is however clear in *On Duties* when he recognizes Stoicism's influence in his own views and dialogues.[57] In this text Cicero discusses the seemingly abstract notion of what he calls the "association"[58] or "fellowship of the entire human race."[59] Indeed for Cicero, our tendencies toward "fellowship and society" are traceable to the "ultimate" purpose of our natures.[60] As we have just seen with Hierocles, Cicero also emphasizes our ties with our closest relations. These closest relations form the basis of the entire fellowship that radiates among humans, in that our sense of our connections with others is "preserved if the closer someone is to you the more kindness you confer" on them.[61] Cicero's presentation of our interpersonal bonds presents most of the same characteristics as Hierocles' cascading structure, moving from the widespread fellowship between all humans to

---

55. Stobaeus in Hierocles, *Hierocles the Stoic*, 91; taken from *Anthology*, 4.84.23.

56. Stobaeus in Hierocles, *Hierocles the Stoic*, 91; taken from *Anthology*, 4.84.23.

57. Cicero particularly emphasizes the importance of the work of the middle era Stoic, Panaetius of Rhodes, and his book also called *On Duties*.

58. Cicero, *On Duties* (2016), 1.50.

59. Cicero, *On Duties* (1991), 1.50.

60. Cicero, *De Officiis* (1928), 1.50.

61. Cicero, *On Duties* (1991), 1.50.

a closer one of the same race, tribe and tongue, through which humans are bound strongly to one another. More intimate still is that of the same city, as citizens have many things that are shared with one another . . . A tie narrower still is that of the fellowship between relations: moving from that vast fellowship of the human race we end up with a confined and limited one.[62]

The similarities between Hierocles' and Cicero's models are readily apparent. They both recognize our closer relationships with our most immediate family members and peers, while also positing a fellowship with the entirety of humanity. This does not mean that they are identical conceptions though. Cicero will later add to his model the detail that nothing transcends the importance of our relationship with our nation state or "commonwealth."[63] This detail is not a feature of Hierocles' structure. Cicero will indeed then even trump this relationship with another level that includes our bonds with the gods, describing how "duties are owed first to god, secondly to one's country, thirdly to one's parents and then down the scale to others."[64] You might notice how our duty to ourselves, to our personal outcomes and individual identities, is not even mentioned. This does not mean that individualized outcomes are unrecognized. It just reflects, as we have seen from the Stoics themselves, that individualized ends are far from our rational priorities. What is individually rewarding manifests, or is made possible, during a grander sense of servitude to, or implication in, the whole from which individuals and parts manifest.

We have addressed how this servitude or duty to the whole might even involve sacrificing our lives. What is at stake in such an act for the Stoics is an appreciation of our role in a rationally interconnected whole. Such interconnection is better maintained, according to certain accounts that we reviewed earlier, by a well-reasoned exit from life than it is by a less-reasoned ongoing existence. I have qualified this point with the clarification that the Stoics do not actually want anyone to suicide. They instead intend for everyone to live rationally. The best way to live rationally is to live with a consciousness of oneself as a part in a whole, and to correlatively contextualize everything about ourselves—our thoughts, actions, identities—as derivative of, or borrowed from, that whole. Robin Hard's recent translation of Epictetus' *Discourses* interestingly translates this kind of directive as where we as individual "parts yield to the whole."[65] This yielding does

---

62. Cicero, *On Duties* (1991), 1.53.

63. Cicero, *On Duties* (2016), 1.57.

64. Cicero, *On Duties* (1991), 1.160.

65. Epictetus, *Discourses* (2014), 4.7.7.

not mean foregoing the possibility of our individual or personal interests. We have seen after all that the interests of the whole and the interests of the individual are identical for much of Stoic theory. Such individualized interests can only manifest though during the activation of the interests of the whole, of which we are each a part. Preserving ourselves means preserving this bond with the source of ourselves by always orienting ourselves toward that source of ourselves. The Stoic sense of self-preservation is thus complex, intertwined with what appears to be self-sacrificial demands, but that in fact represents a wisdom of how we are universally produced and ordered individuals.

This universally systematized shaping of ourselves does not mean that we should entirely discount the reality of our localized relations. Such relations must however always be contextualized within the world's grander web of all rational beings. Despite how distinctly Cicero distinguishes our different kinds of relations with the various categories of people in our lives, he is also receptive to how our immediately surrounding circumstances will force us to reprioritize our respective duties with people. Someone who you do not really know, might suddenly need your support in an emergency for example. This could take precedence over your being able to immediately exercise the bonds you share with your closest family members by attending a dinner they have organized. The mutual connections between all humans surface here, indicating that there will be occasions where our most pressing obligations or relations can be "to a stranger."[66]

Cicero's evaluation of our duties to those outside our most inner circles is thus clear. Evidencing Cicero's Stoic influences, this notion perpetuates what in Stoicism we know as *cosmopolitanism*—the belief that every human in the world is part of a single community. If you subscribe to cosmopolitanism, you hold that the universe is one society, in which we are all fellow citizens. We have seen elements of this view presented in the previous chapter by Marcus Aurelius' conception of the entire world as a single community, not to mention in Cleanthes' and other Stoics' descriptions of the world as one city. Such accounts have impressed on us the interpretation that with a universal fellowship comes associated universal responsibilities, inferring that you and every other person share reciprocal duties.

It is really through Hierocles' Stoicism however that we see this concept of cosmopolitanism come to life. Hierocles, as we have raised, studies how we relate to the people in our various circles of familiarity. Given how differently we associate with people from each circle, part of Hierocles'

66. Cicero, *On Duties* (1991), 1.51.

considerations concerns the question of what constitutes the proper way to treat or interact with the people of any circle?

The question of "proper function" emerges in Stoicism as early as Zeno. Diogenes Laërtius informs us of this when reporting on Zeno's sense of the related concept of *kathēkonta*.[67] This will be the last of the technical terms that we encounter in this chapter, a journey that has taken us from hormê, to oikeiôsis, to now kathēkonta.

Kathēkonta refers to the acts and functions that are "appropriate" or "reasonable" for us. Such acts or functions can be rationally determined to fit or be "proper" for the entity that expresses them, whether that entity is human, nonhuman animal, or even plant. Diogenes describes how for Zeno, kathēkonta in the human regard represents our "activity appropriate to constitutions that accord with nature" and reason.[68] In this definition, the Stoic correlation of an individual's rationality with an overall universal order again becomes apparent, as we are impelled to practically enact our own choices in ways that accord with our grander nature.[69] The functions that are appropriate to our nature are in this regard not exactly "ours," but rather are adopted from and practically enacted within a universally rationalized system.

One way in which we practically enact kathēkonta for Hierocles concerns how we treat people or act toward them. This involves not just people in our inner circles but all kinds of people. Most interestingly and adventurously during this process, Hierocles considers what constitutes acting properly to people in our outer circles, the people with whom we are not well acquainted or do not know at all?[70]

Possibly surprisingly, acting properly, which means acting in accordance with our rational nature, in this context for Hierocles does not mean obeying established protocols of politeness or what is normalized as proper. The imperative is not to maintain a courteous distance between ourselves and others. Such established rules instruct, for example, that we avoid

---

67. Diogenes Laërtius in Long and Sedley, *Hellenistic Philosophers*, 59C; taken from *SVF*, 3.493.

68. Diogenes Laërtius in Long and Sedley, *Hellenistic Philosophers*, 59C; taken from *SVF*, 3.493. Brennan ("Reasonable Impressions," 318–34) provides a comprehensive analysis of how the Stoics define kathēkonta, attending to what constitutes kathēkonta's reasonable functions.

69. Sedley ("Stoic-Platonist Debate," 128–52) reviews the differences between Stoic and Platonic interpretations of the practical enactment of appropriate or proper functions.

70. Stobaeus in Hierocles, *Hierocles the Stoic*, 89–91; taken from *Anthology*, 4.84.20.

demanding the attention, time, or conversation, of people we do not know well.

Hierocles instead wants us to create closer relations with these people with whom we are otherwise relatively unfamiliar. We should actively seek out, in Hierocles' opinion, people that we do not know well and get to know them. Doing this will mean that we can properly activate and exercise our rational predisposition toward cosmopolitan life and its universally inclusive population. As we have seen with Cicero, this kind of approach might require inviting "strangers," as well as other people that we do not know very well, more thoroughly into our lives. Hierocles even argues that a properly developed Stoic personality has the responsibility to bring closer those people from our outer circles. Our interactions with those people should reflect the more intimate relations and interactions that we share with people from our inner circles. The imperative is to "draw" the people from all our circles "together," by converting people from being members of our outside circles into people that we know better as members of our inside circles.[71]

Numerous current scholars provide appraisals of the intentions of this contraction of our circles. One such example is the commentary of Malin Grahn-Wilder, who posits that Hierocles offers the most well-known argument there is for Stoicism's "ethic" of "cosmopolitanism."[72] Cosmopolitanism, remember, refers to the belief that every human is part of the one community. Grahn-Wilder recognizes a certain egalitarian imperative accordingly in Hierocles' demand to reduce the differences in how we treat our fellow humans. Hierocles wants to coerce an "equality between all humans," where we are impelled to act as "ethical agents," as well as required to be open to others' requests to be closer to them. This latter function means that with such openness we are not only moral agents in our actions, but also in how we make ourselves available as the "objects of moral action" for others.[73] All the hallmarks of Stoic mutual and social responsibilities manifest accordingly.

While Hierocles encourages us to equalize our social relations with our fellow humans, he understands that this is not our normal approach. It can in fact feel strange and counterintuitive, he appreciates, to approach people that we do not know in new ways. He duly warns that it will be quite an "effort" at first to "assimilate" strangers into our closer circles. This will require a shift in how we view each other, given that it seems natural that

71. Stobaeus in Hierocles, *Hierocles the Stoic*, 91; taken from *Anthology*, 4.84.23.

72. Grahn-Wilder, *Gender and Sexuality*, 277.

73. Grahn-Wilder, *Gender and Sexuality*, 277.

when we are not related to someone, we instinctively feel less "goodwill" toward them.[74]

He strongly holds though that it would not be consistent with our rational natures to ignore our commitments to, and bonds with, all other people. Stoic understandings of human life radiate around a belief in our collective existence, and for Hierocles this reflects a universal communal instinct in all humans. Even if the idea does not seem natural regarding bringing strangers into our communal existences, for Hierocles it is an expression of our shared rationalities with which we are born, meaning that every single human is "naturally disposed to community."[75]

In explaining the day-to-day mechanics of how a community manifests, Hierocles points to marriage and family. His sense of what is naturally communal about family becomes apparent when he describes of our immediate family members, how when we are born, nature has provided us with a collection of instant collaborators.[76] In going beyond the immediate family though, Hierocles proposes a technique that can assist us with practically enacting our cosmopolitan natures. The ethos of this approach is undoubtedly well-intentioned. Its application sounds odd though. This is because this technique asks us to call our cousins "brothers," our uncles "fathers," and our aunts "mothers."[77] He presents this as a stepping-stone to the grander task of developing family-like relations and interactions with people we have never met. During that process we can begin to refer to people in our local communities, to whom we are not related at all, by familial terms. We can even expand this broadened sense of family to people outside our local communities.

How should we evaluate the practical utility of this instruction? The actions and purposes are easy to understand, telling us not to treat people as entirely unconnected to us, but rather via language to build an entire human community of closer relations. Such a practice is not absolutely alien to us in the present day in fact. A word in Chinese Mandarin for aunt (ayi) is commonly used to address females older than oneself to whom one is not related.[78] The Philippine language similarly has expanded the use of the terms for one's blood-related aunt (tita) and uncle (tito) to include people from older generations to whom one is not related.[79] On this topic we must

74. Stobaeus in Hierocles, *Hierocles the Stoic*, 93; taken from *Anthology*, 4.84.23.

75. Stobaeus in Hierocles, *Hierocles the Stoic*, 73; taken from *Anthology*, 4.67.21.

76. Stobaeus in Hierocles, *Hierocles the Stoic*, 89; taken from *Anthology*, 4.84.20.

77. Stobaeus in Hierocles, *Hierocles the Stoic*, 93; taken from *Anthology*, 4.84.23.

78. Chen et al., *Chinese Primer*, 78.

79. Bankston, "Filipino Americans," 199.

also consider the prevalent use of the term "brother," which in numerous contexts and societies is applied informally to indicate a close or respectful association with someone who is not one's actual sibling, a usage that seemingly has biblical and theological legacies.[80]

Through more liberally using the titles we otherwise reserve for our closest relatives, Hierocles believes a contraction of all our circles will begin that will reduce feelings of distance in the relationships that we share with others.[81] Hierocles even broadcasts the moral obligation of such a pursuit, describing how it is something every rational individual "should" fulfil. If we exercise the contraction of our circles we will live with greater "fairness"[82] in his view, where if something is to be truly fair it must not simply be a theoretical discussion. Consistent with Stoic imperatives around the practical action and realization of philosophical ideas, fair ideas must be enacted.

Aside from the earlier mentioned, culturally specific, contemporary examples, it still seems doubtful though that such an instruction would have a genuine practical efficacy. Would calling your uncle "father" really change your relationship with your uncle to something more like that which you share with your actual parent? Would doing this confuse the relations you share with your actual father? While the titles might change, even becoming newly normalized over proceeding generations, might the different, entrenched types of interaction that are typically instilled from spending more time from birth with fathers versus uncle-fathers mean that not much would change in terms of how you felt about each? Hierocles does not really discuss in enough detail, at least in the works of his that have survived, the practical challenges of this new naming technique.

Philosopher Julia Annas recognizes the admirable intention in Hierocles' model, respecting his objective that we conceive of all our fellow humans "impartially" and afford everyone the same respect and concern.[83] Despite this drive, the approaches that Hierocles offers would not really change anything for Annas either, because using a title such as mother cannot replicate the actual feelings that are associated with the primary mother relationship.[84] Our already existing protocols regarding how we refer to someone reflect something about how their privileged role in our life makes us feel about them. Is Hierocles calling for us to contradict the differentiated

---

80. Hackett (*Illustrations of Scripture*, 118–19) provides one account of the influence of biblical applications of the term.

81. Stobaeus in Hierocles, *Hierocles the Stoic*, 93; taken from *Anthology*, 4.84.23.

82. Stobaeus in Hierocles, *Hierocles the Stoic*, 93; taken from *Anthology*, 4.84.23.

83. Annas, *Morality*, 268.

84. Annas, *Morality*, 268.

feelings associated with the various roles that people have in relation to each other? In terms of these differentiations, for Annas our relations to people in our closer circles are inherently "partial," and could never be conversely impartial, because we share "commitments" with them that we "cherish."[85]

Our relations with certain people are closer because we create a partiality toward them, we preference them. By bringing other people closer, by preferring them, an identical or even comparable *im*partiality across all our interpersonal relationships would not result. Even if Hierocles' intentions were realizable, more instances or forms of "increased partiality" would instead simply occur for Annas, more instances of increased preference for the people we draw into the closer circles.[86] The conclusion we arrive at through Annas is that Hierocles' imperative would therefore increase rather than decrease partial interpersonal relations.

Aristotle has similarly expressed concern about trying to draw in too many people too closely. In *Politics II*,[87] Aristotle argues that expanding our sense of who is in our family does not actually produce a bigger family unit. Such a change contrarily weakens the bonds of our established family unit by deprioritizing the attachments we share with each family member.[88] While it is not apparent if Hierocles is familiar with this feature of Aristotelian philosophy, he does exhibit an awareness of this adverse ramification. Hierocles conservatively cautions that when inviting or drawing in people who are socially distanced from ourselves, we should not forego or relinquish the connections of our most inner circle relations. This evokes the earlier reviewed demand from Cicero that during any enactment of our cosmopolitan natures we should always keep our "closest" interpersonal bonds guaranteed. Hierocles even describes how it would go against nature and be unwise to invite others into our lives to whom we have no connection, while "neglecting" our immediate family members.[89] While it is in our nature to share cosmopolitan relations of fellowship with all humans, it is in those close family relations given to us by birth that nature has provided us with our first "allies."[90]

With such conditions Hierocles exhibits our cosmopolitan nature's rational *orderliness* when he carefully, not recklessly, asks us to invite a world of

85. Annas, *Morality*, 268–69.

86. Annas, *Morality*, 269.

87. Aristotle, *Politics*.

88. Saunders (in Aristotle, *Politics*, 114) commentates on this as having the effect of "thinning" family relationships.

89. Stobaeus in Hierocles, *Hierocles the Stoic*, 91; taken from *Anthology*, 4.84.23.

90. Stobaeus in Hierocles, *Hierocles the Stoic*, 89; taken from *Anthology*, 4.84.20.

fellow humans into our lives. Our integration with a Stoic cosmopolitanism, a universal singular community of fellow rational beings, must be rationally ordered and systematically discriminated. This duly raises the question of how exactly to order our openness to others. If our rational social ordering does not comprise unreflectively just inviting anyone and everyone into our lives, of what should we be conscious to be truly rationally communal for Hierocles?

Recognizing Ourselves in Each Other

The link between what is rational and what is social in Hierocles' cosmopolitanism becomes overt when we exercise what is common or kindred about rationality. Exercising our social rationality requires living with a consciousness of ourselves and others as ordinary parts of a superior whole. Through the ordered and consistent application of this consciousness, not through unpredictable or reckless goodwill, we enact our mutual bonds with all rational others as collaborators, as they likewise exercise their cosmopolitan impulses toward us:

> Reason [rationality] . . . is a great aid, which appropriates strangers and those wholly unrelated to us by blood and provides us with an abundance of allies.[91]

Hierocles' perspective is that when activating our communal nature by integrating people unrelated to us into our lives, we should do so with a consciousness of our common rational natures. Such an orientation duly requires simultaneous inward and outward perspectives. This is because when Hierocles impels us to reduce the distance between ourselves and others, he wants us to be conscious of our internal selves, while also recognizing our internality in a world of other people.

This directly returns us to this chapter's topic of self-preservation. We have seen that for the Stoics an appreciation of what is common about us all, what is common about our shared rationalities and our matching compulsions to self-preservation, speaks to the mutual rather than to the personal conditions underpinning our individual self-preservation. By understanding self-preservation and fellowship together, a relationship becomes apparent that activates the earlier encountered Stoic principle of oikeiôsis.

We should remind ourselves that this principle, oikeiôsis, refers among other things to what we believe accords with us, what benefits us, what belongs to us. If what belongs to and benefits us is our rational nature,

---

91. Stobaeus in Hierocles, *Hierocles the Stoic*, 89; taken from *Anthology*, 4.84.20.

and this rational nature is what also belongs to and benefits other rational human beings, then what belongs to us is not exclusively individualized or personalized. What belongs to us instead also belongs to all rational beings in a kindred way. Rationality is itself a kindred mind, as we might recall Marcus Aurelius describing it. By recognizing what it is about the world that is rational to which we belong, we accordingly recognize a fellowship.

A feature of this fellowship is still undoubtedly for the Stoics our orientation toward our own welfares. We might be explicitly discussing self-preservation's communal qualities, but what we learn from the surviving fragments of Hierocles' *Elements of Ethics* is that initially this self-preserving impulse presents in Hierocles' view as somewhat of an inauguration of our individual selves. This is not too surprising in an everyday regard, given that self-preservation conventionally refers to what appears to be our individual well-being and survival. We can also describe it in this way for Hierocles, where self-preservation is in his thesis activated by each of us as we first perceive the world and our distinction from it:

> An animal, when it has received the first perception of itself, immediately becomes its own and familiar to itself and to its constitution.[92]

The point Hierocles is making is that early in our existence we perceive ourselves as distinct from the world, and from this distinction we begin to care about ourselves. This might remind us of aspects of Cicero's similar sense of our innate self-orientation, where in each "creature . . . nature bestows . . . from the beginning a desire for self-preservation and for maintaining itself in the best possible state according to nature."[93] In the views of Hierocles and Cicero it is in our nature to incline toward our own well-being. Depending on the nuances of the theory of each, this inclination originates from the moment we are born (according to Cicero), or from the moment we first perceive something about ourselves and become aware of ourselves (according to Hierocles).

Where this moves from a self-preserving inclination that is occupied with our individual well-being, to a grander orientation toward collective well-being, concerns our identification of, and our identification with, others. This insight arises from the heart of the principle of oikeiôsis, which involves a process where we develop an appreciation that what belongs to, or benefits, or is affiliated with, ourselves individually, also belongs to, or benefits, or is affiliated with, our fellow humans. We see a rational order

92. Hierocles, *Hierocles the Stoic*, 19; taken from Hierocles, *Elements of Ethics*, 1.6.50.

93. Cicero, *On Moral Ends*, 5.24.

and patterns in the behaviors of others that resemble our own ordering and behaviors.

Hierocles' *Elements of Ethics* is the most useful Stoic account of oikeiôsis.[94] After our initial realizations about ourselves, as we mature we become more aware of our environment and of other people, particularly of people who show us care. We recognize what our parents and ourselves share or reciprocate in terms of behavior and needs, before then further appreciating consistencies between ourselves and other people in our communities. These kinds of comparisons extend progressively to fellow people in our countries, with whom we identify less-directly but nevertheless can acknowledge our mutual affinities or commonalities. As our self-reflection grows to its most rational point, we can recognize what we share with all humans.[95] The stages via which our self-preserving tendencies radiate from ourselves to a cosmopolitan appreciation of all humans are:

1. Born.

2. Recognize self.

3. Recognize family and those caring for us.

4. Recognize fellow community members.

5. Recognize fellow country members.

6. Recognize fellow humans universally.

Self-preservation is an interpersonally or socially conditioned process for the Stoics. As we move through the stages of recognizing others, we likewise progressively view ourselves as "akin" or similar to them. Our self-belonging and self-preserving impulses expand to involve a comparative sense of belonging to all humans, and to feeling invested in their ongoing preservation as they are in our own. We do not develop through these stages alone either, our fellow humans likewise have the same experience. As these reciprocated recognitions spread among all humans, so for the Stoics the bonds of mutual aid manifest that we have seen Cicero discuss for humanity generally.[96]

---

94. Reydams-Schils ("Philosophy and Education," 566) likewise describes *Elements of Ethics* as the "best evidence on the highly sophisticated Stoic notion of 'appropriation' (oikeiosis)."

95. McCabe ("Extend or Identify," 432) notes that Hierocles' application of oikeiôsis will insist that "we feel for other people just where we are the other people." See also how Reydams-Schils ("Becoming Like God," 146) asserts that the imperative of oikeiôsis is to feel the same kind and amount of appropriation toward our fellow rational humans that we feel toward ourselves.

96. Cicero, *On Moral Ends*, 3.63.

Through these ongoing recognitions of ourselves in others we concurrently develop a matured appreciation of ourselves and our belonging in the world. This is a considerable part of the reason that, as we have seen in preceding chapters, the Stoics believe that personal benefits and individual well-being only arrive via shared relations and conditions. In a way we reveal our own rational ordering through a consciousness of how our group is rationally ordered, where the largest of such groups is all of humanity. Our understanding of self-preservation and self-care builds for Hierocles through the knowledge that being a "sociable animal" means being conscious of the mutual "needs" and natures of all humans.[97]

In either Cicero's or Hierocles' account therefore, we can identify an association of fellowship and self-preservation. Our shared rationality conditions this fellowship. In exercising the closest possible relations with other humans, such relations must equal the affinity we have with the seat of our own rationality, our mind. Stoicism asks us to relate to others in the same way that we relate to our thinking and reasoning selves. Other people are rational minds, of the same rationality, from the same rationally ordered source as our rationality, so in a way we already know each other.

It is only through this kind of insight that I believe we can exactly define the intentions of Hierocles' version of cosmopolitanism. The purpose is not to generate bigger personalized communities for each of us, constituting hundreds of family members and thousands of friends, all requiring our company. A world of altruistic selflessness in which we extend ourselves to each other simply for the sake of the other is not necessarily the focus either. As I have indicated, the point for Hierocles is not to recklessly bring every single human into our lives and try to associate with them all regularly, in the way that we might with our closest people. That would be impractically impossible, and Stoic philosophy's emphasis is that philosophy should be practical, not impractical.

Hierocles instead deftly brings our attention to the universal and mutual affiliations and connections of which humans should always be aware. This rational bond between all of us already exists. Hierocles' considerations of our concentric circles of association highlights this existing bond between all people. It is through identifying the shared origins of all humans that Hierocles reminds us of an ongoing universal fellowship to which we have responsibilities and on which we can rely. We all furthermore have the same parent according to Hierocles in his essay "Parents," in that our

---

97. Hierocles, *Hierocles the Stoic*, 29; taken from Hierocles *Elements of Ethics*, fragments.

biological parents are always merely "images" of "Zeus."[98] Zeus, remember, is a Stoic term for God. And the Stoic God is the rationally ordered world. The singular and divine parent for all of us, to which Hierocles refers, is thus what the Stoics call the rational order that pervades everything, and what we might in the current day recognize as the physical, causal world.

If we already share the same origin, any instruction to offer a family-like closeness or intimacy to people, even to people we do not know, is not really expecting us to integrate absolute "strangers" into our lives. A universal human fellowship, the cosmopolitan condition, means that we are already involved in kinship relations with others, complicating the possibility that anyone is ever this kind of stranger.

Factors that seem to estrange humans are duly reconceived according to this underlying principle. Geographical distance for instance cannot compromise the rational communion that we share, Hierocles demanding that as rational beings we are "a great benefit to one another even if the distance is enormous."[99] This seems to have considerable real-world relevance in the era of a global pandemic, particularly in terms of our awareness of the grander responsibilities we all embody when infections spread throughout the world. Our primary responsibility for the Stoics is not to our individual preservation. It is instead to an ordered world with which we are interconnected and from which our individual self derives. We have a responsibility not just to our families, friends, and neighbors, but to people from whom we are incredibly physically distanced and will likely never even meet. This dispersed sense of responsibility and affiliation for the Stoics is consistent with the cosmopolitan view that we are each a part of the same community despite living streets, towns, states, or countries apart. Hierocles conceptually contracts our circles to bring attention to how this universal fellowship already exists, rather than offers a template for how we can construct such a fellowship in a world that lacks it. Through this rational appreciation of the common conditions for our own well-being, we find in Stoicism the intentions, ends, outcomes, and benefits of an individual's orientations toward self-care and self-preservation. Our discussion will now lead us toward considerations of how we learn to live in these communally oriented, Stoic ways, and what our motivations are when we study Stoic philosophy.

98. Stobaeus in Hierocles, *Hierocles the Stoic*, 83; taken from *Anthology*, 4.79.53.
99. Stobaeus in Hierocles, *Hierocles the Stoic*, 89; taken from *Anthology*, 4.84.20.

5

Knowledge,
a Social Education

Well-being from Living Locally and Thinking Universally

STOIC PHILOSOPHY UNDERSTANDS THE individual as a trace of an ordered system. We have reviewed how for the Stoics, our rationalities, our minds, our bodies, even our self-preserving tendencies, are all fragments of something grander. Everything about us is a part of a universal, collective system. What might initially appear simply to be our individually oriented behaviors and personally targeted outcomes, are instead for the Stoics linked to and borrowed from what is shared about our existence. The Stoics describe the entire universe as the most primary of sources from which we derive our attributes and characteristics. We are born rational for the Stoics. This is a belief that we have identified across all the philosophy's ancient eras.

Despite rationality being our default nature, we still need to *learn* according to the Stoics about how to live rationally, and most crucially about how our rationality interconnects us with other humans and the universe. A Stoic education to this extent not only teaches us what constitutes rational thoughts and actions, it also trains our consciousness to appreciate our implication in a rationally ordered or systematized world. To give you an indication of where we are heading regarding this theme, while in previous chapters we have discussed the primacy of rational actions, in this chapter we will complementarily be assessing how we learn to act rationally for the Stoics.

The topic of education can spark conventional ideas concerning how study facilitates personal or individual development. Consistent with the reading of Stoicism through which I am leading us that extends beyond individualized outcomes though, this chapter's considerations will attend to the extent to which Stoic philosophy's education of individuals prioritizes processes occupied with social or communal developments. This focus will ask us to review whether in Stoicism an individual's formal or informal education occurs with intentions that exceed the development of that individual. Or more specifically, does the Stoic education of individuals always have a social fabric as its intended beneficiary.

This educational development for the Stoics often concerns how we each transcend a previous state of relative ignorance. The topic of ignorance is a favorite of Seneca, who we have already encountered.[1] We will be engaging a series of letters that Seneca writes on a range of everyday topics, through which he weaves Stoic instructions and principles. He addresses these letters to Gaius Lucilius, who at the time was a high-ranking public official. These letters have been famously anthologized as *Letters from a Stoic* (among other titles). One everyday topic that Seneca's Stoicism here explores, in constructing an argument about our ignorance, is travel. When incorporating this type of philosophical reflection from Seneca we must take into account how easily he was able to travel due to his immense wealth.[2] Seneca was not the typical Roman citizen, either in terms of his considerable notoriety, significant participation and influence in public life, or financial fortune.

It is from a position of relative wealth, and with a keen interest in the application of Stoic ideas toward rectifying our various forms of ignorance, that Seneca discusses his fondness for travelling to his "villa at Nomentum." In one letter, Seneca explains how his most recent trip to Nomentum occurred in response to a "fever that . . . had cast its hold" on him.[3] Travelling to a more serene countryside environment helps with his condition, in that after having left "the city's heavy atmosphere" with its "noxious fumes" he felt his health immediately improve.[4]

It appears that Nomentum's environment is responsible for this change in Seneca's condition. He does after all report enthusiastically on the grassy terrains, animals, and peacefulness that had now surrounded him. As he

1. As with Cato, Seneca carries a "Younger" title because an elder relative, in this case his father, was already well-known by the same name.

2. Wilson (*Greatest Empire*, 127–41) provides an account not only of the size of Seneca's wealth, but also of its source, and of how he was perceived by his contemporaries.

3. Seneca, *Letters on Ethics*, 104.1.

4. Seneca, *Letters on Ethics*, 104.6.

goes into more detail however, we find that the environment had little to do with this improvement. Seneca instead asserts that the principal factor in his better health is his own mind, or more specifically his mental calmness. His mind's tendency to be calm regardless of the environment is the quality on which he leans most heavily to maintain well-being:

> Location is of no avail unless the mind makes time for itself, keeping a place of retreat even amid busy moments. On the contrary, if you're always choosing remote spots in a quest for leisure, you'll find something to distract you everywhere.[5]

Mental well-being, intimately connected with our peace and tranquility, is for Seneca not dependent on the external physical world or surroundings. Certainly for some people, such environments can make it easier to be mentally calm. To approach a truly Stoic mindset though for Seneca, one's mental state will not be bound to its environmental conditions at all. Seneca laments from this that people who travel or move regularly in seeking mental peace and relaxation will be unlikely to experience it. Despite a change in scenery for a holiday or a different place to call home, such people "will in every place they visit find something to prevent them from relaxing."[6] Going overseas or moving to a new city will do nothing for a person's mental state according to Seneca, if they have not already developed the capacity for a mental calmness that is not dependent on their environment.[7]

Seneca feels that often we travel just because we see others doing it, and that we grow up in a culture that normalizes such practice. Travel, or journeying around, becomes understood as a standard way to provide mental relaxation and personal growth. In opposing the idea of following what others do, Seneca instead wants us to think differently.[8] If mental

5. Seneca, *Letters on Ethics*, 104.7.

6. Seneca, *Letters from a Stoic*, 104.6–11.

7. Seneca, *Letters on Ethics*, 104.8. For analyses of Seneca's view that travel will not resolve internal issues that we carry with us, see Graver, *Stoicism and Emotion*, 99–101; Inwood, *Reading Seneca*, 317; Montiglio, "Conflict in Seneca's Thought," 553–86.

8. This position is consistent with Seneca's general concern about the uninterrogated authority of others over our minds. Seneca (*Ad Lucilium Epistulae Morales*, 113.23) here invokes Chrysippus' contestation to certain beliefs held by his teacher, Cleanthes. This indicates a Stoic tradition in which for Seneca we must learn about anything with a certain mental "freedom." Modern commentators have communicated this message regularly. See Reydams-Schils ("Authority and Agency," 299) for observations of Seneca's admiration that a Stoic mind will not without inspection obey an authority figure. Beyond just observing Seneca's instruction, Pigliucci ("Disagree," paras. 1–5) describes how one can apply its ethos to accept or reject what Seneca himself teaches. Also relevant to this topic is Seal (*Philosophy and Community*, 86–88), as well as what Asmis ("Stoic Individualism," 224) describes as Seneca's views on the "right to dissent."

tranquility is what we both lack and seek, we should remain where we are, and reflect on what it is about ourselves that is preventing that tranquility.[9] In typical Stoic fashion, what prevents us from mental tranquility are said to be our irrationally inclined existences, distancing us from our nature. Seneca duly relies on the orthodox Stoic definition of our nature as humans as "rational animals," whose "rationality requires" that we "live in accordance with this nature."[10]

As I have articulated repeatedly, the primary way in which we can live in accordance with our rational nature for the Stoics is to think and act with the consciousness that we are universally and communally interconnected beings. Seneca does not discuss these universal bonds to the extent that other Stoics we have studied do. He is nevertheless emphatic that we live irrationally when we are unaware or unaccepting that we each exist as a part of a greater collective. Rationality for Seneca demands an awareness of, and an intention toward, interpersonally shared ends and outcomes, rather than merely personal ones. Being conscious of our responsibilities, not just to ourselves but to our fellow humans, means that in being rational we have concurrently been "summoned to assist those in need." If you conversely lack this awareness and dedicate your life only or even mainly to your own prosperities, if you "wander off" on your own and do not "help" when all "those around you are reaching their hands in your direction," for Seneca you irrationally neglect your systematized role and participation in the world's "highest good."[11] That highest good is our shared, rational nature.

A desire to be individually wealthy, for example, to acquire many riches for oneself rather than living rationally and civically, would be irrational in Seneca's view. He states in *On the Shortness of Life* that having wealth is not in-itself anti-Stoic. Being born wealthy does not prevent someone from living with a Stoic mindset. Even choosing to be financially wealthy rather than poor is not necessarily contrary to Stoicism. What is most important though is that we are indifferent to any wealth we might have, rather than unhealthily desire, or be affected by, it. This reflects money's status as a "preferred indifferent" in Stoicism, meaning that given the choice we might *prefer* money in order to live comfortably, however we will be mentally and emotionally *indifferent* to that lifestyle if we have it.[12] Accepting our poverty can for Seneca allow us to "demonstrate" rather than "merely say" that we live in accordance with the universal order of things. If we find ourselves

9. Seneca, *Letters on Ethics*, 104.8.

10. Seneca, *Letters on Ethics*, 41.8.

11. Seneca, *Letters on Ethics*, 48.8–10.

12. Seneca, *Letters on Ethics*, 20.10–13.

to be poor and have no problem with that, we show an understanding that much of our life is not up to us because it is instead systematically arranged by a whole world of causes. Being rationally indifferent to the wealth we do have however could be an even greater indication of the Stoic mind in Seneca's view, if it activates a form of indifference from us to a feature of external being that people in poverty do not likewise have the opportunity to activate.[13]

Another feature of our mental and emotional lives that prevents our tranquility or well-being according to Seneca is our fear of death.[14] Travelling somewhere new will not make us fear death less in his view, a point to which he rhetorically asks, "does the character of the place make any difference?"[15] Seneca believes that we fear death primarily as a result of observing others die and experiencing the resulting emotions. We have reviewed in previous chapters how for the Stoics knowledge about the world can be empirically, or observationally, derived and rationalized. It is due to this Stoic correlation of what is empirical with what is rational that for Seneca our unpleasant emotional responses when observing the deaths of others is not entirely irrational. Seneca hence accommodates rather than negates features of our emotional life that are associated with our rationalized observations of the world around us.[16]

Numerous contemporary Stoic commentators further recognize that being Stoic does not require an unemotional existence.[17] As such analyses communicate, what Stoicism instead directs us toward is a better management of the irrational modes that overwhelm or dominate us through unpleasant emotions. In such modes we are irrational in Stoicism as we have seen because we avoid accepting that what happens to us is systematically

13. Seneca (*Letters on Ethics*, 20.10) describes how "there is greatness of spirit also in the person who sees wealth heaped up around him and laughs long and loud for sheer amazement that it has come to him. Others tell him it is his; on his own he scarcely realizes it. It is a great thing not to be corrupted by living amid riches; great is the man who is a pauper in his wealth." Inwood (*Reading Seneca*, 317) and Sellars ("Introduction," 1–14) both observe that through positions like Seneca's we see how for the Stoics choosing wealth is fine as long as you understand it. See Dealy (*Stoic Origins*, 29–37, 293–99) for ancient impressions of the Stoic dual indifference to, and accommodation of, wealth.

14. Seneca, *Letters on Ethics*, 104.10–12.

15. Seneca, *Letters on Ethics*, 104.8.

16. It is because of this accommodation that Seneca (*Letters on Ethics*, 9.2) distinguishes aspects of Stoicism from Epicureanism. The Stoic in Seneca's view "conquers all adversities, but still feels them." The Epicurean approach to emotions is for Seneca conversely concerned with not even feeling them.

17. Becker, "Stoic Emotion"; Farren, "Stoicism & Star Trek," 196–98; Robertson, *Art of Happiness*, 35–36; Sellars, "Stoicism and Emotions," 48.

ordered as part of a greater whole. Feeling our emotions instead through an appreciation of our part-to-whole existential relations will lead to reasonable experiences for the Stoics. Seneca indeed expects us to feel emotions around death. If we desperately construct an alternative sense of self in which we avoid emotions altogether, what will occur in Seneca's view is a repression rather than an acceptance of our inevitable mortal condition. Everyone can, after all, understand their inevitable mortality, or as Seneca puts it, "no matter how naïve a person is, they know they must die sometime."[18] By repressing the fact of our mortality and living ignorantly though, we will for Seneca not be consciously present with our rationally ordered natures.[19] In *On the Shortness of Life*, he duly asks us to be aware of our mortality, to accept that we live only for a certain time, and to waste less of that time.[20]

Seneca's message here is that we should not let fears about our own or others' deaths control our emotional states. Fear can serve our self-preservation well in certain contexts. It can steer us away for example from a danger that if encountered might cause needless harm. Fearing death however can contradict our self-preservation for Seneca if it irrationally reflects that our emotional life is overly concerned with our individual bodily or physical existence.[21] This is not an unexpected assertion given that as we learned in the last chapter, self-preservation correlates with rationality but not necessarily with personal bodily existence. To be emotionally overwhelmed by concerns regarding the continuation of our own bodily existence would conversely indicate our ignorance regarding Stoic prioritizations of the self-preservation of our rational rather than physical state. Such irrationality might also neglect the insights we developed in chapter 3 around how our bodies materially interconnect with all other bodies as "limbs" of a universally ordered body, and as such never physically perish upon dying but rather change and disperse among that universal body. Concerns about the individual body are here not diminished, they are instead contextualized within a grander appreciation of the perpetually reconstructing singular body of the universe of which we are each a part. To focus on our individual physiologies, our own bodies, to the neglect of this greater composition, would contradict our connection with the source of ourselves and therefore compromise our rationally self-preserving concerns. Given this alienation, the resulting adverse mental anxieties that come from thinking in an overly

18. Seneca, *Letters on Ethics*, 77.11.

19. Seneca, *Letters on Ethics*, 104.12.

20. Seneca, *Shortness of Life*, 5. See also where Pigliucci ("How to Be a Stoic," 7) recognizes the Stoic view that because death is universal and inevitable, there should be nothing especially fearful about it.

21. Seneca, *Letters on Ethics*, 104.10–12.

individualistic way about ourselves, or about our own bodily states and lives, would not surprise Seneca or other Stoics.

It is evident then that Seneca believes one way we avoid rationally reflecting on our fears, such as those concerning our mortality, is by travelling. This is not to suggest that travelling is always or only used as a distraction from our fear of death. "Changing places" or "wandering all over the world"[22] is nevertheless for Seneca a significant example of how we live without an awareness of the relationship between ourselves and the universal whole. Seneca's grander point here is that we undertake frivolous activities to avoid thinking about the nature of being human. Travelling in this mode, visiting various places just to see somewhere different, does not make us more knowledgeable for Seneca consequently. Such travel instead contributes in his view to us remaining "ignorant" of our "just" and "honorable" duties.[23] Seneca proposes that rather than travelling we should stay where we are and dedicate our time to learning to live rationally via philosophical education. We can explore our ties with the world not by moving geographically and seeing more of it but by reflecting rationally.

Community Is the Common Interest

As with other Stoics that we have reviewed, myriad interpersonal conditions emerge for Seneca when we attend to our rational and mental lives. Seneca's focus is not as regularly dedicated to discussions of our social constitutions as that of a thinker like Marcus Aurelius. His attention to how socially oriented we are as rational creatures nevertheless becomes apparent in his demands regarding our duties to others.

Seneca presents the same dual positions regarding our social existence that we have encountered in other Stoics. On the one hand he directs us to be indifferent to contingent social matters such as reputation and social status, remarking that "only an absolute fool values" someone else according to "their social position, which after all is only something that we wear like clothing."[24] He repeatedly warns not to let our minds be dictated by the popular trends found in crowds,[25] and also discusses passionately in another letter the general dangers that other humans can present to us.[26]

22. Seneca, *Letters on Ethics*, 104.18–19.

23. Seneca, *Letters on Ethics*, 104.16.

24. Seneca, *Letters from a Stoic*, 47.14–19.

25. Seneca, *Letters on Ethics*, 7.1–12; 8.1–2.

26. Seneca, *Letters on Ethics*, 103.

On the other hand though, Seneca emphasizes that we bear responsibilities and duties to other humans and to the common nature of humans.[27] That common nature, as we have seen Seneca declare, is that we are a rational animal. Friendship for Seneca is accordingly a state shared between fellow rational humans because it is an attribute and an expression of our common rational condition. Friends are rational, and notably for my focus on Stoicism's priorities beyond individualistic ends, friends for Seneca are also mutually aware that we participate in collective ends and outcomes rather than individualized ones:

> If a thing is in your interest it is also in my own interest. Otherwise, if any matter that affects you is no concern of mine, I am not a friend. Friendship creates a community of interest between us in everything. We have neither successes nor setbacks as individuals; our lives have a common end. No one can lead a happy life if he thinks only of himself and turns everything to his own purposes. You should live for the other person if you wish to live for yourself.[28]

We need to reflect here on how this might relate to oikeiôsis, and what is rationally self-preserving about recognizing and regularly activating our affinities with others. While we might share these affinities with all rational beings, Hierocles and Cicero have both reminded us that the foundations of a cosmopolitan structure are our most familiar and close interpersonal relationships. Seneca indicates something similar in his attention on our friendship. While he is referring to the bonds shared by all humans, Seneca gives extra attention to the relationships we share with those we know best. We become aware of these mutual bonds by staying where we live with such people, as we develop an appreciation of their presence in our lives through what a Stoic education teaches about mentally recognizing our rational interconnections.

It is with this direction that Seneca actually endorses one kind of travelling; a journey toward a greater rationality. Seneca's understanding of rational travel concerns moving ideologically from an ignorant state to a knowledgeable state, a shift that occurs by moving to better "company." Seneca plays with the subtly different senses of the word "move" here. Instead of moving geographically he wants us to move internally, which we can activate through the wisdom acquired from philosophical teachings. Seneca accordingly advises the individual who is caught in irrational behavioral cycles to "attach" themselves to philosophers such as "Socrates and

27. Seneca, *Letters on Ethics*, 48.8–11.
28. Seneca, *Letters from a Stoic*, 48.1–6.

Zeno."[29] Rather than moving to another town or country to learn about different places in the world, Seneca believes we will learn more about how enmeshed we are with the world, and attain a "practical . . . knowledge of humans and the universe," if through studying and enacting what we study we "live with Chrysippus, live with Posidonius."[30]

The message is to focus your attention inwards. Seneca like most Stoics identifies rationality as an internal feature of the self. We have covered extensively for the Stoics how interwoven our internal rationality is with a rationally ordered universe. This sense becomes apparent in Seneca, in his clarifications that when looking inward we will find that our "individual spirit" is "a spirit very like the universe."[31] Our internal spirit, our rationality, cannot be *identical* with the universe, a point that should remind us of the distinction held in Stoicism between the divine whole and the parts. Given that as individuals we always exist as that part or trace of the universal rational spirit, there is no advantage to being in one location of the universe versus another. All that matters is that we live with a rational awareness of our relationship with others and with the universe as a whole.[32]

This is not to say that there is anything wrong with travelling once one has learned to live rationally and knowledgeably. The apparent knowledge that travels typically afford though, such as the acquisition of facts about other countries, does not really comprise knowledge or even education in Seneca's view. This feature of travel instead just provides us with contingent facts that we can remember, and with which we can exhibit our apparent worldliness to others.[33] While such "knowledge" often seems to help us transcend the limited perspectives of the local communities in which we live, true knowledge involves the awareness that living rationally constitutes a universal interconnection that is never restricted to localized factual trivialities. On this point Seneca reminds us of the priority of moving to the company of Zeno, Socrates, and the like while remaining in our current environments, which will give us more than stories to share when "speaking charmingly and captivating an audience."[34] Stoic philosophy in this mode is concerned not with how as individuals we can exceed our local communities. It is instead invested in how we immerse ourselves learnedly and participatorily within them.

29. Seneca, *Letters from a Stoic*, 104.19.
30. Seneca, *Letters from a Stoic*, 104.19.
31. Seneca, *Letters from a Stoic*, 104.26.
32. Seneca, *Letters from a Stoic*, 104.19.
33. Seneca, *Letters from a Stoic*, 104.12.
34. Seneca, *Letters on Ethics*, 104.22.

Through philosophy we receive an education that marks a development of self-awareness. This awareness is not just occupied with apparently individualized or personalized goals however, the concerns instead are our roles within and duties to an interpersonal system. So inescapable is this orientation for each of us that Seneca defines how "a sense of companionship links all human beings to one another" through which we live with a primary commitment to "a common law of humankind."[35] This companionship trumps what we might feel or want as personal concerns, Seneca capitalizing that "no one can have a happy life if they look only to themselves" for "neither good times nor bad affect just one of us."[36] Our lives, and our experiences of our lives, have a common law because they are shared, and they are shared because they are commonly ordered.

Much like Epictetus, Seneca attributes the source of what is common and shared about this existence to our rationality, and therefore to the rationally systematized order of the universe itself. We have just seen this in his comparison of individual and universal spirits, and he further discusses it later in the same letter when describing how "Nature brought us forth" with "a spirit that closely resembles that of the universe."[37] Just as with any relation of part to whole, we as parts are not identical by degree to the whole, but instead we resemble the whole by being of the same kind of phenomenon. Our knowledge of the whole is duly an internally connected, part-perspective's, knowledge of it. What we know individually always lies somewhere beyond each of our localized minds, for our knowledge, which is rational, is inextricable from a universal system of knowledge. This is a counterintuitive sense of "beyond" though. It does not refer to a world that is external to or outside us, but rather designates a world that is the source, spark, and constitution of our own internality.

Seneca's appraisal of knowledge covers the later stages of how it develops in each of us. To illustrate what I mean by this, I propose that knowledge for the Stoics occurs in three steps, where we firstly:

1. Derive information about the world through observations of it, then we . . .

2. Develop knowledges of the world by rationally reflecting on those observations of the world, before we . . .

3. Consciously apply those knowledges through practical action.

---

35. Seneca, *Letters on Ethics*, 48.3.
36. Seneca, *Letters on Ethics*, 48.2.
37. Seneca, *Letters on Ethics*, 104.23.

Seneca shows us the importance of philosophical instruction in step 2. His encouragement of course is that we study philosophical observations of the world, we correlate them with our own observations, and we reflect on the consequent knowledges that we have developed. He also indicates how we should rationally apply our new knowledges of ourselves and of the world (step 3) through actions and intentions oriented toward the well-being of others.

Before we can review further ways in which the Stoics propose we satisfy the learning of Stoic principles as part of step 2, what we are lacking in our understanding of this model is a thorough account of how the information that we derive about the world becomes knowledge. This marks the transition from step 1 to step 2. To consider more about this feature of Stoicism's epistemological structure, we can re-invite Epictetus to our discussion.

Learning How to Know

Questions of how we develop an understanding of the world speak to the link Stoicism makes between observation and knowledge production. A foundational example of this interpretation, as we have already touched on, is Epictetus' assertion regarding the Stoics' observations of the world's ordered, physical patterns. The conclusion Epictetus derives from those observations is that there is an overall, systematic, rationalized order to things.[38] We know the world is rationally ordered or systematized because we observe it behaving predictably and repeatably. How though do these observations become knowledge? What are the mechanics of the transition from our observations of the world and receiving sensory information or data about it, to reflecting on that information or data and generating knowledge? Detailing these mechanics will not only target the current, just identified, gap in our understanding of Stoic knowledge claims, but will also evidence further common, shared, and collective conditions for the Stoics regarding the knowledges that we individually have.

While we can study Stoic beliefs around knowledge acquisition and production through Epictetus, such an analysis proves to be more comprehensive when also incorporating the refutations of Stoic knowledge claims made by the Pyrrhonist sceptic, Sextus Empiricus.[39] The Pyrrhonist school,

---

38. Epictetus, *Discourses* (2014), 1.14.4.

39. For further comparisons of Stoic knowledge claims with those of other schools, see where Bonazzi ("Platonist Appropriation," 120–41) considers the relationship between Stoic epistemological beliefs and those of Platonists.

established by the early Greek skeptic Pyrrho, interrogates how our pre-existing judgements and beliefs participate or linger in our observations and evaluations of the world. Sextus' skepticism indeed demands that we cannot defer unconditionally to perceptual and empirical foundations for knowledge, due to this ongoing infiltration of our preconceived ideas. Because we might unwittingly hold numerous different ideas (preconceptions) about a thing in the world that could shape our experience of it, we must for Sextus consciously "suspend belief" about whether we really know the truth of a thing.[40] As this is the only reasonable solution for the skeptics, it is also in their view a source of mental tranquility. Sextus refers to this process of skepticism and suspension of claims of knowledge as an "ability or mental attitude, which opposes appearances to judgements" and from which we feel a consequent "unperturbedness or quietude."[41] Both Sextus' own philosophy, and skepticism generally, refute the belief that what we observe is reliable enough to underpin knowledge claims, a view that he strongly articulates in his work *Against the Logicians*.[42]

Despite this apparent opposition, the Stoics and Sextus agree on key aspects regarding our knowledge claims. The most relevant Stoic belief in this regard is that before observing, experiencing, or investigating anything, we require a "prior notion" or preconception of it in order to know it.[43] According to this view we never have an entirely unfamiliar experience with the world and its things. This is a position with which Sextus Empiricus agrees, disputing that someone could "investigate" anything without already having a preconception of what is "being investigated."[44]

Our preconceptions inform how we view and know the world. Sextus' concern with these preconceptual conditions for observation and investigation is that when perceiving a thing in the world, how do we know which of our preconceptions matches the thing in reality? When we perceive the world for Sextus we are steered, usually unknowingly, by "many" different preconceived ideas of it.[45] Without knowing which preconception and consequent conception is correct though, how can we make claims about

---

40. Gill (*Structured Self*, 393) conveys that Pyrrhonist skepticism comprises an unfulfilled search for truth about the world.

41. Sextus Empiricus, *Outlines of Pyrrhonism*, 1.8. Annas and Barnes (in Sextus Empiricus, *Outlines of Scepticism*, 1.8) likewise translate this as where skepticism, by setting more rigorous conditions for knowledge claims and the supposed relations between appearances and judgements, induces feelings of "tranquility."

42. Sextus Empiricus, *Against the Logicians* (2005).

43. Sextus Empiricus, *Against the Logicians* (2005), 2.331a.

44. Sextus Empiricus, *Against the Logicians* (2005), 2.331a.

45. Sextus Empiricus, *Against the Logicians* (2005), 2.332a.

knowing the world? This problem leads to the aforementioned suspension of belief for Sextus. We have no choice but to suspend belief in our knowledge of the thing we are perceiving or investigating, because we are incapable of "discriminating" between our preconceptions to determine which is correct.[46]

Given that Epictetus delivers his lectures on this topic just chronologically prior to Sextus' intervention, it is possible that Sextus is directing much of his attention toward Epictetus' school of thought. There are two features of Epictetus' account of knowledge for the Stoics that are important in distinguishing Stoic and Skeptic understandings. Both these features orient our considerations toward how each of us in Stoicism is a collectively shared, rather than an independent or individualized, set of attributes and functions.

The first feature to discuss concerns how Epictetus proposes that the preconceptions we have of the world are universal. We all have the same preconceptions in each of our minds, they are "common to all" humans because they derive from the same universal, rational nature. As we each live with these universal preconceptions and perceive the world through them, we commonly enact what they assume about the world. Epictetus argues that one proof of their universality concerns the preconception around what is good and just:

> Who among us doesn't assume that the good is beneficial and desirable, and that we should seek and pursue it in every circumstance? And who among us doesn't assume that what is just is honourable and appropriate?[47]

When Epictetus says "assume" here, he is referring to how we are preconfigured to think about an experience or thing in the world through our preconceptions of that experience or thing. We all share the same preconfiguration in this regard. The universal rational order that we have discussed, orders us, as in systematically produces us, to direct ourselves toward the same rationally good existence. This rational preconfiguration is our nature, we have seen Stoicism posit this from its earliest incarnations in Zeno and Chrysippus.

The second shared feature that we need to discuss about the preconceptual apparatus through which we observe and experience the world

---

46. Sextus Empiricus, *Against the Logicians* (2005), 2.332a. See also how Bury (in Sextus Empiricus, *Against Logicians* [1935], 2.332a) translates that of any thing we perceive we "have so many notions and preconceptions of it, and that it is because of our inability to decide between them and to discover the most cogent amongst them."

47. Epictetus, *Discourses* (2014), 1.22.1.

for Epictetus concerns his belief that our rational nature *is* capable of distinguishing between correct and incorrect preconceptions. This of course differs from Sextus' belief that we are unable to exercise such distinctions. Crucially this means that Sextus does not recognize the educationally developmental features of the rational self in the way that the Stoics do. Epictetus for example does not suggest that we are simply born with the capacity to distinguish between *all* preconceptions. We instead for the Stoic learn to make such distinctions[48] through the various instructions we receive informally from peers and authority figures, as well as via formal philosophical study and education. Dual components are therefore in operation regarding our discernment of our preconceptions according to Epictetus. These components comprise our inherent rational natures, and an array of socially structured, philosophically educational processes:

> We have need of education, so as to be able to apply our preconceptions of what is reasonable and unreasonable to particular cases in accordance with nature.[49]

Though our education we developmentally discern how to steer our judgements in a manner that the Stoics have described as "appropriate" in the previous chapter's analysis of self-preservation. The appropriate discrimination of our judgements, a discrimination that is in accordance with an interconnected and ordered self and world, is in this context for Epictetus where our preconceptions do not mutually contradict or conflict.[50] We can instead rationally identify which preconception matches which worldly presentation.

Sextus does not agree with the Stoic belief in our ability to discriminate between our preconceptions. Unlike the Stoics he does not place the same degree of emphasis on the collective or shared nature of each of our rationalities. His fear as a result is that we will each discriminate between preconceptions in significantly different and individualized ways. Sextus' additional concern is the conditional quality of the Stoic trust in our cognitive impressions of the world. This addresses how particularly for the "later Stoics" according to Sextus, the cognitive impression of a thing in the world

---

48. Numerous contemporary scholars affirm that for Epictetus, we learn and develop our capacity to distinguish between our preconceptions and impressions. See Brennan, *Stoic Life*, 29–30; Crosbie, *Revenge Tragedy*, 252–53; Gill, "School Roman Imperial," 43–44; Jackson-McCabe, "Stoic Theory"; Johnson, *Role Ethics*, 118; Long, *Epictetus*, 80; Long, "Socratic Imprint," 21.

49. Epictetus, *Discourses* (2014), 1.2.6.

50. Epictetus, *Discourses* (2014), 1.22.1.

that we have in our mind will only meet the "criterion of truth . . . provided that it has no obstacle."[51]

Sextus might be exaggerating how much more emphatic this condition is in later versus earlier Stoic theses, given that the school's considerations of obstacles to our mental access to the truth of the world begin with Zeno. Our perceptions when developing a trustworthy "cognitive impression" of the world for the earliest Stoics are complemented rather than impeded by our preconceptions only if the consequent impression manifests with "clear and distinct" conditions.[52] Either way, the possibility, readily admitted by the Stoics, that there might not be such clarity because of preconceptual impediments,[53] means for Sextus that neither they nor we can trust perceptual conditions for knowledge. If the resulting cognitive or mental impression that we have of a thing when perceiving it is "not the criterion of truth unconditionally,"[54] then in Sextus' view we must discount the Stoic understanding of there being a reliable relationship between preconception-conditioned perception and knowledge or truth.

Earlier I indicated we would discuss the actual mechanics of this relationship between perception and knowledge in Stoicism. Zeno's initial conception of it, portrayed by a series of gestures, is famously described by Cicero in *On Academic Skepticism*. Zeno begins by representing our perception (impression) of the world, or the data given to us by our senses, with an open palm. This follows with Zeno closing his fingers, which refers to our subsequent mental agreement with, or what he calls "assent to," that perceptual or sensory impression. These stages are, as we have seen, guided by our preconceptions of what we are perceiving. We mentally agree to what our senses tell us, and that agreement occurs via our rational adjudication of which preconception matches the perception. The next stage involves Zeno closing his fingers into a fist, signifying a more developed stage of mental "comprehension" of the perception. Here we are moving out of the preconception stage and into the conception stage. Having reached the point of having a conception of the world that we are perceiving, Zeno finishes by

---

51. Sextus Empiricus, *Against Logicians* (1935), 1.253.

52. Diogenes Laërtius in Long and Sedley, *Hellenistic Philosophers*, 40C; taken from *SVF*, 2.53. See also where Cicero (*On Academic Skepticism*, 1.67) acknowledges the Stoic belief that the wise person will be capable of distinguishing between false and true impressions.

53. Diogenes Laërtius in Long and Sedley, *Hellenistic Philosophers*, 40C; taken from *SVF*, 2.53.

54. Sextus Empiricus, *Against Logicians*, 1.257.

covering his fist with his other open hand, the coming together of which declares the coherence of "knowledge."[55]

Breaking down knowledge production into these stages validates our beliefs in the reliability of our knowledges for Zeno. This does not mean that for the Stoic *every* perceptual experience accesses the truth of what it senses. Zeno would therefore agree with some of Sextus' concerns around how unconditionally we might link our preconceptions, perceptions, and knowledge. Zeno would however strongly disagree with Sextus that our senses and associated perceptions cannot condition, or be involved in, much knowledge. Contrarily for Zeno, what he refers to as "sensation" is indeed trustworthy on this matter,

> not because it apprehended all the features of its object, but on the ground that it omitted nothing detectable by it . . . [N]ature had given apprehension as a standard and starting point for scientific knowledge of the world: it was the source from which our conceptions of things were later stamped on our minds, which in turn give rise not just to the starting points but to certain broader paths for discovering reason.[56]

Zeno's confidence that a relationship exists between perception and knowledge provides a foundation for Epictetus' later belief that we can naturally, rationally reach truth claims by distinguishing what is true about preconceptions and sense-impressions.[57] We even see a further similarity between the two Stoics in Zeno's qualification that our perceptual experiences are however not always trustworthy. Cicero is again our source here, informing us of Zeno's view that of "sense presentations" we must concede that "some . . . but not all" of them can be false.[58] Somewhat relatedly, Epictetus grants that conflict does sometimes occur between preconceptions, such as when we erroneously apply preconceptions to what he calls "particular cases."[59] This conflict depends on how educated we are in applying our universally

55. Cicero, *On Academic Skepticism*, 2.145.

56. Cicero, *On Academic Skepticism*, 1.42.

57. Epictetus (*Discourses* [2014], 1.28.1–5) argues that if we doubt the legitimacy of sensory experiences we should try to convince ourselves during the day that it is, conversely, the night. Because your perceptions, your sense-impressions, will defy this belief, Epictetus holds that they duly can provide adequate bases for knowledge production. We should not for Epictetus withhold assent therefore when it comes to sensory conditions for knowledge, but rather educate ourselves to identify which sensory experiences are adequate. For Sextus, of course, "adequate" impressions will not lead to knowledge.

58. Cicero, *Nature of Gods*, 1.70.

59. Epictetus, *Discourses* (2014), 1.22.2.

held preconceptions to specific circumstances. When we develop a false impression of something in the world because we have associated that thing with an incorrect preconception, the issue for Epictetus is not with the preconception itself but in how rationally we apply preconceptions to specific aspects of our lives.

This is where education and the development of knowledge, particularly self-knowledge, becomes so important for the Stoics. Epictetus advises that to avoid incorrectly applying our preconceptions, we must learn to employ them to particular cases in accordance with our rational nature.[60] As we have covered at length, the primary mode of living in accordance with our rational nature is thinking and acting as parts of an interconnected whole. To know ourselves is to know that we are parts of an ordered system. Marcus Aurelius, following Epictetus, will later correlate our assent to correct and rational impressions, with our orientation toward this consciousness of our entwined and therefore communal/social state:

> To a nature endowed with reason, this means assenting to no impression that is misleading or obscure, giving rein to no impulse toward actions that are not social.[61]

Knowledge for the Stoics is therefore more than a matter of remembering facts about the world from which we might personally gain via accolades, social standing, and/or fortune. Because knowledge comprises the consciousness that everything about us is a part derived from a whole, it underpins our living and acting in accordance with a communally beneficial nature. Epictetus describes this social nature in virtuous terms as the "nature of the good."[62] What we can now crucially therefore observe in such a claim is that the Stoic correlation of rational assent with knowledge and collective goods incorporates a value orientation.

This link between value and knowledge is readily apparent in *Discourses*, when Epictetus defines knowledge as well-being, in that in the "conduct of life, there must be a science to living well"[63] or a "knowledge of the art of living."[64] What does the "art" of "living well" mean? Put simply, it refers to thinking and acting in accordance with a rational nature. As we have seen via Seneca and Epictetus, knowledge guides us in that pursuit. Stobaeus

60. Epictetus, *Discourses* (2014), 1.22.9.

61. Marcus Aurelius, *Meditations* (1964), 8.7. See also the translation by Hard (in Marcus Aurelius, *Meditations* [2011], 8.7), which interprets the final line in terms of a rational nature that "directs its impulses only to actions that further the common good."

62. Epictetus, *Discourses* (2014), 1.23.2.

63. Epictetus, *Discourses* (2008), 4.1.63.

64. Epictetus, *Discourses* (2014), 4.1.63.

informs that numerous Stoics express this value-laden understanding of knowledge, for whom "knowledge is a cognition" that operates only in the "virtuous."[65] We do not acquire knowledge about the physical world primarily to be able to scientifically know the world from a distance and then control it through that knowledge. While we have reviewed how the Stoics are committed to empirically understanding the ordered ecological patterns they see around them, Stoic knowledge is not primarily a tool that we can use to manipulate our physical environments for our own benefit, or to medicate our physical bodies for an elongated physiological existence. The acquisition of knowledge is rather an education and an exercise in learning the *limits* of our control. This is a mode that we have reviewed from the outset in this book, a mode that I have characterized as deriving from a fundamental consciousness of ourselves as communally and universally embedded entities. By understanding that we are not separately self-determining individuals, but instead are ordered parts in a systematized whole, we appreciate the boundaries of what is up to us individually. In this chapter we have seen the assertion that formal philosophical education, paired with the informal application of what we have learned, develops our appreciation of these limits.

With this emphasis on the role of education in our ongoing rationalization though, I am prompted to question just how universal our rational natures can be. The rationalities that we each embody have a shared source and composition in Stoicism. If these rationalities are developed and matured through education, training, and learning however, will this mean that the knowledge required to continually live in accordance with our rational nature could be *unavailable* to some? Not everyone has access to proper educational structures or philosophical instruction. Might some humans have the default inclinations to live in accordance with nature but not the chance to learn how? Or in other words, even if the universe is one collective society for the Stoics, is it a society that is not collectively educationally egalitarian?

What I mean by egalitarianism in this context concerns the questions of (i) who receives the chance to be educated, by either formal or informal instruction, and (ii) what are the respective outcomes and benefits that emerge in people's education and instruction. While the first element refers to opportunities to access education, the second identifies whether someone can apply their education to improving their own life and others' lives. I am interested in how Stoic understandings of education relate to these kinds of

---

65. Stobaeus in Long and Sedley, *Hellenistic Philosophers*, 41H; taken from *SVF*, 3.112. Sextus Empiricus (*Against the Professors*, 7.151–57) makes the same observation of the Stoics.

questions, in determining how universal the opportunities are for humans to be trained to hold a consciousness of our systematically interconnected existences.

We can consider such themes by intersecting Stoic conceptions of education and gender. One reason for targeting gender is that in the roughly two and a half thousand years since the inception of ancient Stoicism, most societies have not been educationally egalitarian. Access to formal study has regularly not been available to women around the world.[66] Men have by default dominated most societies' professional, political, commercial, legal, academic, and other structures that typically require the kinds of knowledges and networks developed during the studies from which women have been restricted. How then, we can now ask, might a philosophy that identifies a common rationality among all of us, position the human study of this common rationality when considering the gendering of such study opportunities?

The Social Rules and Expectations for Educational Equality

When appreciating a history of the exclusion of women from educational and vocational structures, we might not expect nor demand much to be different in ancient Greek and Roman cultures. In the middle to later era Stoicism of Gaius Musonius Rufus however, we possibly find a surprising gender egalitarianism regarding educational opportunities. This concerns Musonius' belief that women and men deserve the same education. Before beginning with Musonius, I should clarify that his is not the only ancient philosophical voice to have considered themes around gender. Through Diogenes Laërtius we learn for example that Zeno's text *Republic* instructs us to view men and women as equally rational and "commonly wise."[67] Epictetus, who we have learned Musonius teaches, in his *Discourses* also discusses how the wife of a wise man will similarly be wise.[68]

Possible connections between the Stoics and Socrates are also traced through common ideas around gender.[69] Part of the speculation around this connection is fueled by Diogenes' account of Antisthenes' assertions

66. Brown and Zong (*Global Perspectives*) provide a historical and global analysis of women's educational opportunities. Complementarily, UNESCO (*Gender Equality*) reports the international developments in improving access to education for women who have otherwise previously been excluded from studying.

67. Diogenes Laërtius, *Lives and Opinions*, 7.66.

68. Epictetus, *Discourses* (2014), 3.22.68.

69. Plato (*Republic* [2007], 6.456a) conveys Socrates' beliefs that women are no less philosophical than men.

that virtue is identical for men and women.[70] Because Antisthenes was educated by Socrates, and then himself educated Zeno's mentor, Crates of Thebes, a link between Socratic and early Stoic thinkers is proposed.[71] Moving to the present day, perhaps the most comprehensive recent portrayal of Stoic discussions of gender comes in Malin Grahn-Wilder's *Gender and Sexuality in Stoic Philosophy*. Of relevance to our impending attention on Musonius is Grahn-Wilder's observation that given the Stoic first principle of a common rationality across the human species, Musonius' assertion of equal educational opportunities for women and men coheres with Stoicism's fundamentals.[72]

With that background, we can now analyze Musonius' position. Stobaeus reports on Musonius lecturing to an audience about the reasons that daughters and sons should receive identical educations.[73] When certain audience members interrogate Musonius about this, he justifies his position by proclaiming that there is no difference between the genders in the capacity to be rational. This is consistent with what Grahn-Wilder has just observed about Stoic philosophy. If in Stoicism the universe is rational, and human rationalities and associated mental functions are traces of this universe, then male *and* female humans must have this rational trace. Women are as rationally oriented as men for Musonius and share the "same reasoning power."[74] Because of this common rational nature, women are likewise as geared as men are toward an existence of "virtue."[75]

Earlier we attended to Seneca's equation of rationality with ongoing philosophical study. We must already be rational to benefit from what we learn philosophically, however it also helps to dedicate ourselves to spending time with philosophy in order to understand how to live rationally. Having recognized that men and women have the same rational capacities, Musonius duly criticizes the belief of the time that philosophical study was more suited to men. If philosophy allows us to understand how to live rationally

70. Diogenes Laërtius, *Lives and Opinions*, 6.5.

71. Dudley (*History of Cynicism*, 2–4) counters claims of any real links between the two eras though, asserting that the Stoics constructed stories of the links between Antisthenes and Zeno to create the impression of an unbroken sequence between Socrates and the early Stoics.

72. Grahn-Wilder, *Gender and Sexuality*, 10.

73. Stobaeus in Musonius Rufus, *Lectures & Sayings*, 4.1–8.

74. Stobaeus in Musonius Rufus, *Lectures & Sayings*, 3.1.

75. Stobaeus in Musonius Rufus, *Lectures & Sayings*, 3.1. Nussbaum ("Incomplete Feminism," 290) reads a belief from Musonius here that women and men share the same predisposition regarding how to rationally integrate oneself within a collective ethical order.

and honorably,[76] and the universe has rationally ordered women as it has done with men, why should society exclude women from an education that trains them in how to be conscious of that.

Consistent with our interest in this book in the insight that Stoicism's primary focus is on communal and universal outcomes rather than on individualized or personalized ends, this demand from Musonius is not merely designed to benefit or liberate women individually. Musonius envisages that once young women receive the same philosophical education as men, society as a whole will enjoy a greater, collective prosperity. Through this attention we encounter signs that a Stoic impulse toward more equally available educational structures is concerned with social ends.

Musonius' prerogatives indeed appear to be surprisingly socially progressive, and able to be synced with many present-day ideas around equalizing educational and associated vocational opportunities for all genders. There are nevertheless concerns about how Musonius details the enactment of these philosophical and educational opportunities, both by the newly educated women, and by the societies in which they live. These concerns will contradict aspects of the egalitarian potentials of his work.

To examine this, we firstly need to consider Musonius' suggestion that philosophically educated women would be more "just" than women without such an education. This portrayal becomes less than egalitarian when he qualifies how the newly educated women would practically enact or use this "justness," that being to serve their husband and children.[77] The proposed social applications of women's education emerge in clearly unequal ways compared to how men can exercise their own education, if being educated means that women will be expected to better perform their duties as "a careful guardian of husband and children, entirely free from the love of gain or grasping for too much."[78]

A philosophical education seems in this characterization to serve the purpose of tempering the women's desire for anything more from her immediate family members than the chance to service them. The motivation of the newly educated woman would be to always "serve her husband" and never to question nor "hesitate" to undertake duties that are otherwise "appropriate for slaves."[79] Musonius recognizes that both women and men are capable of processing philosophical instruction. For women though, their education is designed to help them fulfil already established, labor intensive,

76. Stobaeus in Musonius Rufus, *Lectures & Sayings*, 3.1–2.
77. Stobaeus in Musonius Rufus, *Lectures & Sayings*, 3.4.
78. Stobaeus in Musonius Rufus, *Lectures & Sayings*, 3.4.
79. Stobaeus in Musonius Rufus, *Lectures & Sayings*, 3.5.

socially structured roles (wife, mother). Musonius rhetorically asks his audience, who could be "more just" than a woman who performs her domestic servitude so wisely after having undertaken philosophical study.[80] This justness and wisdom would be attributable to Stoic teachings around our part-to-whole relations with the world. This concerns how we each must rationally accept that our "lot" or situation in life reflects our systematized role or duty in a universally ordered structure. Where the Stoics argue that as individuals we are not unconditionally self-determining and that we are instead the systematically ordered parts of a greater whole, the effect for philosophically educated women would be to perform domestic roles with a consciousness and an acceptance of their role in the universal order, rather than of any desire for their individual liberation.

With this perspective there is no intention therefore in Stoicism to enact a socially equalizing application of educational outcomes. Philosophical instruction is certainly oriented by Musonius toward producing individuals who are conscious of the importance of rationally fulfilling social duties. This is consistent with the characterizations of philosophical study and human rationality that we have seen Seneca forward. For women in Musonius' model, those duties seem restricted to the very domestic service that they were undertaking before being educated.[81] We are obligated in discussing Musonius in this way to note that he never declares an intention to liberate women from existing socially structured responsibilities. Such imperatives could indeed be entirely foreign to this era and context, given that instead his attention is on the practical outcomes that can ensue for society if a greater number of individuals access philosophical education. Here we encounter consistencies with the communal and distributed priorities that have emerged when other ancient Stoics raise what initially might otherwise appear to be individualistic motives or themes.

A further point that Musonius makes on the social ramifications of an individual's educational development sees his philosophy slightly diverge from other Stoics. This concerns the topic of social standing. While

---

80. Stobaeus in Musonius Rufus, *Lectures & Sayings*, 3.4. Nussbaum ("Incomplete Feminism," 296) sympathizes to an extent with Musonius, observing that Musonius was probably conscious of "reassuring" husbands in his audience that their newly philosophical wives would not "stubbornly or boldly" abandon them and their household duties. However, Nussbaum ("Incomplete Feminism," 286) does not let Musonius off entirely, arguing that he does nothing to emancipate educated women from a division of functions that encumbers them with the domestic responsibilities.

81. For more dedicated analyses of what Musonius offers to discussions around women's liberation, see Aikin and McGill-Rutherford, "Stoicism"; Arnold, *Roman Stoicism*; Asmis, "Stoic Individualism"; Grahn-Wilder, *Gender and Sexuality*; Hill, "Feminism and Stoic Sagehood"; Hill, "Were the Stoics Feminists?"

detailing the ways in which a philosophically educated woman would serve society at large via the family unit, he also anticipates their elevated social reputation due to being more philosophical. This differs from the views we have reviewed in Seneca, Epictetus, and Marcus, all of whom have spoken about the indifference we should embody to matters around social standing and reputation. Perhaps not surprisingly for Musonius in any case, this benefit would not begin and end with the educated individual woman. The newfound respect they receive would instead structurally radiate beyond the woman, to also serve her husband's social standing. Being married to a woman of philosophical knowledge is accordingly said to provide the husband with a "great advantage" and "honor."[82]

The social or public effects of education for women therefore transcend their individualized concerns. Their "philosophical knowledge" will not provide access to a different kind of life beyond the private realm, however such knowledge will reverberate with various social effects. If one such effect was a woman's capacity to relinquish her family responsibilities, this would be destabilizing for communities. Musonius here clarifies that he does not want nor expect women studying philosophy "to cast aside their appropriate tasks" such as "sitting at home spinning wool"[83] and "managing her household."[84] Given this expectation of ongoing domestic commitments, the effects in the public realm of her new philosophical status would often be felt without her individual presence to such effects, trapped as she was in the domestic sphere. To be fair to Musonius, he also warns men not to abandon their daily responsibilities when studying philosophy, stating that he does not expect women *or* men to neglect their appropriate daily duties and concern themselves only with philosophizing.[85] The differences in what constitutes an "appropriate task" for men versus women is however where we find what is limited about the possible activation of women's education beyond the domestic context.

These appropriate tasks refer to the division of duties, which in turn concern a conceptual division between how the ancients assign indoor and outdoor labors. Musonius conventionally observes the different physical strengths of the genders as nature's indication that women should be allocated indoor tasks.[86] This direction by default removes women from the

82. Stobaeus in Musonius Rufus, *Lectures & Sayings*, 3.6.

83. Stobaeus in Musonius Rufus, *Lectures & Sayings*, 3.6.

84. Stobaeus in Musonius Rufus, *Lectures & Sayings*, 3.2.

85. Stobaeus in Musonius Rufus, *Lectures & Sayings*, 3.6.

86. Engel ("Gender Egalitarianism," 381) argues that given Musonius' attachment to distinctions between differently gendered, indoor versus outdoor roles, we should not unconditionally associate his philosophy with a gendered egalitarianism.

public realm. Musonius, it must be said, is aware that not all men are stronger than all women, and further indicates that no duty is exclusively the domain of either men or women. Reflecting the Stoic commitment to the belief that all social duties are rational duties, and that each of our rationalities has common or kindred conditions, he likewise recognizes a "common basis" for all such duties.[87] While however Musonius expresses a genuine belief that philosophy "honors equality," women of Musonius' era, philosophically educated or not, are commonly excluded from contributing to grander public and interpersonal forms of social existence in the ways that men can. Strictly according to the Stoic understanding of a universal social fabric, philosophically rational women would always be socially participatory if when they think and act, they do so with a consciousness of their interconnections with the whole world. This is what we have seen Marcus Aurelius call the "city of Zeus." In a localized regard though, their publicly social participation would remain muted.

Musonius does not interrogate this standard, instead perpetuating it by critiquing women who might think to "abandon their house-keeping and go around in public with men and practice arguments."[88] Given that Musonius recognizes that women are no less rational than men, it is not that women are believed to lack the natural capacity to participate in philosophy publicly, they just lack the opportunity to practice it.[89] We have just seen that Musonius assumes men will exercise their argumentative skills in public in order to enact the practical mandates of Stoic philosophy. Philosophy for the Stoics is regularly an outdoor, public, collaborative exercise. To this feature of the philosophy, women just are not invited.

If the educated woman furthermore enacted her new Stoic knowledge, she might only be motivated to perpetuate this marginalization. Where conversely a woman, newly trained in Stoic philosophy, happened to complain, the apparent adverse emotional response could have been interpreted as a sign that she had not been capable of learning and embodying the Stoic indifference to what is beyond one's control. This could in turn have had negative ripple effects throughout communities regarding how people viewed Musonius' call for the suitability of women to philosophical education.

---

87. Stobaeus in Musonius Rufus, *Lectures & Sayings*, 4.6.

88. Stobaeus in Musonius Rufus, *Lectures & Sayings*, 3.6.

89. See Grahn-Wilder (*Gender and Sexuality*, 192) for further discussion on this point.

Training Ourselves to Be Rational,
While Training Others to Be Rational

By raising this point regarding the learning of how to develop a Stoic indifference to what is not up to us, we are obligated to consider how the Stoics propose that we undertake such training. This concerns the regulation or management of our emotional responses. Our interests in this book are Stoicism's attention on social and universal ends rather than individualized ones. Consistent with this theme, this discussion on emotional responses will explore how our self-management of our feelings speaks fundamentally for the Stoics to collective ends and benefits that exceed any personally localized results.

The idea of emotional control via Stoicism has gained much popularity in recent times. As discussed in the opening chapter, self-help industries have thrived by offering techniques designed to teach us how to exercise this kind of self-management. We can review the Stoic bases of these modern applications by returning to Epictetus. This builds on his portrayal of our mental experiences that we have covered. Living rationally, according to Epictetus, involves a constant appreciation of what is within our mental control or up to us.[90] Rather than repeating discussions regarding our mind and thoughts in relation to this directive that we covered in chapter 2 though, we will now extend that study by attending to our feelings that are associated with those thoughts. Of relevance given our current topic of education, are the questions of how we train ourselves to feel certain ways and not others for the Stoics, and whether such feelings are ever simply our own personally.

There is a conventional reading of Epictetus' views on our relationship with our emotions. That reading is that living rationally requires being indifferent, not just mentally but also emotionally indifferent, to what is not up to our own decision-making.[91] Epictetus equates a greater feeling of being emotionally out of control, with being more invested in what is not up to us. Refusing to accept what is beyond our control, namely the systematic ordering of the universe of which we and our lives are mere parts, will in this understanding lead us to feeling in emotional disarray.[92]

We have reviewed what is, versus is not, in our control according to Epictetus' *Enchiridion*. In our control, or up to us, are our mental functions such as judgements and decisions. Conversely not up to us or in our control

---

90. Epictetus, *Enchiridion*, 1.
91. Epictetus, *Discourses* (2014), 1.29.24.
92. Epictetus, *Discourses* (2014), 2.13.1.

is a world of physical objects, other people, and what is classified as "external" to us.[93] Epictetus develops this idea in the lectures found in *Discourses*, criticizing at length how much we value things such as our reputation and other people's opinions of us. When we become personally invested in these kinds of uncontrollable characterizations of ourselves, or in Epictetus' terms when we "love, hate, or fear these things,"[94] we become slaves to what other people think. By "having power" over what emotionally controls us, these people represent "our masters."[95] This is not simply because they might influence how we present ourselves to others in the future, as we attempt to affect or shape others' opinions of ourselves and our reputations. More importantly for Epictetus, they become our masters because they control how we feel about ourselves internally. If what people think of us dictates how we feel about ourselves, those people master our identity and sense of self. From this understanding we see how emotions, which arise through individual feelings, regularly adversely manifest through interpersonal settings for the Stoics.

Despite this terminology of mastery and slavery, Epictetus does not agree that emotional reactions are *imposed* on us by externalities such as other people and their opinions. While these kinds of circumstances set the scene, it is only once we have internally mentally reacted to our circumstances that we experience the emotional reaction prompted by or associated with what we think about the circumstances. Given that we have control over these internal mental reactions, if we have an unfavorable emotional response to our circumstances, the responsibility for the emotion falls not with the circumstances but with ourselves.[96] Managing our emotions for the Stoics therefore requires an inward not an outward perspective, in order to remain aware of what we can internally mentally and rationally control, rather than irrationally "gripe and protest against circumstance[s]" not up to us.[97] This self-management for Epictetus demands constant training of our internal rational functions.

While Epictetus asks us to look internally when regulating our emotional experiences, this is not an inward perspective that marks an individual self-control separate from the world. What is internal is our rationality, and as we have seen, our rationality is a communally and universally dispersed system. To look inward is to look to a kinship with all that is rationally

93. Epictetus, *Enchiridion*, 1.

94. Epictetus, *Discourses* (2014), 4.1.60.

95. Epictetus, *Discourses* (2014), 4.1.60.

96. Epictetus, *Discourses* (2014), 1.2.5–11.

97. Epictetus, *Discourses* (2008), 1.12.20.

ordered. Epictetus does not expect us to always be able to embody a consciousness of this rational nature like a sage would though. In speaking to this chapter's topic of education, he details how we can train ourselves to be conscious that our internal natures are just traces of the universe, by exercising indifference to what happens in that universe that is not up to us.

Earlier we have reviewed Seneca's characterization of the twofold nature of our rationality. We have an innate rational faculty, however that faculty must be educated or developed. Epictetus will endorse a similar model in terms of how we train or work on ourselves to be indifferent to certain emotional stimuli. In evoking Seneca's discussion on the fear of death, Epictetus argues that neither death, nor dying, nor pain, harms us. What does harm us are our fears and anticipations of death and of painful experiences.[98] The same then applies to other aspects of our lives such as our reputations, jobs, wealth, friendships, and so on. Losing any of these things is not necessarily a harm for Epictetus, to the extent that such things are not entirely up to us. Fearing the loss of them is harmful however, given the irrational investment in what is outside our control that such fear indicates.

The Stoic rational response to fear should not involve trying to manage the situations or people that have induced the fear in us and mastered us accordingly. Such things will invariably not be up to us, and we must be conscious of the way in which the world is an ordered system without regard for our personal preferences. We are of course just parts of the whole. We must instead therefore rationally order ourselves so that we remain indifferent to the causes of our fear. This requires transferring our focus from what is outside our mental control to what is inside it, where what is primarily inside our rational mental authority is being conscious of these part-to-whole relations and evaluating everything that occurs through that consciousness.[99] This transfer demands our continual dedication, as we "train" our rationalities in the management of our associated feelings. Epictetus emphasizes that as part of this learning and development you must "talk to yourself, train your thoughts,"[100] to automate responses of indifference to what is external to your mental appreciation of your relation to the world.

This kind of training is a recurring theme in Epictetus' *Discourses*. Epictetus wants our education or training to highlight to us that only how we think and feel about things can hurt us, not the things themselves. What we are educating ourselves toward in focusing internally on how we feel

98. Epictetus, *Discourses* (2014), 2.1.13.

99. Epictetus, *Discourses* (2014), 3.5.4.

100. Epictetus, *Discourses* (2008), 4.4.26.

according to Epictetus is duly a state of "serenity."[101] If only what can harm us is already under our control, then we should feel reassured by the notion that we have at our disposal the capacity to live an emotionally stable existence. This theme of serenity might again remind us of Seneca and his portrayal of the internal tranquility that he experiences in Nomentum. This is a peace that is not dependent on surroundings. It is instead conditioned by one's internalized fragment of a universal rational order.

An education in Stoic philosophy becomes a practice in dealing with adverse external circumstances and is in this regard comparable to physical exposure training. As someone is exposed to harsh environmental conditions, they can learn to endure extreme temperatures for example. Developing a mental resilience to external threats requires a similar developmental process for Epictetus. Just as people can learn to be resilient to "heat and cold," likewise we can develop our mind to be indifferent to external activations of our emotions.[102]

Where Epictetus describes this as "withholding" our investment in sources of our emotions that are not ourselves, we possibly get the sense of the most individualized characteristics of our rational development. There seems to be something personally demanding about the labor we must each invest when learning and ritualizing emotional indifference. Even though our default rational nature is a *common* nature for the Stoics, there is an obligation to each apply ourselves to individually "make progress"[103] toward a truly rational state. No one else can do this for us and the training never ends.[104] This leads Christopher Gill, who we involved earlier, to posit that of all the Stoic thinkers, Epictetus asserts most regularly that it is up to us whether we mentally engage a Stoic education as a therapeutic intervention to our irrationally oriented tendencies.[105]

Despite the apparently individualizing tone of these modes via which we learn and apply our rational indifference, we still find recognitions within such instructions of the underpinning collective intentions and outcomes

101. Epictetus, *Discourses* (2014), 1.4.5.

102. Epictetus, *Discourses* (2014), fragment 20.

103. Epictetus, *Discourses* (2014), 1.4.6.

104. Brittain and Brennan (in Simplicius, *On Epictetus Handbook*, 23) note that such training for Epictetus is a process in which we are always navigating between vice and virtue.

105. Gill, *Personality in Greek*, 451. This is also apparent where Epictetus (*Discourses* [2008], 3.23.30) refers to philosophical lectures as a "hospital," and additionally where Epictetus (*Discourses* [2014], 3.23.30) describes philosophical education as a "doctor's surgery." For more on readings of Stoicism as therapeutic, see Long, "Plato, Chrysippus, and Posidonius"; Robertson, *Cognitive-Behavioural Therapy*; Schofield, "Stoic Ethics," 253–56.

that we have identified throughout Stoicism. Given that our emotional states and responses are regularly interpersonally produced and enacted for example, a more rationally controlled Stoic individual serves communal benefits by contributing to a more rationally cohesive social group. A less emotionally unsettled individual is a more ordered and controlled citizen, able to participate in a collective harmony. This motivates Epictetus to describe how if you have "orderly conduct" you will not "shout out," "jump up," or get upset if displeasing events arise.[106] Our orderly conduct recognizes our role as a part or fragment in an overall rational system. Through our rational self-control we present ourselves as belonging to something harmoniously greater than ourselves.

This is partly why Stoicism from its earliest eras places such emphasis on self-control. As far back as Cleanthes we have fragmented evidence that what is good is what is "well-ordered, just, holy, pious, *self-controlled*, useful, honourable."[107] Our previous studies have similarly revealed that when considering the daimon, what is up to us concerns our rationality, however our rationality has a source that is not separate from other peoples' rationalities. In considerations of what is "up to us," the "us" that is fundamental to our application of the Stoic principles concerned with control and emotional indifference is both an individualized "us" (in terms of how we each train and enact our rationalities), and an indication of a community or fellowship of rational beings. This latter "us" is an "us" of which we are each a part, and with which we share kindred relations. It is because we rationalize only as traces of this universally ordered "us," that for the Stoics the interest of the individual must be shared with the interest of the community.

Stoic honor speaks to the social and universal orderings that are adhered to by minds trained to understand that we only control ourselves as parts of an order that is beyond our control. If we are each able to be indifferent to what is not up to us individually, our own lives become more manageable because we mentally cohere with an overall rationally ordered system. We have seen that fighting against that ordered production of our individual lives not only induces adverse emotions but is also a futile exercise.

Stoicism's communal features are also apparent in the intersecting themes of education and self-control when we appreciate that as we live in controlled ways, we show others how to be Stoic. A practical reading of this would be that with this distributed form of instruction we generate more resilient and less volatile societies. Epictetus indeed posits that the

---

106. Epictetus, *Discourses* (2014), 4.3.9.

107. Clement in Long and Sedley, *Hellenistic Philosophers*, 60Q; taken from *SVF*, 1.557; emphasis added.

interpersonal influence and collective benefits that our own rational control emanates are some of the primary reasons for embodying such control. With self-control we not only cohere with a universal rational order, we also educate and show others how to live as a Stoic:

> To begin with, you have to set a different example with your behaviour. No more blaming God or man. Suspend desire completely, train aversion only on things under your control.[108]

Who do we "set an example" to (or what is otherwise translated as "show" ourselves to)[109] as Epictetus describes in this passage? To our fellow humans, particularly those of our immediate communities and populations, as well as to those humans of the far broader cosmopolis as the example we set ripples through and participates in the ordering of others and their behaviors. Our rational indifference is simultaneously directed both internally and interpersonally, with both personal and impersonal sites. This explains further why I have described our rational internality as what spreads "beyond" our localized selves. This "beyond" does not designate anything external. It instead denotes the dispersal of each of us within a universe that is the source and site of our rational self.

These are themes with which we might already be familiar thanks to our earlier engagement with Marcus Aurelius. So primary is the impulse in each of us to serve common interests according to his philosophy, that when we think or act rationally, we are doing so as an exemplification and a contribution to others. This communal nature is our Stoic nature. When we have "performed some benevolent action or accomplished anything else that contributes to the common good," we have likewise for Marcus done what we were by nature "constituted for."[110] Epictetus has here clearly inspired Marcus again. We see the same description applied in *Discourses* when Epictetus states that God has "constituted the rational animal" in a way that we are designed as individuals to "contribute to the common benefit."[111]

In Stoicism we are educated as individuals via the kinds of training and labor that have the effect of improving individual well-being. These individualized orientations and outcomes however derive from wider interpersonal and social benefits and priorities. While the imperatives of training ourselves to be resilient to external causes of our emotions are often

---

108. Epictetus, *Discourses* (2008), 3.22.13.

109. Epictetus, *Discourses* (1916), 3.22; Epictetus, *Discourses* (2014), 3.22.13.

110. Marcus Aurelius, *Meditations* (2011), 9.42.

111. Epictetus, *Discourses* (2014), 1.19.12.

conceived around themes of personal rationality, a communal ordering is the underlying Stoic motivation and impetus. Because we are each a trace of a rationality in which we all share, any education regarding our enactment of that rationality must address how to cohere with other peoples' rationalities as traces. Learning does not constitute an external instruction that installs new knowledge in us, but instead is a reminder of what our internal rational nature already embodies. With this foundation, we can now consider how the ultimate form of our rational existence is a shared rather than an individualized state.

6

Collective Happiness

Happiness Is Not an Emotion

WE CONCLUDE THESE CONSIDERATIONS of our communal natures with a study of the ultimate end or state for a Stoic, that which is regularly translated in English by the term "happiness." Because we will be exploring an aspect of the philosophy that is referred to as happiness, we will also incorporate further discussions around our emotional existence for the Stoics. Be warned though, this does not mean that what is frequently translated for the Stoics as happiness denotes an emotional state.

Throughout this book we have seen that in Stoicism we share a rational mentality. This commonality is responsible for our communal and social links, our kindred relations, and our mutual bonds. When we think and act rationally as individuals, for the Stoics we do not primarily intend personal benefits and outcomes. We look rather to collective and universal ends. To be rational is to be conscious of how our rationality interconnects us, meaning that our associated internal mental processes are not those of an isolated or separate being.

Where does this equation of rationality with connectivity leave the emotions though? If in Stoicism rational states are communal or social states, and emotional states are not the same as rational states, does this mean that our emotional states inversely separate us from a communal or social existence for the Stoics? To what extent can we be rationally social, according to its Stoic definition of an awareness of our part-to-whole relations with the world and each other, and simultaneously be emotional? We will consider this question by appraising the relations posited by various ancient Stoics between our rationality and our emotions.

Given that I have already indicated a distinction between emotion and what modern English translates from the ancient Stoics as happiness, our first task though is to understand what this happiness means. Consistent with the priorities of the Stoics that we have explored, happiness in Stoicism refers to living in accordance with our rational nature. Living rationally will be what we understand in Stoicism to be a happy existence. There is more to what is translated as happiness for the Stoics therefore than simply feeling a pleasurable way.

Instead for the Stoics, the term that is translated as happiness refers to a well-being, a flourishing, a living well. Both terms, happiness and well-being, incompletely represent what the Stoics mean however. It is worthwhile accordingly to know that the Greek word being translated in this way is *eudaimonia*. An early appearance of the term's stem, "eudaimôn," comes in the ancient poetry of Hesiod. There eudaimôn has the sense of a state of enhanced welfare or well-being that results from having avoided displeasing the gods.[1] Aside from acknowledging Hesiod's application, we should also note that this term has two parts. "Eu" refers to "well" in English,[2] whereas "daimôn" we have encountered in chapter 2 as a divine trace and guardian spirit. Through Epictetus we have indeed learned of the Stoic belief that we each embody a daimôn as the source of our rationality. When we break down this term eudaimôn into its component parts therefore, we see a meaning that is consistent with Hesiod's application of it as living well in accordance with what is divinely ordered.

As this concept develops philosophically, the correlation of eudaimôn with rationality becomes overt. The idea emerges that if we live rationally we can avoid the kind of godly ill will that Hesiod mentions. Where living rationally comprises reflecting on ourselves as rational creatures as we have seen the Stoics mandate, as well as living in accordance with this rationality, so Plato's equation of rational self-reflection with well-being also becomes relevant. This twin Stoic and Platonic relevance makes sense when considering the Socratic influence on the Stoics that we have raised.

Some caution is required when engaging Plato on the topic of happiness, given debates around the terms that Plato uses to describe it.[3] In

1. Hesiod, *Homeric Hymns*, 826–28.

2. Ogilvie, *Student's English Dictionary*, 263.

3. See Bobonich ("Socrates and Eudaimonia," 293–332) or White (*Individual and Conflict*) for discussions on the Socratic application, or not, of the term "eudaimonia." Long (*Stoic Studies*, 182) assists by referring to how Plato uses "cognate words" for eudaimonia. *The Definitions*, a lost ancient book dedicated to explaining key Platonic

the *Apology* though, Socrates famously defines rational self-examination as virtuous, and such virtue as the necessary and sufficient condition of the "greatest good": happiness.[4] This is consistent with other features of happiness that Socrates presents in a manner that suggests the goodness of happiness is unquestionable.[5] Socrates puts rational self-examination on its pedestal here by famously uttering that "the unexamined life is not worth living."[6] We can also find this kind of discussion in Plato's *Meno*[7] and *Phaedo*,[8] where Socrates correlates happiness with living wisely and virtuously.

Not only are Stoics such as Epictetus heavily influenced by the Socratic relationship between self-reflection and rationality, but Stoicism also adopts aspects of the distinction Plato makes between pleasure and happiness. *The Symposium* is one source in which Plato distinguishes the pleasure that wealth brings, from the rational happiness of reflective wisdom. We have of course already seen traces of this influence in our engagement with Seneca on the topic of wealth. In Plato's *The Symposium*, Appollodorus duly expresses how he "feels sorry" for his friends who are overly occupied with their wealth, the "rich money-makers," telling them that the pleasures associated with wealth do not mark an achievement.[9] Appollodorus conveys to them that happiness alternatively occurs by living wisely and virtuously, a process with which Socrates assists him. Socrates also differentiates the pleasures of wealth, from rational well-being, when addressing the people of Athens in the *Apology*.[10] Plato's repeated excursions into this theme duly mark it as a favorite of the Socratic dialogues.

The Stoics likewise do not correlate happiness with pleasure. On this point we can recall from chapter 4 the Stoic account forwarded by Cato and Cicero, in which self-preservation, not pleasure, is our primary function because self-preservation is rational. Cato conveys the Stoic view that

---

concepts but whose author is unknown, apparently describes eudaimonia. It is widely interpreted that Plato's followers in the Academy, not Plato himself, wrote this work.

4. Plato, *Apology*, 38a.

5. Long (*Epicurus to Epictetus*, 182–83) notes that there are certain features of happiness that are considered to be indisputable because when Socrates presents them in argument they are never challenged. These features include happiness being "what everyone desires," that which results from the good not bad, what the gods have, the freedom to live well, and people's "ultimate objective."

6. Plato, *Apology*, 38a.

7. Plato, *Meno*, 88b–89a.

8. Plato, *Phaedo*, 81a–82b.

9. Plato, *Symposium*, 173c–d.

10. Plato, *Apology*, 29e.

happiness as our nature's end or ultimate good is not reducible to any associated "pleasure" and that it is not a human's "nature to seek pleasure but simply to love themselves."[11] We can here readily appreciate the Socratic influence in the Stoic distinction between rationalized happiness and pleasure. Complementing what we have just reviewed on this topic from Plato's *The Symposium*, in the *Gorgias* Socrates further argues that because the difference between good and bad is not the same as the difference between pleasure and pain, what is good and what is pleasure must themselves be different. This is important given the connection of what is good with what is rational, a matter that we will soon discuss in terms of Zeno's recognition of the good flow of a rationally ordered world. For Socrates the difference between good and pleasure is apparent in that something can be good without it being pleasurable, and vice-versa.[12] This is also evident in the *Phaedo*, where for Socrates the soul is "happy" once it has dispensed with externals such as "physical desires and pleasures," and is then only occupied with the well-being of what is rationally internal to it.[13] We will later consider how Plato's *Republic* further unpacks this rational well-being in terms of a supposed harmonious application of the different aspects of our internal selves.

Internal processes of rational self-awareness are integral to these Socratic and Platonic positions regarding our well-being that precede and inform Stoic conceptions. Once we arrive at Aristotle though, we find that while the emphasis on the internal conditions for our well-being is not lost, also included in such eudaimonic well-being are aspects of the world that are external to us. This will present important differences from Stoic beliefs.

Happiness Is an Activity, Not a Target

Aristotelian philosophy explicitly references eudaimonia as well-being. Most prominently discussed in his *Nicomachean Ethics*, Aristotle correlates eudaimonic well-being with activity, specifically virtuous activity, rationally oriented actions, and self-reflection on those actions.[14] When observing how different things in the world have different functions, as well as the different appropriate actions designed to serve those respective functions, Aristotle defines the human function as being rational and categorizes rational *actions* as serving that function best.[15]

11. Cicero, *Moral Ends*, 2.33.
12. Plato, *Gorgias*, 497c–e.
13. Plato, *Phaedo*, 81a–b.
14. Aristotle, *Nicomachean Ethics*, 1.8–9.
15. Aristotle, *Nicomachean Ethics*, 1.7.

While rational activity conditions a range of beneficial outcomes for the self, Aristotle distinguishes for special attention rationality's relationship to our well-being or happiness. This is because for all the ancient Hellenistic schools, living rationally, that is living well or happily, is only done for the sake of living rationally, well, and happily. We orient toward rational activity not to serve anything beyond being rational, rational activity "is always choosable for its own sake and never because of something else."[16] Aristotle duly describes rationalized well-being and happiness as the "final end," the "chief good," and the "self-sufficient" aspect of our being.

An influence on Stoic perspectives regarding the communal purposes and ends of our existences is apparent in Aristotle's clarification that an equation of happiness with self-sufficiency does not infer individuated or autonomous, self-directed human intentions and outcomes. Aristotle's definition of happiness involves in fact a remarkable number of references to our interpersonal and communal existences. To live rationally happily for Aristotle means living socially. Happiness' "self"-sufficiency therefore is a reference to the belief that we need nothing else except its rational existence:

> By self-sufficient we mean not what is sufficient for oneself alone living a solitary life, but something that includes parents, wife and children, friends and fellow citizens in general; for man is by nature a social being . . . A self-sufficient thing, then, we take to be one which by itself makes life desirable and in no way deficient; and we believe that happiness is such a thing.[17]

The Stoics will not only agree with Aristotle that we are social beings, but they will also vigorously pursue the belief that well-being or happiness is an activity, comprising living rationally and virtuously. For both schools, happiness is not an emotional state that we should target with the purpose of feeling personal pleasure. Just as Aristotle positions eudaimonic well-being and happiness as the ultimate end, likewise for the Stoics living rationally well is not an end that serves other ends,[18] whereby instead "being happy is the end for the sake of which everything is done, but which is not itself done for the sake of anything."[19]

16. Aristotle, *Nicomachean Ethics*, 1.7.

17. Aristotle, *Nicomachean Ethics*, 1.7.

18. This is the orthodox reading of commentaries both current and of the last few hundred years. As examples of this transgenerational relevance, see Ackeren, *Companion to Marcus Aurelius*, 421; Annas, "Ethics in Stoic Philosophy," 64; Anthon, *Classical Dictionary*, 1404; Brennan, *Stoic Life*, 35; Hyslop, *Elements of Ethics*, 44–47; Inwood and Donini, "Stoic Ethics," 684; Spence, *Control Problem*, 81–8.

19. Stobaeus in Long and Sedley, *Hellenistic Philosophers*, 63A; taken from *SVF*, 3.16.

Within Stoicism this position can be traced to Zeno's early definition of happiness as "living in agreement" with a "good flow of life."[20] Zeno describes this flow, which is the interconnected, world system, as "good," because it is rationally ordered. As we have indeed seen for the Stoics, there is nothing more perfect than the rational ordering of the universal whole. The subsequent head of the Stoic school, Cleanthes, expands Zeno's definition by implicating our apparent individual rationality within this overall rational order, describing happiness in terms of living in accordance with our own nature. By stating that happiness and well-being are the actions and process of living in accordance with a rational nature, through Cleanthes we receive a clear early Stoic indication that individuals achieve happiness by living rationally, rather than by targeting happiness as a state to feel. Stobaeus further conveys how for Zeno we should not seek happiness via objectives or ends. It is just by living rationally that happiness will manifest as that life.[21]

There is a consistent theme throughout the positions of the early heads of the Stoic school therefore. This continues through to Chrysippus, whose definition we will work with more thoroughly given that ancient commentaries present his wording as the fullest extension provided by the Athenian Stoics. One such commentary comes via Stobaeus, through whom we learn that Chrysippus correlates happiness with a rationally happy life itself, just as we have seen with Zeno and Cleanthes. An insight also emerges here into how durable this definition of happiness becomes for the Stoics, in that Stobaeus reports that Chrysippus and his Stoic "successors" continue to believe that happiness is identical to the act of living happily.[22] The extension of this definition for which Chrysippus is responsible,[23] concerns the assertion that happiness depends on what actually happens, or more specifically "what happens" in accordance with "nature."[24] Happiness in this understanding is not a personal state or feeling that transpires after doing rational things or thinking rationally. The early Stoic sense of happiness instead refers to the rationally ordered "happenings" of a systematically interconnected "nature."

---

20. Stobaeus in Long and Sedley, *Hellenistic Philosophers*, 63A; taken from *SVF*, 3.16.

21. Stobaeus in Long and Sedley, *Hellenistic Philosophers*, 63A; taken from *SVF*, 3.16.

22. Stobaeus in Long and Sedley, *Hellenistic Philosophers*, 63A; taken from *SVF*, 3.16.

23. Boeri, "Cosmic Nature," 177; Gould, *Philosophy of Chrysippus*, 168–70; Jedan, *Stoic Virtues*, 61; Richardson, "Basis of Ethics," 87–97; Striker, *Essays*, 224.

24. Stobaeus in Long and Sedley, *Hellenistic Philosophers*, 63B; taken from *SVF*, 2.75.11–76.8.

We will be living happily and with well-being if we accept that our life accords with nature's ordered happenings.

Aristotle and the Stoics cohere on numerous points regarding happiness. We have seen that it is positioned by both as the ultimate end or good of our rational existence. Happiness for both is never in service of anything subsequent to it, it is not a feeling that we seek, it is rather a rationality that we actively live. This makes happiness for Chrysippus (as conveyed by Diogenes Laërtius, and in employing the same terminology as Aristotle) our nature and "the Chief Good."[25] A particular Stoic signature is then put on this interpretation via their belief that happiness is this ultimate activity because happiness is the rationally ordered world itself, and there is nothing greater than the world. To live happily and with eudaimonic well-being is to live with and as an ordered part of a whole system.

Where this point indicates what is particular about the Stoic worldview, so we begin to see differentiations between the Stoic and Aristotelian conceptions of happiness. This divergence becomes increasingly apparent when considering how each school conceives of the relationship between happiness and externals. We have learned how Stoic happiness, in being bound up with what is internal to our rational nature, is not dependent on the external world of objects, popularized social trends, and so on. We should recall here the Stoic mantra regarding indifference to externals. Our happiness, that is our rational existence, is not perturbed by nor drawn to externals.[26]

Aristotle conversely involves features of the external world within our happiness or well-being. By doing this we find that he differs not only from the Stoics, but also from Plato's presentation of Socratic beliefs. Whereas for the Stoics and Socrates, living virtuously and rationally are necessary and sufficient for our happiness, for Aristotle such orientations provide necessary however not absolutely sufficient conditions for happiness. When we think and act rationally and virtuously, it is in the Aristotelian view often by doing so through external goods that our rationality becomes action and happiness radiates accordingly. External aspects to our lives such as having enough money to buy food, enjoying our daily work, or our friendships,

---

25. Diogenes Laërtius, *Lives and Opinions*, 7.53.

26. Cicero provides many accounts of the Stoic attribution of happiness to internal mental processes rather than to anything external. One such example is where Cicero (*On Duties* [2016], 1.79) posits how the Stoic Cato's "honorable conduct" and consequent rational happiness, are "wholly posited in the care and reflection of the mind." In the translator's instruction, Rackham (in Cicero, *De Natura Deorum*, vii) likewise records Cicero's recognition that for the Stoics, happiness depends on our mental functions.

cannot alone condition happiness in his view. Such externals are, neverthe-less, involved in the activation of our rationalization for Aristotle. Happi-ness is duly an activity that regularly "needs the addition of external goods" in Aristotle's understanding, even if such goods alone cannot be the basis for that happiness.[27]

The Stoics of course mandate that we must be indifferent to material externals. Throughout this book we have seen that externals play no role in Stoic rational processes. It must now therefore be the case that externals are likewise not involved in our rational happiness. Ironically though, it is *because* of this Stoic indifference to externals that complementarily Stoicism will observe that in certain situations it might be more rational to accom-modate externals into our lives, than it would be to irrationally and over-emotionally deny ourselves the externals. This rational accommodation of externals would need however to maintain a resolute indifference to the externals that we are accommodating.

This relates to the already raised category of "preferred indifferents." These are aspects of the world that it can be more rational to elect to live with than without. Such aspects might include choosing to be physically/bodily healthy instead of unwell, or to be rich rather than poor.[28] While Aristotle therefore incorporates externals into our internal structures of happiness in a manner that the Stoics do not, this category of Stoic preferred indifferents possibly exhibits his influence. The just-mentioned Stoic pre-ferred indifferent of health is a probable indicator of such a link. Aristotle specifically situates "goods of the body," for example, between our internal capacities and external objects. Here Aristotle focuses on the involvement of bodily goods such as physical health in our internalized happiness and well-being because it is his opinion that of all the externals, "health is best."[29]

The mention of wealth in the preceding discussion as a Stoic preferred indifferent should remind us of Seneca's argument that a Stoic can live with wealth, provided that they do not irrationally desire wealth. Seneca makes the further point that living with wealth can even demand a more intensive rationalized existence than living without wealth could, given how wealth has the potential to overcome our rational natures if we do not remain re-siliently indifferent to it. The Stoic claim is that we can in this mode treat preferred indifferents such as health and wealth as "adjacent" to our rational

27. Aristotle, *Nicomachean Ethics*, 1.8.

28. Stobaeus in Long and Sedley, *Hellenistic Philosophers*, 58D; taken from *SVF*, 3.124.

29. Aristotle, *Nicomachean Ethics*, 1.8.

ends and goods.[30] In *On Stoic Self-Contradictions*, Plutarch evidences this Stoic affirmation. When relaying positions presented by Chrysippus' *On Good Things*, Plutarch informs us of the Stoic belief that we can integrate "preferred indifferents" where appropriate, and furthermore that we can call them "goods."[31] It is with positions like this that Stoicism presents as motivated to live in accordance with reason, in ways that also reasonably reflect certain material realities of our daily lives.

From the preceding two sections we have considered that the Stoics emerge from a tradition which posits that what is often translated as happiness refers to a rational existence rather than to an emotional feeling. Given that our individual rationality for the Stoics does not originate or operate in isolation, so our rationalized happiness marks how we are oriented toward a universal system or order. Because our happiness is part of this ordered flow of the world, we have also learned that happiness is not a personal outcome to be targeted. Our happiness instead manifests as an activity in which we consciously align ourselves with that order. As we can consider now, this consciousness involves not simply living in accordance with a rationally ordered world, but also anticipating how in the future we might be conversely irrationally and therefore unhappily destabilized.

Visualizing Unhappiness

Understanding happiness as a rational state, distinguished from the conventional sense of a pleasurable or emotional feeling, will prepare us for a later discussion on the possibly collectively or communally lived features of happiness in Stoicism. When happiness is conversely understood as that which makes us feel good, it is a state that can arise in two ways. We can intentionally bring about its pleasurable feeling by identifying its causes and repeating them (such as spending time with people we like). Alternatively, we can inadvertently feel happy by stumbling across something that makes us feel good.

These understandings of happiness as pleasure differ from how the Stoics interpret eudaimonia. The just mentioned impression of an inadvertently derived mode of happiness is especially incoherent with Stoicism. When appreciating Stoic happiness' rationally ordered conditions and system, Epictetus for example would reject the idea that happiness, as eudaimonia,

30. Stobaeus in Long and Sedley, *Hellenistic Philosophers*, 58E; taken from *SVF*, 3.128.

31. Plutarch in Long and Sedley, *Hellenistic Philosophers*, 58H; taken from *SVF*, 3.137.

can ever be accidentally or inadvertently produced. We cannot stumble on happiness for the Stoics. Happiness is the world's intentional order or system, and our happiness is a necessary rather than a contingent expression of it, as we consciously rationally appreciate our position within it.

This becomes apparent in Epictetus' opposition to the Epicurean belief that our rational nature was the result of "accident," or that we are each born rational merely by "chance." Contrary to Epicurus' belief that the world's current arrangement arose through accidental collisions between atoms,[32] for Epictetus we live in a highly ordered, indeed a rationally systematically ordered, world. If an individual's happiness is a rational existence for the Stoics, and any individual form of rationality is a trace of a universal rational order, then it is that ordering of us which conditions our personal forms of happiness. Interpreting aspects of the world, such as happiness, to be accidental, conversely diverts us from the first condition of being rational, which requires being conscious that we are parts of a communal, universal whole. Happiness for the Stoics only results from an intentionally ordered, rational existence, and is the most important state of subjective being.

Part of being intentionally rationally happy for the Stoics involves training ourselves to avoid being inversely irrationally unhappy in the future. This training concerns a technique that is now known as *negative visualization*. Such a technique concerns for the Stoics visualizing the worst possible scenarios that could happen to us in the future and preparing ourselves for how that will feel. The Stoic belief is that this protects us from being shocked by any adverse scenarios that we have premeditated, should they eventuate. What the Stoics are demanding that we prepare ourselves for are not simply the feelings, but more importantly the irrational state that we might experience that is associated with the adverse feelings. This again speaks to the rational conditions for Stoic eudaimonic happiness. If something occurs to us that is not up to us, and that emotionally destabilizes us, our irrational unhappiness will be defined not by how we feel but instead by how invested we are in what is not up to us. In defining unhappiness, the Stoics are much less concerned with the emotions or feelings, and more with the states of irrationality.

Ideas related to what would later become categorized under the theme of negative visualization appear in the records of numerous Stoics. Galen reports that for Posidonius we are unsettled not by absolutely everything that is adverse or "evil," but more specifically by what arrives to us "fresh":

---

32. Epicurus, *Letters and Sayings*, 1–28. Sextus Empiricus (*Against the Physicists*, 2.244) explains how this means that even time is an accidental arrangement for Epicurus.

> If anything we are unprepared for or is strange to us suddenly
> hits us, we are knocked off balance . . . while that which is prac-
> tised, familiarised or prolonged either doesn't disturb us at all to
> give rise to emotionally disturbed movement, or only to a very
> limited extent.[33]

This "practise" involves intentionally visualizing and feeling emotional experiences before they suddenly arrive. The Stoic should in Posidonius' advice "live with things in advance, and treat what is not yet with us as if it were." Galen describes Posidonius' intention here as "prefiguring in our mind what is going to happen." This is an exercise via which we become anticipatorily familiar with future events, as well as develop a lived "habituation" with the associated emotions.[34] Posidonius invokes the methods of Anaxagoras in this discussion, admiring how the Presocratic philosopher viewed his children as mortals when fathering them. This is said to be a practice that would protect Anaxagoras from future distress, should he ever learn of the death of any of his children.

Epictetus' *Enchiridion* features more than one similar kind of discussion about how to use negative visualization techniques to avoid irrationally unstable future states. There is no less explicit example of this than when he instructs us to always be conscious of the mortality of our friends, family, and others to whom we are close:

> If you kiss your child, or your wife, say that you only kiss things
> which are human, and thus you will not be disturbed if either of
> them dies.[35]

While this is an instruction that will prepare you for forthcoming emotional states, another purpose in being conscious of the possible deaths of people we know is that it helps us to develop an appreciation of their presence in our lives while they are still alive.[36] The intention is not to induce a morbid mentality in the present, where we only perceive the people we know through a lens of death. What this instruction should encourage is a way of living in the present that is most fulfilling, by incorporating a consciousness of how that present will change and therefore appreciating it now accordingly.

Seneca likewise develops techniques of negative visualization that are concerned with the theme of perpetual change. In his letter, "Consolation

---

33. Galen in Posidonius, *Fragments*, fragment 165.

34. Galen in Posidonius, *Fragments*, fragment 165.

35. Epictetus, *Enchiridion*, 1.3.

36. Irvine (*Good Life*, 70) describes that one benefit of negative visualization is that it allows us to enjoy our friendships more while we have them.

to Marcia," Seneca writes to a woman who has been unable to overcome the emotional pain of her son's death years earlier. Seneca's advice concerns how she can avoid similar kinds of grief in the future by anticipating the changes and events that cause the grief. This does not mean viewing the present world from a position of hopelessness and with the mindset that all will be inevitably lost. Seneca advocates rather the importance of premeditating how quickly things can change, in order to hope for outcomes that are best, while being "prepared" for what can happen that would be the "worst."[37] An appreciation of our lives as parts of universal change here demands that each of us must remember how, at any moment, the universe can reclaim anything about ourselves that we derived from it. Our lives, our minds, our bodies, all aspects of us are aspects of the universe that are "loans that someday will be recalled."[38]

Through negative visualization techniques we therefore observe that while happiness manifests in accordance with rational rather than emotional or pleasurable prerogatives, being rationally oriented can nevertheless produce more stable emotional states. Living rationally has this effect of feeling emotions better. Eudaimonic happiness and well-being orients toward something about our existence for the Stoics that is grander than our localized selves. It is nevertheless from such orientations, that we feel consequent benefits as localized individuals.

The relationship between an individual's rationality and universal rationality has been a consistent theme in this book. Whether in the context of our own mind, body, self-preservation, or knowledge, we have found that for the Stoics what might rudimentarily appear to be an individualized attribute that we possess, is in fact a grander universal system or order in which we participate. Everything about us is a trace of an ordered world. We can now examine how our happiness, our personal experience of eudaimonic well-being, is no different.

An Individual's Happiness Is a Trace of Universal Happiness

In returning to the early Stoic era of Chrysippus, we find a conception of happiness that adheres to the part-to-whole understanding. Diogenes Laërtius is one source here, conveying the Chrysippean demand that we live in accordance with the entire universe, with nature, because "our individual natures are all parts of the universal nature."[39] Given that we have previously

37. Seneca, *Letters on Ethics*, 24.12.
38. Seneca, *Letters on Ethics*, 74.18.
39. Diogenes Laërtius, *Lives and Opinions*, 7.53.

also seen through Stobaeus that for Chrysippus, living in accordance with this nature is happiness itself,[40] the part-to-whole constitution of a happiness that is at once both individual and universal starts to become evident.

If living happily is defined by living in accordance with a nature grander than ourselves alone, then as we have seen, the source of our happiness for the Stoics cannot be reducible to our individual ends or prosperities. By living rationally, we manifest a happiness that is already a universally common state. Happiness in this sense for Chrysippus is "supervened" on us as individuals, where supervened has the philosophical definition of being consequent on what is not ourselves.[41] This is partly why Chrysippus states that fulfilling an outcome for ourselves is not the cause of happiness, and that we cannot define an individual who targets personally "progressing" to the "furthest" point of an end as happy.[42] By instead living rationally every day, which we have defined as thinking and acting with a perception of ourselves as parts in a whole, happiness actualizes for us. This marks our living in accordance with a universal nature, the conception of the "good flow of life" that we have seen Zeno originate for the Stoics, a good that Chrysippus correlates with happiness by distinguishing it from what is bad/evil:

> Chrysippus admits that good things are entirely different from evil, and it must be so if by the presence of the latter men are straightway made utterly unhappy and by that of the former happy in the highest degree.[43]

If living rationally is living happily then likewise living happily is living virtuously, given that living virtuously is living rationally. It is virtuous, for example, to think and act with a consciousness of common and shared, rather than of personal, outcomes. Plutarch's *On Common Conceptions* apparently informs readers of the ancient eras that Chrysippus emphasizes the connection between virtue and happiness when distinguishing virtue from vice. In defining the "essence" of vice as unhappiness, Chrysippus is said to "maintain in every book of physics and of morals the proposition that to live viciously is the same as to live unhappily."[44]

---

40. Stobaeus in Long and Sedley, *Hellenistic Philosophers*, 63A; taken from *SVF*, 3.16.

41. Levine ("Pantheism, Ethics, and Ecology," 123) defines Stoic "supervened" states in terms of how our individual rationality derives from a pantheistic, rational universe.

42. Stobaeus in Long and Sedley, *Hellenistic Philosophers*, 59I; taken from *SVF*, 3.510.

43. Plutarch, *Moralia*, 8:1042.

44. Plutarch, *Moralia*, 8:1042.

Plutarch's insight that Chrysippus' works on physics all attend to the theme of happiness is notable. Happiness and the topic of ethics would seem understandably matched, but physics? The reason Chrysippus would be discussing happiness and physics in tandem concerns Stoic correlations of happiness with rationality, and of rationality with the physical world. In chapter 3 we learned how the physical, material substance that comprises us, and that also comprises the rest of the universe, is rational. Living rationally involves a physical interconnection with a universal system, where the universe is rational because it is ordered. If happiness therefore is concerned with living rationally, and living rationally involves our physical interconnections, then happiness has physical conditions. These physical conditions are not the external physical goods that we have seen Aristotle posit are involved in happiness. The Stoics are instead referring to the rationally ordered physical substance of all bodies, or more specifically to how bodies interconnect internally with each other and with the overall body of the world, because all such bodies share rationally ordered conditions. The universal aspect of this is also confirmed in the just raised commentary from Plutarch, where he discusses how Chrysippus insists that we should engage the "theory of happiness" from an understanding of Stoic beliefs in a "universal nature" or order, and of that nature's or order's "administration of the world."[45] What is administered according to Chrysippus is rationally ordered happiness, where our individual rational happiness is a "dispensation of the universe."[46]

The phrase "administration of the world" refers to the pantheistic jurisdiction of God,[47] which is the systematic rationality that the Stoics believe causally orders everything. Consistent with what we have learned to this point, this rationality is the "universal nature" that Chrysippus mentions here. Such terminology speaks to the Stoic tendency that we have considered which uses the terms "God" and "Nature" interchangeably.[48] Cicero's *On the Nature of the Gods* brings our attention to a passage where Chrysippus himself unambiguously states that the "universe itself is god."[49]

45. Plutarch in Long and Sedley, *Hellenistic Philosophers*, 60A; taken from *SVF*, 3.68.

46. Plutarch, *Moralia*, 8:1035.

47. Bénatouïl, "Divine Activity in Stoicism," 23–45; Bobzien, *Determinism and Freedom*, 210; Collette, *Stoic Doctrine*, 204–7; Meijer, *Stoic Theology*, 60–65.

48. Lapidge ("Stoic Cosmology," 163–64), and McDonough (*Christ as Creator*, 109–10), both provide useful summaries of how "God" and "nature" act as synonyms in Stoicism. See also where Kooten (*Cosmic Christology*, 17) commentates that for the Stoics, "physics is . . . interchangeable with theology."

49. Cicero, *Nature of Gods*, 1.39.

For Chrysippus the rationalized happiness of the world is singularly administered by what interconnects and causally activates it. God as we have reviewed is another term for this activating and interconnecting "reason" in everything, "the regulator . . . of all existing things."[50]

A ramification of this is that because for the Stoics (not to mention also for Aristotle and others) happiness is the ultimate mode of being, happiness must also be the nature of the ultimate aspect of being; the universe as God. Happiness is our rational nature, and because God as our universe is the rational ordering of our rational nature, God likewise must be rationally happy. Diogenes explains this relationship in the sense that our rational happiness is a version or a part of the universe's happiness, and thus of God as the rational "animal . . . perfect . . . in happiness."[51] God can be described as an animal because as we have covered, what exists is bodied, animals exist (and so are bodied), the universe is an all-encompassing singular body, and God is that universe.

What does this mean though, that God is "perfect" in happiness? To answer this question, we must remember the fundamental Stoic principle that the universe's nature is rational because it is ordered. We as traces of the universe are also rational by nature, whereby it is in our nature to be parts of that overall order. For us to live happily is for us to live rationally, which is to live in accordance with the greater system or Whole. Living rationally means thinking and acting with a consciousness of these interconnected conditions for our being, recognizing that we are parts of a body greater than ourselves. Having that mentality and actively participating in the world in accordance with it, is eudaimonic happiness.

To answer our question at the beginning of the previous paragraph therefore, if we are each rational as a part of a rationalized universe, and nothing is greater in the universe than the universe, then there is no more perfect form of rationality than the universe itself. Just as the body of the universe comprises and entwines all individual bodies, likewise the rational happiness of the universe comprises and entwines every individual form of rational happiness. The universe is perfect in happiness, and God as that universe is likewise perfectly happy.

We might ask here whether everyone has to be individually living rationally for the universe to be perfectly rational at any point in time. This is a difficult question to answer, given that in one regard everything in the world *is* perfectly rationally ordered, in that the world's causal structure rolls on whether we as individuals want it to or not. There are though of

50. Diogenes Laërtius, *Lives and Opinions*, 7.53.
51. Diogenes Laërtius, *Lives and Opinions*, 7.72.

course irrational modes that we can freely exercise, when as we have seen we mentally detach ourselves from this interconnected order or refuse to accept it. This occurs when we do not remain indifferent to what is not up to us or in our control, that being the universe's ordering of us and everything else. We can debate therefore the meaning that Diogenes conveys from the Chrysippean account that the condition of the universe's unified "perfect happiness" is not simply that it comprises all individual rationalities, but that such happiness is when "everything is done according to a harmony."[52] If "done" here refers to what is enacted by the universally rationalized system, then the universe is always perfectly happy because the system always exists. If conversely "done" here refers to every individual always thinking and acting in rational ways, then conversely the universe would probably never be perfectly happy, even if it is the condition of perfect happiness.

Either way, our individual rational happiness is a fragment of the whole rationalized order of the universe. We might on this topic also re-invite our earlier considerations regarding the daimon, described as our guide/guardian/genius, which for each of us is composed both of our own rationality and a universal, rationalized substance. Through this rationality we experience happiness, and such rationality is a universally "dispensed" condition as we have just reviewed Plutarch report on behalf of the Stoics. Our happiness in accordance with this "individual genius" of ours is not an entirely subjective function for the Stoics, but instead must occur "with reference to the will of the universal governor."[53]

For Chrysippus, indeed for Epictetus too, we are implicated in a universe in which our happiness, our rational ordering, is intended, not accidental. This intention, remember, is the reliable, rather than the incidentally random, ordering of the world. We might in the current era call this universal system or order the world's natural, physical laws. Such universal intention marks a universal interconnection, and our appreciation of our presence in that interconnection induces our well-being. Let me repeat that. Our appreciation, our rational appreciation, of our interconnection with the universe, conditions eudaimonic happiness and well-being for the Stoics. A universe that "administers" us rationally and interconnectedly, administers us happily. We each feel part of that collective order, where if we are rational we embody two senses of group belonging; one to our localized communities or human administrations, and the other to a universally singular community and administration. We have studied this dual belonging with Hierocles, not to mention with Cleanthes' notion of the universal city. Our

52. Diogenes Laërtius, *Lives and Opinions*, 7.53.

53. Diogenes Laërtius, *Lives and Opinions*, 7.53.

well-being, our happiness, is our rational accordance with, and our awareness of, these belongings. Having considered the *universally* kindred conditions for our own happiness, we can now turn our attention to what this means for happiness as an interpersonally or *socially* shared mode.

Collective Harmony and Communal Happiness

Rationally ordered well-being is our own nature because it is the nature of the world that orders us. Chrysippus recognizes these dual sites of happiness when establishing the Stoic belief that human "nature" is both "common" to the entire universe and "particular" to humans.[54] In discussing what is common about human and universal rational natures, we should recall Chrysippus' earlier distinction of good from bad things, and association of what is good and happy with what is universally ordered. This is a characterization of happiness that he develops from Zeno's understanding of our nature as living in accordance with the good, which means according with the rationally ordered, causal flow of the universe. It is important that we have this point in mind now because, through Stobaeus, we see that for the early Stoics there is a common prosperity from "good" ends that we share not simply with the rationally ordered universe but also with our fellow rationally ordered humans. Happiness is the ultimate form of such ends, where for those humans who live rationally, "all goods" prove to be "common."[55]

What is rationally good is not described as "common" simply because it is present in all human individuals. More crucially for the Stoics, happiness is a common good because it has a singular source and constitution in which humans participate together. This relies on the communal or collegial conditions and outcomes of rationality that we have acknowledged. Collective rationality, as happiness, as the ultimate good, is said to flourish among a community where "the virtuous benefit one another."[56] "Inferior" or "foolish" individuals who irrationally individuate themselves away from thinking and acting as fragments of a whole, conversely mentally fight against our natural collegiality.[57]

54. Diogenes Laërtius, *Lives and Opinions*, 7.53.

55. Stobaeus in Long and Sedley, *Hellenistic Philosophers*, 60P; taken from *SVF*, 3.626.

56. Stobaeus in Long and Sedley, *Hellenistic Philosophers*, 60P; taken from *SVF*, 3.626.

57. Stobaeus in Long and Sedley, *Hellenistic Philosophers*, 60P; taken from *SVF*, 3.626.

For Anthony Long and David Sedley, this belief in the shared states of rationalized happiness is particularly Stoic. They describe what is "distinctively" Stoic about viewing eudaimonic happiness and well-being in terms of the "mutual" advantages available for individuals who understand happiness through the lens of "community."[58] With a sensitivity to these fundamental features of Stoicism we reach an understanding of an individual's happiness that only makes sense within a harmonious communal body. The collegial conditions for happiness and well-being are the basis on which we think and act for the Stoics if such thoughts and actions are to be rational. Diogenes' accounts of the Stoics broadcast this priority, detailing how to be "happy" requires "doing everything" with a consciousness of the "concordance" between ourselves and our fellow rational humans.[59] Via Diogenes we here see that when we do anything, if while doing that we are aware of what we share with others, then our happiness and well-being is ordered in tandem with the happiness and well-being of others. For the Stoics, individuals' ends are indeed mutually beneficial ends.

Marcus' belief, as we have also reviewed, is that we orient this way from birth. Our happiness, our well-being, is conditioned not by pursuing our individual ends, but instead reflects how each of us is made "unselfish"[60] and "for the sake of one another."[61] If we are each "born for community"[62] or "made for society"[63] as he also states, then we have a socially natural mode for the Stoics that is not contingently ordered by trends or patterns, desirous of constant companionship, or defined by concerns about reputation, status or gossip. Our social nature instead reflects how we are by default systematically ordered in a way that implicates each of us with others' orderings. It can only be that the goods of happiness, which are these systematic orderings of us as parts of a whole, manifest collectively. This invokes Marcus' associated assertion that the "good for the reasonable animal is society"[64] and "fellowship with others."[65] Had Chrysippus lived contemporaneously with Marcus, I can imagine him endorsing such a worldview. Chrysippus has exhibited a belief, we should not forget, in the coherence of individual and universal

---

58. Long and Sedley, *Hellenistic Philosophers*, 377.

59. Diogenes Laërtius in Long and Sedley, *Hellenistic Philosophers*, 63C; taken from *SVF*, 3.178.

60. Marcus Aurelius, *Meditations* (2002), 5.16.

61. Marcus Aurelius, *Meditations* (2011), 5.16.

62. Marcus Aurelius, *Meditations* (2006), 5.16.

63. Marcus Aurelius, *Meditations* (1900), 5.16.

64. Marcus Aurelius, *Meditations* (1900), 5.16.

65. Marcus Aurelius, *Meditations* (2011), 5.16.

natures and happiness. The importance of pairing Chrysippus and Marcus in this way is that we highlight a consistency in the Stoic school's conception of happiness that spans almost its entire ancient timeline.

When we consider happiness for the Stoics, we must appreciate a universal web, not restricted to an individual's localized fortunes. There are interpersonal, collegial, and systemic conditions for our own well-being. We might even say that the Stoics highlight the universally impersonal structures according to which personal happiness seems to come to individuals, is experienced by individuals, and is shared by individuals. Individualized happiness here occurs beyond what we might strictly define as the self, in that we are immersed in or participate in our happiness, because our happiness is rationality, and rationality is the world's nature in which we are likewise immersed. This is quite different from the impression that our happiness is our experience alone, that we exclusively feel or possess internally.

To be rationally happy is to live with a consciousness that we are interconnected expressions of the world. Even in a conventional, non-Stoic understanding of happiness, that could seem reasonable in terms of it countering feelings of isolation. While Stoic eudaimonic happiness does not preclude feeling positive emotions though, its primary conditions concern our rational and communal functions. We can recall that via Hierocles, Cicero, Epictetus, Marcus, in fact seemingly with every Stoic or ancient commentator of Stoicism that we have encountered, a rational individual is both a civically minded individual and an individual who is in control of their emotions. It appears that this notion of a civically oriented, emotionally regulated, individual, matches common beliefs that a civil society rationally and reliably regulates or controls its population. If someone breaks away from collective agreements around how to behave, perhaps by acting unlawfully and violently attacking someone else, the more civilized a society is the less likely it will be to seek retribution against that unlawful rebel through an impulsive and impassioned mob reaction. The collectively rationalized and ordered response, concerned with outcomes that are just, is instead methodically reasoned and controlled. Legally this will involve carefully appraising the facts of the transgression of law, consulting witnesses, and making comparisons with other cases. The civil state operates according to its structured reasons and orders, not according to how it impulsively feels.[66]

66. See Blumenthal ("Law and the Emotions," 1) for a discussion about the suitability of emotions in legal processes. Also relevant is where Kelsen (*Law and State*, xvi) distinguishes law from political ideology on account of the latter's supposed roots in volition instead of cognition. Numerous voices however argue against the interpretation that legal processes lack emotional impulses. For two examples of this, see Bornstein and Weiner, "Emotion and the Law," 1–12; O'Donovan, "Engendering Justice," 127.

Such a reading mirrors the typical advice that we should not make important decisions while we are upset. When we have calmed down, when we are thinking "straight" and rationally, then we can proceed. Emotions and passions here present almost as enemies to our true selves, or at the very least we categorize such states as self-induced interferences to our mental and rational states. The idea either way is that only once our instinctively impulsive emotional states are under control, can our rational states be exercised. Often the interpretation is that while it is natural for us to get angry and upset, we need to be self-aware of this aspect of our nature, we must be present with our natural emotions if we are to control them when they arise.

Stoicism challenges the reduction of our nature to what is emotionally impulsive though. We have instead covered comprehensively how the Stoics equate our natural state with rationality. Every era of ancient Stoicism imparts the message that our natural instinct, our default impulse, is to be rational and reasoned and that this is an attribute in which we all share. Note the language I use there . . . rationality is not simply something *that* we share. Rather, rationality is shared because it is of the world, rationality is that world *in which* we all share. We can refer to any of the ancient Stoics that we have covered for confirmation that rationality is our default, communal and kindred nature. Marcus describes it typically succinctly though, in the terms that our "nature is rational and social."[67]

We have acknowledged more than once in this book that Stoicism does not require an entirely unemotional existence. Seneca for instance has indicated that we can expect to experience positive and negative emotions around death and that not all these states are a problem. On the other hand however, Seneca, along with Epictetus and other Stoics, have also demanded that we rationally control our unhealthy and indeed unnatural emotional states. Such states are for Stoicism unnatural or unhealthy if they contradict our rational natures. This irrationality typically results from our lack of acceptance that we are each a part of a rationally ordered whole, and that what happens to us is beyond our own authority because it is a part of the whole system. Regulating our emotional states emerges as a necessary Stoic requirement if we are to live in accordance with what we share with others as ordered, systemic parts. This indeed was a theme apparent in Hierocles' cosmopolitanism. We can further recall on this matter Epictetus' sentiments in *Discourses*, where he instructs us to recognize and relinquish our servitude to our emotions that arise via our interactions with the world around us:

---

67. Marcus Aurelius, *Meditations* (1900), 6.44. Marcus Aurelius, *Meditations* (2006), 6.44.

> I liberate myself from my master—which is to say, from the
> emotions that make my master frightening—what troubles can
> I have? No human is my master any longer.[68]

For the Stoics our nature is rational. Our nature is common to all other
rational beings, meaning that our nature is communal. We live naturally
when we live harmoniously, rationally. What does this mean for our emotional existence though? When we are emotional rather than rational, are we
therefore excluded from the collective fellowship that rationality conditions
for the Stoics? Alternatively, can we be both rational and emotional, and
therefore emotional and Stoically social, simultaneously? To explore these
questions, we will have to consider ancient understandings of the relations
between rationality and emotion.

If Our Rationality Is Communal,
When We Are Emotional Are We Still Part of the Group?

Stoic conceptions of the relations between rationality and emotions, or
reason and passion as these states are also respectively referred to, crystal-
lize through the ideas of Epictetus, Chrysippus, and the Greek politician,
scientist, and Stoic philosopher, Posidonius of Rhodes. I will use the terms
"rationality" and "reason" interchangeably during this discussion, an approach that I will also take with the transferability of the terms "emotions"
and "passions." This is so that when I cite the Stoics, I match the grammati-
cal preferences of each as closely as possible. Such a method correlates with
what I believe is the most sensible interpretation; that the ancient Stoics use
these terms entirely interchangeably.

Epictetus' *Discourses* appraises these relations by holding that while
our rationality and emotions, our reason and passions, are not in total opposition, they still operate in a hierarchized structure. We have discussed
that for Epictetus our rationality orders or controls our emotions, where
each of us lives according to our nature if we rationally regulate and "tend to
our passions."[69] This is not to say that we cannot live with both states if there
is a "healthy" rational regulation, as Epictetus describes it, of our emotions/
passions. Epictetus laments though that regularly our emotions adversely
affect us in ways that we find too difficult to rationally control, leading us to
think and act irrationally.

---

68. Epictetus, *Discourses* (2008), 1.29.63. Matheson (in Epictetus, *Discourses* [1916],
1.29.63) translates this as where "if I feel that these things are nothing to me, . . . Who
is there left for me to fear, and over what has he control?"

69. Epictetus, *Discourses* (2008), 1.17.4.

This suggested mode in which rationality presides over emotions might indicate that for the Stoics, emotions are absolutely different from rationality and that emotions originate from an entirely separate part of the self. We can here recall how intimately Epictetus and other Stoics associate rationality with our daimon, as an aspect of our internal self that is a trace of a world beyond the self. We have not identified any such interconnected source for our emotions.

Yet in distinguishing rationality from emotions, Epictetus is not conceiving that emotions derive from a separately dedicated, irrational part of ourselves. We do not have both a rational daimon and a complementary irrational part. The position that he forwards is instead that when we are irrationally emotional, we are simply acting less rationally than we would be when acting rationally.[70] Acting rationally therefore does not indicate for Epictetus the result of a successful internal battle between rational and irrational parts of the self. What Epictetus proposes is that when living rationally, our singular internal, rational faculty, has coordinated ourselves well, rather than lost control of the self with irrational behavior ensuing.[71]

The basis of this interpretation that we have only a rational faculty, and not a complementary irrational faculty, concerns the Stoic use of the Greek word *pathê*. Everyday Greek language and terminology employs pathê to refer to the bodily states that we experience and possibly even endure. Within philosophical contexts the term deviates though to incorporate a spectrum of meanings, designating emotional, spirited, and desiring impulses. Categorized under such impulses are our feelings of joy, sadness, anger, frustration, excitement, as well as of hunger, thirst, and urges for sex.

Galen describes Chrysippus as referring to pathê in accordance with these kinds of impulses.[72] Despite not sounding very rational, these impulses for Chrysippus are modes of our rationalizing capacity. As is true for Epictetus, rationality in the Chrysippean understanding is our "central agency," our "coordinating faculty," for everything about us, including our

---

70. Pratt (*Seneca's Drama*, 59) agrees, arguing that when we behave irrationally for Epictetus, such behaviors are internally motivated and enacted, however they do not arise from an exclusively "non-rational" site within the self. See Long (*Epictetus*, 244–46) for further discussion on this distinction.

71. Epictetus, *Discourses* (2014), 1.17.1.

72. There are certain consistencies between pathê, and the term hormê/hormai that we have encountered in chapter 4. These consistencies become apparent when Cicero (*Nature of Gods*, 2.58) refers to how for the Stoic Balbus, just as the universe has its "impulses and desires" called hormai that impel it be one way versus another, likewise so do we (as traces of this universe), which is shown when our "spirits and emotions" motivate us.

desirous or emotional impulses.[73] Galen's *On Hippocrates' and Plato's Doctrines* details how for Chrysippus, we think *and* feel from the same internal part of ourselves. In this theory our "commanding faculty" incorporates functions of the various "passions," which occur in the same "region" as the "mind" that the passions "affect."[74]

Through Galen's accounts therefore, our impression is that Chrysippus does not view the source of our emotional or passionate modes as distinct from our rational modes.[75] What instead occurs as we think and act, are fluctuations in how completely we live in accordance with the rational features of our internal source of thinking and acting. Galen reports that in a Chrysippean work called *On Passions* this position is explicit. There Chrysippus explains how our rational inclinations come from the same aspect of ourselves as our emotions, the latter of which if too impassioned or impulsive will from time to time "exceed" our rational order.[76]

Even though our rationality and emotions manifest from the same internal aspect or faculty of the self for Chrysippus and Epictetus, when we are uncontrollably emotional in their view we are not acting in accordance with the nature of this internal aspect or faculty of ourselves. In these irrational modes we do not accord with the universe's nature as whole, which is its rationally consistent ordering, and so can be mentally cut off from our internally conditioned bonds with our fellow rational beings. By not thinking and acting with our universal, rational interconnections as our focus, we emotionally exclude ourselves from the rational fellowship that the Stoics identify. While we might each only have a singular internal aspect or faculty, this faculty cannot in this view be both rational and irrational simultaneously. Irrationality instead arises, before it is tamed and defined as rational, before once again we are overcome irrationally, before our rational orientations return, and so on. In this view there is no real sense of connection with a rationalized world order when we are emotional. The dichotomy instead holds that we are interconnected when rational, and often disconnected when overly emotional and irrational.

While Posidonius maintains the same unerring belief in the role of rationality, he does not agree with these kinds of conceptions of our internal structure. For Epictetus and Chrysippus, rationality/reason and emotions/passions come from the same internal aspect/faculty of the self. The

---

73. See also Gill (*Naturalistic Psychology*, 97) for whom this understanding that we have a central or controlling function denotes not just the site of our reason, but also that of our impetus and "hormê."

74. Galen in Long and Sedley, *Hellenistic Philosophers*, 65H; taken from *SVF*, 2.886.

75. Galen in Posidonius, *Fragments*, fragment 166.

76. Galen in Long and Sedley, *Hellenistic Philosophers*, 65J; taken from *SVF*, 3.462.

understanding we will see from Posidonius alternatively is that these func-tions come from differently dedicated internal aspects/faculties of the self.

I will qualify this distinction between Posidonius and the other Stoics with the advisory that we should be careful about unconditionally adopt-ing the view that Posidonius absolutely differs from what at the time was the preceding Chrysippean conception. Such care is required because our source on this aspect of Posidonian philosophy is Galen, whose views gen-erally critique Chrysippean philosophy when instead supporting certain contrasting positions of Plato.[77] Galen shows this selected commitment on numerous themes, one example being his considerations of how humans can be shaped by proper values. This is a topic that Galen believes Plato has explained with typical "precision," whereas Chrysippus' account is said to be "unsound" and contributes nothing for other philosophers to develop.[78]

When not comparing with Plato, Galen still often exhibits a lack of respect for the views of Chrysippus. In discussing Chrysippus' *On Emo-tions*, Galen commentates on how despite its length, his analysis of it took a relatively small amount of effort.[79] Part of Galen's study laments that Chrysippus' philosophy of emotions has nevertheless become the dominant Stoic position on the topic. Galen duly criticizes how "all the Stoics" aside from Posidonius seem to accommodate Chrysippus' "errors" and ignore the truth.[80]

This "truth" is Galen's reference to Plato's understanding that we have a multi-part internal self, a theory presented in Book IV of Plato's *Republic*. In considering whether our "soul," what is internal to us, is composed of more than a singular faculty, Plato asks "do we learn with one part of us, feel angry with another, and desire the pleasures of eating and sex and the like with another?"[81] In setting up a comparative study, Plato recognizes the alternative understanding (that Chrysippus would support), in which inversely "we employ the mind," our rational faculty, for all such functions.[82] While Plato might raise this latter possibility of a singular faculty for all our modes, he does not agree with it. This puts Chrysippus, and eventually Epictetus, in opposition to Plato.

---

77. See Gill ("Galen and the Stoics," 111–14) for a brief overview.

78. Galen in Posidonius, *Fragments*, fragment 31.

79. Galen in Posidonius, *Fragments*, testimonia 63.

80. Galen in Posidonius, *Fragments*, testimonia 59. Also relevant is how Galen (in Posidonius, *Fragments*, fragment 164) interrogates entire generations of present and past Stoics for not having been able to answer Posidonius' questions.

81. Plato, *Republic* (2007), 4.436a.

82. Plato, *Republic* (2007), 4.436b.

The reason Plato disagrees with the idea of a singular faculty is that sometimes we think and feel in contradictory ways at the same time. An example is where we might strongly desire to eat something tasty and unhealthy, however when thinking about the health ramifications we decide not to. In such a situation we feel one way about a situation yet think a different way about it. A singular faculty of our thoughts and emotions could not accommodate this simultaneously split set of functions for Plato, which means that by recognizing such contradictions we determine that our internal self has more than one faculty.[83] Ultimately this becomes a three-part model for Plato, comprising internal faculties that he calls reason (rationality), spirit, and appetite. Emotions and passions derive from the faculties of spirit and appetite. Much like Stoic understandings of the hierarchy of rationality over emotions, in the Platonic model the rational faculty can overrule these other faculties.[84] Plato also confirms this in the *Timaeus*, discussing how our appetitive faculty operates at a lower level than our reason, often functioning as a mere image of reason and subservient to it.[85]

Raising the controlling function of rationality leads us to a consideration of how happiness relates to this internal structure of the self for Plato. In the *Republic*, Plato describes happiness as a state that manifests from the virtuous or just application of our three parts or faculties. A virtuous or just application involves our rational faculty leading our other parts or faculties, so happiness still has necessarily rational conditions for Plato. This application also requires however that each of our three internal faculties is responsible for the specific or respective function for which it is designed. Our emotional, appetitive faculty for instance is not designed to reason, it is instead designed to desire. Plato compares this divided but united function of our three internal faculties, to a harmonious division of functions between the various classes of people in a city state.[86]

It is through this Platonic reading of plural internal faculties that Posidonius views the structure of our rationality and emotions. Given these Platonic roots, the conceptual distinction of multiple parts of our internalities also represents Galen's own beliefs.[87] Galen's further appraisal is that Chrysippus, by allocating all our modes to a singular all-commanding faculty, counters not only what we observe to be true about humans, but

83. Plato, *Republic* (2007), 4.436c.

84. Plato, *Republic* (2007), 4.441e–442b.

85. Plato, *Timaeus*, 71a–b.

86. Plato, *Republic* (2007), 4.441d–443e.

87. Galen in Posidonius, *Fragments*, fragment 160.

also contradicts the early Stoic positions of Zeno and Cleanthes.[88] From this insight we learn that when we earlier reviewed Galen's criticism of "all other Stoics" for following Chrysippus, Galen must have been referring predominantly to those Stoics who lived contemporaneously with Chrysippus, and not to their Stoic predecessors. Galen conversely portrays Posidonius heroically, as defending the Stoic school's original (Zeno's) position.[89] We do not have much surviving material to verify this claim of Galen's. Cleanthes' *Hymn to Zeus* as reported by Galen does though distinguish between reason and passion:

> What is it. Passion, that you want? Tell me this.
> I want. Reason? To do everything I want.[90]

The distinction here seems hardly emphatic enough to evidence that Cleanthes' believed we internally house dedicated rational and irrational faculties. We can agree that Cleanthes *distinguishes* between reason and passion, and that they are in Posidonius' appraisal "two different" ways of being for Cleanthes.[91] Cleanthes though is operating in an era in which most Stoics believed that our internal faculty is solely rational.[92] From the little that survives of Cleanthes' work (not to mention that of Zeno), and when taking into account Galen's Platonic investments, we possibly do not have enough proof that the earliest Stoics were in complete agreement with Posidonius about whether we have a dedicated irrational internal faculty.

88. Galen in Posidonius, *Fragments*, fragment 166.

89. See Nock, "Posidonius," 2.

90. Galen in Long and Sedley, *Hellenistic Philosophers*, 65I; taken from *On Hippocrates' and Plato's Doctrines*, 5.6.34–37. Or as Kidd (in Posidonius, *Fragments*, fragment 166) translates Galen: "What do you want, Anger? Tell me that. Me, Reason? To do anything I want."

91. Galen in Posidonius, *Fragments*, fragment 166.

92. See where Tieleman (*Galen and Chrysippus*, xxiv) describes this as the "unitarian rational" view of our internality for the early Stoics. Kidd (in Posidonius, *Fragments*, 21) observes that if our psychologies are solely rational, how can we ever be internally oriented otherwise. The Stoics of course will argue that we internally compromise our rational faculty through our less than diligent activation or application of it. Given that a Stoic cannot blame any consequent irrationality on their external circumstances though, Kidd's question remains regarding how what is only rational can ever be anything but rational. Posidonius conversely can attribute aspects of this internal shift to an irrational human faculty, an interpretation that is not open to Chrysippus. Kidd recognizes this, however is also careful to note that this does not mean that in Posidonian philosophy we have an evil "daimon" that complements our rational daimon. See the second chapter of this book for a discussion on the daimon. Also see Reydams-Schils ("Posidonius and the *Timaeus*," 474) for further points concerning why a belief in an evil daimon would erroneously characterize Posidonius as a dualist.

What we can be certain of though, as we have seen throughout this book, is that all eras of Stoicism posit that we are internally responsible for our irrationality. While external circumstances might prompt us to think irrationally, and to feel adverse emotions, the source of those emotional states and our responses to such circumstances are never imposed on us. We have reviewed how Epictetus and Seneca criticize us in this regard for how we blame our emotional hardships on what occurs to us, or on the people around us. That hardship though is due to our own irrational impulses. As I have detailed, the primary way in which we live this irrationality is by thinking and acting without an appreciation of ourselves as parts of a greater whole, and therefore ignoring our communal and universal default states. When we think of ourselves as separate individuals and become overly invested in hyper-localized situations and personalized stakes, we lose momentary sight of the world of which we are each a trace and feel the consequent unease.

To find the source of emotional irrationality, where unhappy emotions refer to the irrational self before they denote any resulting adverse feelings, we must look to the internal self. That is clear for the Stoics. The currently unresolved question is whether such emotions manifest from a dedicated internal faculty that is not our rational faculty. This is important in terms of our lingering inquiry in this chapter, given that our communal or social natures have to this point been associated exclusively with our rational modes. As we have asked, given that to be rational is to be interconnected, where does this leave us when we are irrationally emotional? Are we really detached from the rationally ordered fellowship that the Stoics have endorsed? Alternatively, is our emotional existence not entirely separate from our rational existence? This is what is at stake when determining the internal structure and relationship of our rational and emotional faculties for the Stoics.

Our Emotions Are Regulated

A new angle on this question concerns how Chrysippus describes impassioned thoughts and actions, our irrational passions, as forms of "judgement."[93] This makes sense in terms of the Chrysippean understanding of a singular, all-encompassing commanding faculty, which given its monopolization of our internal responses must be the source of both our rational and our irrational decisions and impulses. While our decisions and

---

93. Galen in Posidonius, *Fragments*, fragment 34.

impulses source from a rational faculty, not all will always perfectly accord with the rational ordering of ourselves and the world.

Posidonius identifies that this characterization of passions as judgements is a significant error of the Chrysippean singularization of the source of reason and passion. If judgements are from the same faculty as passions, and judgements are also associated with reasoning and rationalizing, then nonhuman animals that we have seen the Stoics believe do not have rationality, must also be without passions or desires. To put this logic another way, if nonhuman creatures do not have a rational faculty, and judgements are from a faculty that administers both rationality and the passions, then nonhuman creatures must have no internal faculties. Posidonius posits that the strange and unacceptable outcome of this is that a theory of a singular faculty "deprives irrational animals of emotions."[94] Given that we do see nonhuman "non-rational" animals living in appetitive, emotional, and desiring ways according to Posidonius,[95] Chrysippus must be mistaken in singularizing rationality and emotions.

In characterizing emotions as akin to judgements, Chrysippus is possibly building on a preceding position from Zeno. While we do not have records of Zeno ever describing passions and emotions as faulty judgements in the manner of Chrysippus, Zeno does evidently believe that passions and emotions are the "results"—the misdirected results—of certain judgements.[96] These judgements of course would be our less than rational decisions and actions. We might recognize this understanding in much of this chapter's discussion. Unhappiness is in Stoicism not an emotional state, it instead is an irrational state. This does not mean though that what we conventionally understand as unhappy emotions will not result from living less than entirely rational states. Unhappy emotional states from living irrationally are indeed to be expected and can serve as an indication that we need to live more rationally.

Zeno's terminology that emotions can be irrational results of judgements also proves to be too singularizing for Posidonius though. He concurs with Zeno's assertion that passions or emotions are not identical to rationality or reason. Complementarily however, Posidonius must contest the Stoic founder's conception that the passions and emotions "follow judgement." The reason for this contestation, as Galen presents it, is that judgement is the domain of rationality in Posidonian philosophy, it does not venture

94. Galen in Posidonius, *Fragments*, fragment 33.
95. Galen in Posidonius, *Fragments*, fragment 33.
96. Galen in Posidonius, *Fragments*, fragment 34.

into the emotional modes that we experience and is just judgement alone.[97] Posidonius' distinction from the Chrysippean position duly becomes as sharp as his differentiation from Zeno's. Galen repeatedly asserts that the passions or emotions for Posidonius derive from a dedicated "competitive and appetitive faculty," and that such a faculty is distinct from the processes of judgements and reasoning.[98]

It appears then that rationality or reason, and emotions or passions, are for Posidonius mutually exclusive modes derived from differently dedicated parts or faculties of ourselves. Despite this appearance however, Posidonius' conception is not that simple. To explain why, we need to consider another Posidonian perspective that is not exclusively reported by Galen. This will lead us into more complex relations between rationality and emotions for Posidonius than Galen's Platonic commitments can permit Galen to acknowledge.[99]

Even though Posidonius believes that rationality and emotions derive from differently dedicated faculties within the self, this does not mean for Posidonius that emotions are entirely lacking the modes of judgement that we otherwise associate with rationality and reason. One source for this reading is Plutarch, who in a surviving fragment describes how for Posidonius our "affections" such as our "desires, fears, angers . . . are those connected with judgements and suppositions."[100] These affections, what Galen elsewhere reports Posidonius as calling "mental emotions,"[101] occur with both impassioned irrational, and discerning rational, features. Lactantius' *A Treatise on the Anger of God* further indicates an assumption of this intersection for Posidonius. The early Christian author here reports that Posidonius

97. Galen in Posidonius, *Fragments*, fragment 34.

98. Galen in Long and Sedley, *Hellenistic Philosophers*, 65K; taken from *On Hippocrates' and Plato's Doctrines*, 4.3.2–5.

99. Additional commentators have addressed concerns around the objectiveness or legitimacy of Galen's reporting of Posidonian philosophy. Gill ("Did Galen Understand?," 113) argues that there are more coherences between Plato's three-part internal structure of the self and "both Chrysippean and Posidonian" understandings than Galen is willing to recognize. Cooper ("Posidonius on Emotions," 71) acknowledges Posidonius' critique of Chrysippus' singularization of reason and emotion, and converse admiration for Plato's understanding that our internal self comprises plural faculties. Cooper is unsure, however, whether we can say that Posidonius strictly differs from Chrysippus' "standard" Stoic beliefs regarding the site of our emotions. Gill ("Galen and the Stoics," 88–120) encompasses numerous themes on how the ideas of Galen, Posidonius, and Chrysippus relate. Gill ("How Stoic and How Platonic?," 192) further attends to how through later Hellenistic thinkers such as Posidonius, we can reconsider how straightforward are comparisons between Platonism and Stoicism.

100. Plutarch, *Moralia*, 15:48.

101. Galen in Posidonius, *Fragments*, fragment 34.

observes a general belief that judgements, thoughts, and the mind are involved in the emotions, particularly in how everyone defines anger:

> As the desire of punishing him by whom you think that you have been unfairly injured. Some have thus defined it: "Anger is an incitement of the mind to injure him who either has committed an injury, or who has wished to do so."[102]

Through accounts like Plutarch's, we further understand that for Posidonius there are different kinds of emotion. Some emotions are purely bodily, whereas others are purely mental, and others even involve a mixture.[103] What we derive from this categorization is that for Posidonius, certain emotional processes involve the judgements and decisions typically associated with the mind.[104] This is an interpretation that Lactantius' portrayal of Posidonius' characterization of anger has just supported. Posidonius is not proposing that how we experience emotions or passions is identical to how we make judgements. Emotions are not thoroughly rational or reasonable. In certain modes though, our emotions or passions always follow reasoning processes. Emotions involve ordered patterns, the incorporation of choices and mental reflections, and are not simply impulsively instantaneous.

We should pause to remember that if rationality and emotions are not entirely inconsistent modes of being, then perhaps there are aspects of our emotional existences that communally connect us with a whole universe. This of course is a reference to how the Stoics equate our rational modes with our fellowship. In one regard, Posidonius definitely describes our passions and emotions as driven personally, bodily, and at times feverishly by our competitive and appetitive faculties.[105] In another regard though, what we find when we explore the intersection between emotion and judgement further is that Posidonius also discusses how our passionate part, our appetitive or spirited faculty of the self, can self-regulate and "calm down its

---

102. Lactantius, "Anger of God," 274.

103. Plutarch, *Moralia*, 15:48.

104. Sorabji (*Emotion and Peace*, 105) also recognizes this, stating that while Posidonius refuses to acknowledge the presence of judgement in all categories of emotions, Posidonius does believe that judgement is involved in our standard emotions.

105. Galen in Long and Sedley, *Hellenistic Philosophers*, 65P; taken from *On Hippocrates' and Plato's Doctrines*, 4.7.24–41.

own movement"[106] when it is "satisfied."[107] This does not mean, as I have indicated, that rationality and emotions are identical for Posidonius, nor that they derive from the same source as Chrysippus might argue. What it does mean for Posidonius though, is that just like reason, our emotive, passionate faculty is to some degree systematically ordered. Our emotional life is not always haphazard and impetuous, but more expansively "has its own proper natural goals."[108]

In Posidonian Stoicism we have dedicated parts of our internal selves from which our passionate or emotional modes arise. While such parts are not rational, they nevertheless enact certain rationally regulated and ordered qualities. This regulation is necessary in the Posidonian view, given how overwhelmingly excessive our emotional states could otherwise be.[109] Recognizing the reality that we experience unhealthy excesses of emotions forms another part of Posidonius' challenge to Chrysippus' belief in a singular source of both rationality and irrationality. How could this excessive experience ever be of a rationally regulated faculty, he asks Chrysippus rhetorically:

> What is the *cause* of the excessive impulse. For reason, whatever else, could not exceed its own business and measures. So it is obvious that there is some other distinct irrational faculty as cause of the impulse's exceeding the measures of reason.[110]

Posidonius' understanding of how we regulate these excessive impulses continues the Stoic interest in the developmental and educational features of our rational modes. The novel twist in the Posidonian model though is how he situates such self-developmental features within our supposedly irrationally dedicated faculties. Posidonius does this by recognizing that our

106. Galen in Long and Sedley, *Hellenistic Philosophers*, 65P; taken from *On Hippocrates' and Plato's Doctrines*, 4.7.24–41. See where the translation of Galen by Kidd (in Posidonius, *Fragments*, fragment 165) reports that in Posidonius' view, even for Chrysippus our emotional self becomes "sated of emotional movements" when "the emotion takes pause and quietens down."

107. Galen in Posidonius, *Fragments*, 165.

108. Galen in Posidonius, *Fragments*, 165. In a similar fashion, Galen (in Long and Sedley, *Hellenistic Philosophers*, 65P; taken from *On Hippocrates' and Plato's Doctrines*, 4.7.24–41) observes Chrysippus' position that "the causes of the passions' ceasing are not beyond reason." The difference between the Posidonian and Chrysippean readings is that "not beyond reason" for Chrysippus refers to the all-encompassing authority of reason to preside over unruly passions, whereas for Posidonius it observes the passions' capacity to self-regulate.

109. Galen in Posidonius, *Fragments*, fragment 165.

110. Galen in Posidonius, *Fragments*, fragment 34.

irrational faculties are self-reflective enough to learn to avoid an "excess" of their own irrational impulse.[111] Given the adverse experience that we have with such excess, our irrationally emotional mode is said to be trained to become "satiated" with its own sensation, and learns to prevent itself surpassing a proper emotional level.[112] Our emotional and appetitive faculties here are understood to develop in a manner akin to the self-aware capacities of our mind and rationality that we have reviewed in earlier chapters. Ironically this means that irrational activity improves our irrational faculties.

Such improvement is necessary, given that for Posidonius our emotionally excessive states represent a "mental" health disorder.[113] While Posidonius encourages us to learn how to regulate our emotions, his argument however is never that a Stoic existence is emotionless. He confirms this by supposing an internal structure to ourselves which includes dedicated irrational and emotional faculties. This is arguably a greater recognition of our inescapably emotional lives than is present in the accounts of any other Stoics, for whom emotional states are often faulty manifestations of our singular, rational faculty.[114]

The learning processes that condition this development or improvement of our irrational faculties underpin Posidonius' conception of the best education for children and young adults. In his view, from an early age we should be "trained" about knowing that we have different faculties for our rational and emotional modes, and this education should occur while we are taught about the "rule" of reason over the irrational faculties.[115] Part of this teaching would duly need to incorporate recognitions of reason's judgmental processes in emotional modes.

In considering themes of education and knowledge we have likewise revealed that for the Stoics, knowledge refers to being rational, and being rational refers to a communal orientation. Knowledge is a fellowship for the Stoics. When therefore Posidonius argues that the self-reflective development of our irrational modes moves us through stages of "knowledge and ignorance" from which we "benefit,"[116] our emotional and passionate existences become implicated in our knowledge. If as we have seen for the

---

111. Galen in Posidonius, *Fragments*, fragment 165.

112. Galen in Posidonius, *Fragments*, fragment 166.

113. Galen in Posidonius, *Fragments*, fragment 164.

114. Stobaeus (in Inwood and Gerson, *Stoics Reader*, 138; taken from *Anthology*, 102.10a) reports that for Chrysippus, what is irrational will not obey nor accommodate rationality. Schofield ("Stoic Ethics," 36–38) provides further reflections on this point.

115. Galen in Posidonius, *Fragments*, fragment 31.

116. Galen in Posidonius, *Fragments*, fragment 162.

Stoics knowledge is a shared activity, then suddenly our emotional life and development does seem implicated in our social existence.

The "benefits" of this journey through knowledge that Posidonius describes are conditioned by the apparently rationally oriented, self-reasoning qualities of our irrational faculties. Such conditions and such benefits must therefore at least for this Stoic thinker be communally directed and participatory. How could the self-regulating, self-reasoning, tendencies of our emotional faculties be anything but socially constituted for this perspective, given the Stoic equation of what is rational, reasoned, and ordered, with what is social and communal? Beyond Posidonius, where Stoics across the ancient eras recognize self-regulating capacities in our irrational faculties, so they too would venture into the territory of acknowledging what is shared and kindred about our emotional states.

In response to our original question in this chapter therefore, we here reach a Stoic position in which our emotional states do not absolutely separate us from a communal or social existence. If there is something self-regulating and self-reasoning about our emotional, passionate lives, so a common ground emerges between rationality and emotions, and therefore between irrational states and the fellowship that rationality conditions. This similarity of course relies on how, through this developing self-awareness, we become less irrationally emotional and more rationally regulated. Emotional self-regulation must be part of an ongoing activity of thinking and acting rationally.

What Posidonius describes as the "cause" of the "calming" of our emotions[117] is therefore also in this view the cause of why our emotional modes are not completely detached from our rationally interconnected modes. We have indeed earlier seen Posidonius describe our self-regulating emotional faculties as having proper "natural" ends. When considering how the Stoics posit being socially oriented as our natural end, this presents an intersection between our emotional and social conditions. It is natural that we will be emotional or impassioned. It is however in our nature to be, and to learn to be, rationally indifferent to the uncontrollable causes to such internal states.

Posidonius' conception of our irrational, emotional modes, orients us toward a final Stoic recognition of our shared constitutions. This fellowship is underpinned by our common rationality. We also have in common an irrational faculty that, as Posidonius has described, is not beyond the ordering and systematization of rationality. What is not beyond rationality is duly not beyond our internal links to our fellow rational beings and the universe that orders us together. This evokes the Stoic sense of "beyond"

---

117. Galen in Posidonius, *Fragments*, fragment 166.

that I have already proposed, which does not infer a world that is externally outside us, but rather indicates a world to which our internality can be traced. Stoicism does not restrict the individual to a locally self-determining mind and body, it recognizes the individual as a fragment of a communal and universal, systematically ordered, mind and body. Your thoughts, your actions, your body, your self-preserving tendencies, your knowledge, your education, your emotions, your well-being, your goals, and your outcomes, are conceived, motivated, activated, and experienced by a system of which you are a part.

Bibliography

Ackeren, Marcel van. *A Companion to Marcus Aurelius*. Blackwell Companions to the Ancient World. Malden, MA: Wiley-Blackwell, 2012.

Aikin, Scott, and Emily McGill-Rutherford. "Stoicism, Feminism, and Autonomy." *Symposium* 1 (2014) 9–22.

Alter, Alexandra. "Ryan Holiday Sells Stoicism as a Life Hack, without Apology." *New York Times*, December 6, 2016. https://www.nytimes.com/2016/12/06/fashion/ryan-holiday-stoicism-american-apparel.html.

Annas, Julia. "Ethics in Stoic Philosophy." *Phronesis* 52 (2007) 58–87.

——. *The Morality of Happiness*. New York: Oxford University Press, 1993.

——. *Platonic Ethics, Old and New*. New York: Cornell University Press, 2013.

Anthon, Charles. *A Classical Dictionary*. New York: Harper & Brothers, 1841.

Aristotle. "On the Cosmos." In *On Sophistical Refutations. On Coming-to-Be and Passing-Away. On the Cosmos*, edited by T. Page et al., translated by David Furley, 344–409. Loeb Classical Library 400. Cambridge: Harvard University Press, 1955.

——. *History of Animals*. Vol. 1, *Books 1–3*. Translated by A. L. Peck. Loeb Classical Library 437. Cambridge: Harvard University Press, 1965.

——. *The Metaphysics*. Translated by Hugh Lawson-Tancred. London: Penguin, 1998.

——. *The Nicomachean Ethics*. Translated by J. Thompson. London: Penguin, 2004.

——. *Physics: Books III and IV*. Translated by Edward Hussey. Oxford: Clarendon, 1993.

——. *Politics: Books I and II*. Translated by Trevor Saunders. Oxford: Clarendon, 1995.

Arnold, Edward. *Roman Stoicism: Being Lectures on the History of the Stoic Philosophy with Special Reference to Its Development within the Roman Empire*. Cambridge: Cambridge University Press, 1911.

Asmis, Elizbeth. "Seneca's *On the Happy Life* and Stoic Individualism." *Apeiron* 23 (1990) 219–55.

——. "The Stoics on Women." In *Feminism and Ancient Philosophy*, edited by Julie Ward, 68–92. New York: Routledge, 1996.

Balkhi, Syed. "How Stoicism Can Improve Your Leadership Skills." *Forbes*, July 2, 2021. https://www.forbes.com/sites/theyec/2021/07/02/how-stoicism-can-improve-your-leadership-skills/?sh=425ba758123a.

Baltzly, Dirk. "Stoic Pantheism." *Sophia* 42 (2003) 3–33.

Bankston, Carl L., III. "Filipino Americans." In *Asian Americans: Contemporary Trends and Issues*, edited by Pyong Gap Min, 180–203. Thousand Oaks, CA: Pine Forge, 2006.

Batuman, Elif. "How to Be a Stoic." *New Yorker*, December 19 & 26, 2016. https://www.newyorker.com/magazine/2016/12/19/how-to-be-a-stoic.

Becker, Lawrence. *A New Stoicism*. Rev. ed. Princeton: Princeton University Press, 2017.

———. "Stoic Emotion." In *Stoicism: Traditions and Transformations*, edited by Steven Strange and Jack Zupko, 250–76. Cambridge: Cambridge University Press, 2004.

Bénatouïl, Thomas. "How Industrious Can Zeus Be? The Extent and Objects of Divine Activity in Stoicism." In *God and Cosmos in Stoicism*, edited by Ricardo Salles, 23–45. Oxford: Oxford University Press, 2009.

Berry, Sarah. "Why Stoicism Is Changing People's Lives for the Better." *Sydney Morning Herald*, February 10, 2016. http://www.smh.com.au/lifestyle/life/why-stoicism-is-changing-peoples-lives-for-better-20160209-gmptyy.html.

Blumenthal, Jeremy. "Law and the Emotions." *Indiana Law Journal* 80 (2005) 159–238.

Bobonich, Christopher. "Socrates and Eudaimonia." In *The Cambridge Companion to Socrates*, edited by Donald Morrison, 293–332. Cambridge Companions to Philosophy. New York: Cambridge University Press, 2010.

Bobzien, Susanne. *Determinism and Freedom in Stoic Philosophy*. Oxford: Clarendon, 1998.

Boeri, Marcelo. "Does Cosmic Nature Matter?" In *God and Cosmos in Stoicism*, edited by Ricardo Salles, 173–200. Oxford: Oxford University Press, 2009.

Bonazzi, Mauro. "The Platonist Appropriation of Stoic Epistemology." In *From Stoicism to Platonism: The Development of Philosophy, 100 BCE—100 CE*, edited by Troels Engberg-Pedersen, 120–41. Cambridge: Cambridge University Press, 2017.

Bornstein, Brian, and Richard Weiner. "Emotion and the Law: A Field Whose Time Has Come." In *Emotion and the Law: Psychological Perspectives*, edited by Brian Bornstein and Richard Weiner, 1–12. New York: Springer, 2009.

Brennan, Tad. "Reasonable Impressions in Stoicism." *Phronesis* 41 (1996) 318–34.

———. *The Stoic Life: Emotions, Duties, and Fate*. Oxford: Clarendon, 2005.

Brown, Elenor, and Guichun Zong. *Global Perspectives on Gender and Sexuality in Education: Raising Awareness, Fostering Equity, Advancing Justice*. Charlotte, NC: Information Age, 2017.

Buck, Ross. "The Genetics and Biology of True Love: Prosocial Biological Affects and the Left Hemisphere." *Psychological Review* 109 (2002) 739–44.

Byers, Sarah Catherine. "Augustine's Debt to Stoicism in the *Confessions*." In *The Routledge Handbook of the Stoic Tradition*, edited by John Sellars, 56–69. Routledge Handbooks in Philosophy. London: Routledge, 2016.

Chen, Ta-tuan, et al. *Chinese Primer, Volumes 1–3 (Pinyin)*. Rev. ed. Princeton: Princeton University Press, 2020.

Cicero, Marcus Tullius. *On Academic Scepticism*. Translated by Charles Brittain. Indianapolis: Hackett, 2006.

———. *On Divination*. Translated by David Wardle. Oxford: Clarendon, 2006.

———. *On Duties*. Edited by M. T. Griffin and E. M. Atkins. Cambridge: Cambridge University Press, 1991.

———. *On Duties*. Translated by Benjamin Newton. Ithica, NY: Cornell University Press, 2016.

———. *De Finibus Bonorum et Malorum*. Translated by Harris Rackham. Loeb Classical Library 40. London: Heinemann, 1914.

———. *On Moral Ends*. Edited by Julia Annas. Translated by Raphael Woolf. Cambridge: Cambridge University Press, 2004.

———. *De Natura Deorum*. In *De Natura Deorum. Academica*, translated by Harris Rackham, 2–387. Loeb Classical Library 268. Cambridge: Harvard University Press, 1967.

———. *The Nature of the Gods*. Translated by Peter Walsh. New York: Oxford University Press, 1998.

———. *De Officiis*. Translated by Walter Miller. Loeb Classical Library 30. London: Heinemann, 1928.

———. *De Oratore: Book III. De Fato. Paradoxa Stoicorum. De Partitione Oratoria*. Translated by Harris Rackham. Loeb Classical Library 349. Cambridge: Harvard University Press, 1942.

Collette, Bernard. *The Stoic Doctrine of Providence: A Study of Its Development and of Some of Its Major Issues*. Issues in Ancient Philosophy. London: Routledge, 2022.

Cooper, John. "Posidonius on Emotions." In *The Emotions in Hellenistic Philosophy*, edited by Juha Sihvola and Troels Engberg-Pedersen, 71–112. Dordrecht: Springer, 1998.

Crosbie, Christopher. *Revenge Tragedy and Classical Philosophy on the Early Modern Stage*. Edinburgh: Edinburgh University Press, 2019.

Dealy, Ross. *The Stoic Origins of Erasmus' Philosophy of Christ*. Toronto: University of Toronto Press, 2017.

Derinbogaz, Ceyhun. "How Learning Stoicism Helped Me in the Age of Anxiety." *Medium*, April 8, 2020. https://cderinbogaz.medium.com/how-learning-stoicism-helped-me-in-the-age-of-anxiety-4bb0b784e429.

Dillon, J. T. *Musonius Rufus and Education in the Good Life: A Model of Teaching and Living Virtue*. Lanham, MD: University Press of America, 2004.

Diogenes Laërtius. *The Lives and Opinions of Eminent Philosophers*. Translated by Charles Yonge. London: Bohn, 1853.

Dudley, Donald. *A History of Cynicism: From Diogenes to the 6th Century A.D.* London: Methuen, 1937.

Dudley, Susan, and Amanda Fine. "Kin Recognition in an Annual Plant." *Biology Letters* 22 (2007) 435–38.

Dyson, Henry. "The God Within: The Normative Self in Epictetus." *History of Philosophy Quarterly* 26 (2009) 235–53.

Eastman, Susan Grove. *Paul and the Person: Reframing Paul's Anthropology*. Grand Rapids: Eerdmans, 2017.

Eliasson, Erik. *The Notion of That Which Depends on Us in Plotinus and Its Background*. Philosophia Antiqua 113. Leiden: Brill, 2008.

Engel, David. "The Gender Egalitarianism of Musonius Rufus." *Ancient Philosophy* 20 (2000) 377–91.

Epictetus. *Discourses and Selected Writings*. Translated by Robert Dobbin. Oxford: Penguin, 2008.

———. *The Discourses and the Manual: Together with His Writings*. Translated by Percy Ewing Matheson. Oxford: Clarendon, 1916.

———. *The Discourses as Reported by Arrian, the Manual, and Fragments*. Edited by T. Page et al. Translated by William Oldfather. London: Heinemann, 1961.

———. *Discourses, Fragments, and Handbook*. Translated by Robin Hard. Oxford: Oxford University Press, 2014.

———. *Enchiridion*. Translated by George Long. New York: Dover, 2004.

Epicurus. *The Epicurus Reader: Selected Writing and Testimonia*. Edited and translated by Brad Inwood and L. P. Gerson. Indianapolis: Hackett, 1994.

———. *Letters and Sayings of Epicurus*. Translated by Odysseus Makridis. New York: Barnes and Noble, 2005.

Erskine, Andrew. *The Hellenistic Stoa: Political Thought and Action*. Ithica, NY: Cornell University Press, 1990.

Evans, Jules. "The Stoic Mayor." In *Stoicism Today: Selected Writings I*, edited by Patrick Ussher, 87–93. CreateSpace, 2014.

Farren, Jen. "Stoicism & Star Trek." In *Stoicism Today: Selected Writings I*, edited by Patrick Ussher, 196–200. CreateSpace, 2014.

Feloni, Richard. "11 Timeless Lessons from a Book That Changed Billionaire CEO Elizabeth Holmes' Life." *Business Insider Australia*, July 3, 2015. https://www.businessinsider.com/lessons-from-elizabeth-holmes-favorite-book-meditations-2015-7.

Flood, Alison. "Dress Rehearsal for Catastrophe: How Stoics Are Speaking to Locked-Down Readers." *Guardian*, April 16, 2020. https://www.theguardian.com/books/booksblog/2020/apr/16/how-stoics-are-speaking-to-locked-down-readers.

Frede, Michael. "Stoic Epistemology." In *The Cambridge History of Hellenistic Philosophy*, edited by Keimpe Algra et al., 295–322. Cambridge: Cambridge University Press, 1999.

Freud, Sigmund. *New Introductory Lectures on Psychoanalysis*. Edited and translated by James Strachey. London: Hogarth, 1949.

Gill, Christopher. "Did Galen Understand Platonic and Stoic Thinking on Emotions?" In *The Emotions in Hellenistic Philosophy*, edited by Juha Sihvola and Troels Engberg-Pedersen, 113–48. Dordrecht: Springer, 1998.

———. "Galen and the Stoics: Mortal Enemies or Blood Brothers." *Phronesis* 52 (2007) 88–120.

———. "Marcus Aurelius' *Meditations*: How Stoic and How Platonic?" In *Platonic Stoicism, Stoic Platonism: The Dialogue between Platonism and Stoicism in Antiquity*, edited by Mauro Bonazzi and Christoph Helmig, 189–208. Ancient and Medieval Philosophy 1/39. Leuven: Leuven University Press, 2007.

———. *Naturalistic Psychology in Galen and Stoicism*. Oxford: Oxford University Press, 2010.

———. *Personality in Greek Epic, Tragedy, and Philosophy: The Self in Dialogue*. Oxford: Clarendon, 1996.

———. "The School in the Roman Imperial Period." In *The Cambridge Companion to the Stoics*, edited by Brad Inwood, 33–58. Cambridge Companions to Philosophy. Cambridge: Cambridge University Press, 2003.

———. *The Structured Self in Hellenistic and Roman Thought*. Oxford: Clarendon, 2006.

Glassborow, Nigel. "Without the Divine, There Is No Stoicism: A Polemic by Nigel Glassborow." *Modern Stoicism*, February 15, 2015. https://modernstoicism.com/a-polemic-by-nigel-glassborow/.

Goodhill, Oliva. "Silicon Valley Tech Workers Are Using an Ancient Philosophy Designed for Greek Slaves as a Life Hack." *Quartz*, December 17, 2016. https://

qz.com/866030/stoicism-silicon-valley-tech-workers-are-reading-ryan-holiday-to-use-an-ancient-philosophy-as-a-life-hack/.

Gould, Josiah. *The Philosophy of Chrysippus*. Philosophia Antiqua 17. Leiden: Brill, 1971.

Grahn-Wilder, Malin. *Gender and Sexuality in Stoic Philosophy*. New York: Palgrave MacMillan, 2018.

Graver, Margaret. *Stoicism and Emotion*. Chicago: University of Chicago Press, 2007.

Griffin, Miriam. "Philosophy, Cato, and Roman Suicide: I." *Greece & Rome* 33 (1986) 64–77.

Guthrie, W. K. C. *A History of Greek Philosophy*. Vol. 1, *The Earlier Presocratics and the Pythagoreans*. Cambridge: Cambridge University Press, 1962.

Hackett, Horatio Balch. *Illustrations of Scripture: Suggested by a Tour through the Holy Land*. Boston: Heath & Graves, 1856.

Hankinson, R. J. "Explanation and Causation." In *The Cambridge History of Hellenistic Philosophy*, edited by Keimpe Algra et al., 479–512. Cambridge: Cambridge University Press, 1999.

Harriman, Benjamin. "Disjunctions and Natural Philosophy in Marcus Aurelius." *Classical Quarterly* 69 (2020) 858–79.

Heraclitus. *Fragments: A Text and Translation with a Commentary by T. M. Robinson*. Translated by T. M. Robinson. Toronto: University of Toronto Press, 1987.

———. *Fragments: The Collected Wisdom of Heraclitus*. Translated by Brooks Haxton. New York: Viking Penguin, 2001.

Hesiod. *The Homeric Hymns and Homerica*. Translated by Hugh Evelyn-White. Loeb Classical Library. Cambridge: Harvard University Press, 1982.

Hierocles. *Hierocles the Stoic: Elements of Ethics, Fragments, and Excerpts*. Edited by Ilaria Ramelli. Translated by Ilaria Ramelli and David Konstan. Atlanta: Society of Biblical Literature, 2009.

Hill, Lisa. "Feminism and Stoic Sagehood." In *The Routledge Handbook of Hellenistic Philosophy*, edited by Kelly Arenson, 410–21. Routledge Handbooks in Philosophy. London: Routledge, 2020.

———. "The First Wave of Feminism: Were the Stoics Feminists?" *History of Political Thought* 22 (2001) 13–40.

Holiday, Ryan. *The Obstacle Is the Way: The Timeless Art of Turning Trials into Triumphs*. New York: Penguin, 2014.

———. "The Stoic Scholar: Interview with Professor Anthony Long." *The Daily Stoic*, July 15, 2017. https://dailystoic.com/anthony-long/.

Holiday, Ryan, and Stephen Hanselman. *The Daily Stoic: 366 Meditations on Wisdom, Perseverance, and the Art of Living*. London: Profile, 2016.

———. *Lives of the Stoics: The Art of Living from Zeno to Marcus Aurelius*. London: Profile, 2020.

Humphreys, Joe. "Five Lessons of Stoicism: What I Learned from Living for a Week as a Stoic." *Irish Times*, October 29, 2020. https://www.irishtimes.com/culture/five-lessons-of-stoicism-what-i-learned-from-living-for-a-week-as-a-stoic-1.4392422.

Hyslop, James Hervey. *The Elements of Ethics*. Edinburgh: Blackwood & Sons, 1895.

Inwood, Brad. *Ethics and Human Action in Early Stoicism*. Oxford: Clarendon, 1985.

———. "The Legacy of Musonius Rufus." In *From Stoicism to Platonism: The Development of Philosophy, 100 BCE–100 CE*, edited by Troels Engberg-Pedersen, 254–76. New York: Cambridge University Press, 2017.

―――. *Reading Seneca: Stoic Philosophy at Rome*. Oxford: Clarendon, 2005.

Inwood, Brad, and Donini, Perluigi. "Stoic Ethics." In *The Cambridge History of Hellenistic Philosophy*, edited by Keimpe Algra et al., 675–738. Cambridge: Cambridge University Press, 1999.

Inwood, Brad, and Gerson, Lloyd, eds. and trans. *The Stoics Reader: Selected Writings and Testimonia*. Indianapolis: Hackett, 2008.

Irvine, William. *A Guide to the Good Life: The Ancient Art of Stoic Joy*. Oxford: Oxford University Press, 2008.

―――. "Putting the Greek Back into Stoicism." *BBC News*, July 3, 2015. https://www.bbc.com/news/magazine-33346743.

Jackson-McCabe, Matt. "The Stoic Theory of Implanted Preconceptions." *Phronesis* 49 (2005) 323–47.

Jedan, Christoph. *Stoic Virtues: Chrysippus and the Religious Character of Stoic Ethics*. London: Continuum, 2009.

Johnson, Brian. *The Role Ethics of Epictetus: Stoicism in Ordinary Life*. Lanham, MD: Lexington, 2013.

Johnson, Ryan. *Deleuze, a Stoic*. Edinburgh: Edinburgh University Press, 2020.

Kelsen, Hans. *General Theory of Law and State*. Translated by Anders Wedberg. Cambridge: Harvard University Press, 1945.

Kennedy, Vincent. "Stoicism Saved My Life." *The Daily Stoic*, November 14, 2016. https://dailystoic.com/stoicism-saved-my-life/.

Kooten, Geurt Hendrik van. *Cosmic Christology in Paul and the Pauline School: Colossians and Ephesians in the Context of Graeco-Roman Cosmology, with a New Synopsis of the Greek Texts*. Tübingen: Mohr Siebeck, 2003.

Lactantius. "A Treatise on the Anger of God." In *Anti-Nicene Fathers: The Writings of the Fathers down to A.D. 325*, edited by Alexander Roberts et al., 7:259–80. Buffalo: Christian Literature, 1885.

Lampert, Dan. "An Interview with Donald Robertson." *Stoicism in Action*, December 18, 2018. https://medium.com/stoicism/an-interview-with-donald-robertson-44f76758f68b.

Lapidge, Michael. "Stoic Cosmology." In *The Stoics*, edited by John Rist, 161–86. Berkeley: University of California Press, 1978.

LeBon, Tim. *Achieve Your Potential with Positive Psychology*. London: Hodder & Stoughton, 2014.

―――. "Interview: Tim LeBon." *Modern Stoicism*, October 9, 2016. https://modernstoicism.com/interview-tim-lebon/.

Levine, Michael. "Pantheism, Ethics, and Ecology." *Environmental Values* 3 (1994) 121–38.

Lombardi, Jamie. "Marcus Aurelius Helped Me Survive Grief and Rebuild My Life." *Aeon*, February 28, 2020. https://aeon.co/ideas/marcus-aurelius-helped-me-survive-grief-and-rebuild-my-life.

Long, Anthony. *Epictetus: A Stoic and Socratic Guide to Life*. Oxford: Clarendon, 2002.

―――. *From Epicurus to Epictetus: Studies in Hellenistic and Roman Philosophy*. Oxford: Clarendon, 2006.

―――. "Plato and the Stoics on Limits, Parts, and Wholes." In *Plato and the Stoics*, edited by Andrew Long, 80–105. Cambridge: Cambridge University Press, 2013.

——. "Plato, Chrysippus, and Posidonius' Theory of Affective Movements." In *From Stoicism to Platonism: The Development of Philosophy, 100 BCE–100 CE*, edited by Troels Engberg-Pedersen, 27–46. Cambridge: Cambridge University Press, 2017.

——. "The Socratic Imprint on Epictetus' Philosophy." In *Stoicism: Traditions and Transformations*, edited by Steven Strange and Jack Zupko, 10–31. Cambridge: Cambridge University Press, 2004.

——. "Soul and Body in Stoicism." *Phronesis* 27 (1982) 34–57.

——. "The Stoic Concept of Evil." *Philosophical Quarterly* 18 (1968) 329–43.

——. "Stoic Philosophers on Persons, Property-Ownership, and Community." *Bulletin of the Institute of Classical Studies Supplement* 68 (1997) 13–31.

——. "Stoic Psychology." In *The Cambridge History of Hellenistic Philosophy*, edited by Keimpe Algra et al., 560–84. Cambridge: Cambridge University Press, 1999.

——. *Stoic Studies.* Berkeley: University of California Press, 1996.

Long, Anthony, and David Sedley, eds. and trans. *The Hellenistic Philosophers.* Vol. 1, *Translations of the Principal Sources, with Philosophical Commentary.* Cambridge: Cambridge University Press, 1987.

Love, Shayla. "The Revival of Stoicism." *Vice*, June 29, 2021. https://www.vice.com/en/article/xgxvmw/the-revival-of-stoicism.

Lovejoy, Arthur. *The Great Chain of Being: A Study of the History of an Idea.* Cambridge: Harvard University Press, 1964.

Maclean, Paul. "The Limbic System with Respect to Self-Preservation and the Preservation of the Species." *Journal of Nervous and Mental Disease* 127 (1959) 1–11.

Marcus Aurelius. *Meditations.* Translated by Martin Hammond. London: Penguin, 2006.

——. *Meditations.* Translated by Gregory Hays. New York: Modern Library, 2002.

——. *Meditations.* Translated by Maxwell Staniforth. London: Penguin, 1964.

——. *The Meditations of Marcus Aurelius Antoninus.* Translated by George Long. New York: Lupton, 1900.

——. *Meditations (with Selected Correspondence).* Translated by Robin Hard. London: Penguin, 2011.

McCabe, Mary. "Extend or Identify: Two Stoic Accounts of Altruism." In *Metaphysics, Soul, and Ethics in Ancient Thought: Themes from the Work of Richard Sorabji*, edited by Ricardo Salles, 413–43. Oxford: Clarendon, 2005.

McDonough, Sean. *Christ as Creator: Origins of a New Testament Doctrine.* Oxford: Oxford University Press, 2009.

Meijer, P. A. *Stoic Theology: Proofs for the Existence of the Cosmic God and of the Traditional Gods: Including a Commentary on Cleanthes' Hymn on Zeus.* Delft: Eburon, 2007.

Miller, Jon. *Spinoza and the Stoics.* Cambridge: Cambridge University Press, 2015.

Montiglio, Silvia. "Should the Aspiring Wise Man Travel? A Conflict in Seneca's Thought." *American Journal of Philology* 127 (2006) 553–86.

Musonius Rufus. *Musonius Rufus: Lectures & Sayings.* Edited by William Irvine. Translated by Cynthia King. CreateSpace, 2011.

Nock, Arthur. "Posidonius." *Journal of Roman Studies* 49 (1959) 1–15.

Nussbaum, Martha. "The Incomplete Feminism of Musonius Rufus, Platonist, Stoic, and Roman." In *The Sleep of Reason: Erotic Experience and Sexual Ethics in Ancient Greece and Rome*, edited by Martha Nussbaum and Jula Sihvola, 283–326. Chicago: University of Chicago Press, 2002.

O'Donovan, Katherine. "Engendering Justice: Women's Perspectives and the Rule of Law." *University of Toronto Law Journal* 29 (1989) 127–48.

Ogilvie, John. *The Student's English Dictionary: Literary, Scientific, Etymological, and Pronouncing.* Edited by Charles Annandale. London: Blackie & Son, 1895.

O'Grady, Jane. "Is Stoic Philosophy the Answer to Your Lockdown Blues." *The Telegraph*, January 10, 2021. https://www.telegraph.co.uk/books/what-to-read/stoic-philosophy-answer-lockdown-blues/.

Orange, Donna. "A Pre-Cartesian Self." *Journal of Psychoanalytic Self Psychology* 8 (2013) 488–94.

Overby, Andrew. "How Stoicism Helped Me Overcome Depression." *Modern Stoicism*, September 19, 2015. https://modernstoicism.com/how-stoicism-helped-me-overcome-depression-by-andrew-overby/.

Owen, Huw Parri. *Concepts of Deity.* Berlin: Springer, 1971.

Pearce, David. "Foundations of an Ecological Economics." *Ecological Modelling* 38 (1987) 9–18.

Pearson, A. C., ed. and trans. *The Fragments of Zeno and Cleanthes: With Introduction and Explanatory Notes.* London: Clay and Sons, 1891.

Pigliucci, Massimo. "Becker's *A New Stoicism*, II: The Way Things Stand, Part 1." *How to Be a Stoic*, September 9, 2017. https://howtobeastoic.wordpress.com /2017/09/29/beckers-a-new-stoicism-ii-the-way-things-stand-part-1./

———. "The Growing Pains of the Stoic Movement." *How to Be a Stoic*, June 5, 2018. https://howtobeastoic.wordpress.com/2018/06/05/the-growing-pains-of-the-stoic-movement/.

———. "How to Be a Stoic." *New York Times*, February 2, 2015. https://opinionator.blogs.nytimes.com/2015/02/02/how-to-be-a-stoic/.

———. *How to Be a Stoic: Using Ancient Philosophy to Live a Modern Life.* New York: Basic, 2017.

———. "What Do I Disagree about with the Ancient Stoics." *How to Be a Stoic*, December 26, 2017. https://howtobeastoic.wordpress.com/2017/12/26/what-do-i-disagree-about-with-the-ancient-stoics/.

Pigliucci, Massimo, and Gregory Lopez. *A Handbook for New Stoics: How to Thrive in a World Out of Your Control.* New York: Experiment, 2019.

Plato. *Apology.* In *Five Dialogues: Euthyphro, Apology, Crito, Meno, Phaedo.* Translated by George M. A. Grube. Indianapolis: Hackett, 2002.

———. *Gorgias.* Translated by Terence Irwin. Oxford: Oxford University Press, 1979.

———. *Meno.* Translated by George Grube. Indianapolis: Hackett, 1980.

———. *Phaedo.* In *Five Dialogues: Euthyphro, Apology, Crito, Meno, Phaedo.* Translated by George M. A. Grube. Indianapolis: Hackett, 2002.

———. *Republic.* Translated by Desmond Lee. London: Penguin, 2007.

———. *Republic.* Translated by C. D. C. Reeve. Indianapolis: Hackett, 2004.

———. *Sophist.* In *The Dialogues of Plato: Volume IV*, translated by Benjamin Jowett, 281–408. London: Oxford University Press, 1871.

———. *The Symposium.* Edited by M. C. Howatson and Frisbee Sheffield. Translated by M. C. Howatson. Cambridge: Cambridge University Press, 2008.

———. *Timaeus and Critias.* Translated by Robin Waterfield. Oxford: Oxford University Press, 2008.

Plutarch. *Moralia.* Vol. 8, *Part 2.* Translated by Harold Cherniss. Loeb Classical Library 470. Cambridge: Harvard University Press, 2004.

———. *Moralia*. Vol. 15, *Fragments*. Edited and translated by F. H. Sandbach. Loeb Classical Library 429. Cambridge: Harvard University Press, 1987.

Posidonius. *Posidonius*. Vol. 3, *The Translation of the Fragments*. Edited by J. Diggle et al. Translated by I. G. Kidd. Cambridge: Cambridge University Press, 1999.

Pratt, Norman. *Seneca's Drama*. Chapel Hill: University of North Carolina Press, 1983.

Rendall, Gerald. "Immanence, Stoic and Christian." *Harvard Theological Review* 14 (1921) 1–14.

Reydams-Schils, Gretchen. "Authority and Agency in Stoicism." *Greek, Roman, and Byzantine Studies* 51 (2011) 296–322.

———. "'Becoming Like God' in Platonism and Stoicism." In *From Stoicism to Platonism: The Development of Philosophy, 100 BCE–100 CE*, edited by Troels Engberg-Pederson, 142–58. Cambridge: Cambridge University Press, 2017.

———. "Philosophy and Education in Stoicism of the Roman Imperial Era." *Oxford Review of Education* 36 (2010) 561–74.

———. "Posidonius and the *Timaeus*: Off to Rhodes and Back to Plato?" *Classical Quarterly* 47 (1997) 455–76.

———. *The Roman Stoics: Self, Responsibility, and Affection*. Chicago: University of Chicago Press, 2005.

Richardson, W. "The Basis of Ethics: Chrysippus and Clement of Alexandria." In *Studia Patristica*, edited by F. L. Cross, 9:87–97. Berlin: Akademie-Verlag, 1966.

Robertson, Donald. *How to Think Like a Roman Emperor: The Stoic Philosophy of Marcus Aurelius*. New York: St. Martin's, 2018.

———. *The Philosophy of Cognitive-Behavioural Therapy (CBT): Stoic Philosophy as Rational and Cognitive Psychotherapy*. London: Karnac, 2010.

———. *Stoicism and the Art of Happiness*. London: Teach Yourself, 2014.

Sambursky, Samuel. *Physics of the Stoics*. London: Routledge and Paul, 1959.

Schofield, Malcolm. "Stoic Ethics." In *The Cambridge Companion to the Stoics*, edited by Brad Inwood, 233–56. Cambridge Companions to Philosophy. Cambridge: Cambridge University Press, 2003.

———. *The Stoic Idea of the City*. Cambridge: Cambridge University Press, 1991.

Seal, Carey. *Philosophy and Community in Seneca's Prose*. Oxford: Oxford University Press, 2021.

Seddon, Keith. *Epictetus' Handbook and the Tablet of Cebes: Guides to Stoic Living*. London: Routledge, 2005.

Sedley, David. "The Stoic-Platonist Debate on Kathekonta." In *Topics in Stoic Philosophy*, edited by Katerina Ierodiakonou, 128–52. Oxford: Oxford University Press, 1999.

Sellars, John. *The Art of Living: The Stoics on the Nature and Function of Philosophy*. 2nd ed. London: Bloomsbury, 2009.

———. "Introduction." In *The Routledge Handbook of the Stoic Tradition*, edited by John Sellars, 1–14. Routledge Handbooks in Philosophy. New York: Routledge, 2016.

———. "Stoicism and Emotions." In *Stoicism Today: Selected Writings II*, edited by Patrick Ussher 43–48. CreateSpace, 2016.

Seneca, Lucius Annaeus. *Letters from a Stoic*. Edited and translated by Robin Campbell. London: Penguin, 1969.

———. *Letters on Ethics*. Translated by Margaret Graver and Anthony Long. Chicago: University of Chicago Press, 2015.

———. *On the Shortness of Life*. Translated by Charles Costa. London: Penguin, 1997.

——. *Seneca, Ad Lucilium Epistulae Morales: Volume 1*. Edited and translated by Richard Gummere. Loeb Classical Library 75. London: Heinemann, 1962.

Sextus Empiricus. *Against Logicians*. Translated by R. G. Bury. Loeb Classical Library 291. Cambridge: Harvard University Press, 1935.

——. *Against the Logicians*. Translated by Richard Bett. Cambridge: Cambridge University Press, 2005.

——. *Against the Physicists*. Translated by Richard Bett. Cambridge: Cambridge University Press, 2012.

——. *Against Professors*. Translated by R. G. Bury. Loeb Classical Library 382. Cambridge: Harvard University Press, 1949.

——. *Outlines of Pyrrhonism*. Translated by R. G. Bury. Loeb Classical Library 273. Cambridge: Harvard University Press, 1933.

——. *Outlines of Scepticism*. Edited and translated by Julia Annas and Jonathan Barnes. Cambridge: Cambridge University Press, 2000.

Sharpe, Matthew. "How It's Not the Chrisippus You Read: On Cooper, Hadot, Epictetus, and Stoicism as a Way of Life." *Philosophy Today* 58 (2014) 367–92.

——. "Stoicism 5.0: The Unlikely 21st Century Reboot of an Ancient Philosophy." *The Conversation*, July 13, 2017. https://theconversation.com/ stoicism-5-0-the-unlikely-21st-century-reboot-of-an-ancient-philosophy-80986.

——. "When Life Gives You Lemons . . . 4 Stoic Tips for Getting through Lockdown from Epictetus." *The Conversation*, August 23, 2021. https://theconversation.com/ when-life-gives-you-lemons-4-stoic-tips-for-getting-through-lockdown-from-epictetus-166487.

Sharples. R. W. *Stoics, Epicureans, and Sceptics: An Introduction to Hellenistic Philosophy*. London: Routledge, 1996.

Sherman, Nancy. "If You're Reading Stoicism for Life Hacks, You're Missing the Point." *New York Times*, May 14, 2021. https://www.nytimes.com/2021/05/14/opinion/ stoics-self-help.html.

——. *Stoic Wisdom: Ancient Lessons for Modern Resilience*. New York: Oxford University Press, 2021.

Simplicius. *On Epictetus Handbook, 1–26*. Translated by Charles Brittain and Tad Brennan. London: Bloomsbury Academic, 2014.

Snyder, H. Gregory. *Teachers and Texts in the Ancient World: Philosophers, Jews, and Christians*. London: Routledge, 2000.

Sorabji, Richard. *Emotion and Peace of Mind: From Stoic Agitation to Christian Temptation*. Oxford: Oxford University Press, 2000.

——. *Self: Ancient and Modern Insights about Individuality, Life, and Death*. Chicago: University of Chicago Press, 2006.

Spence, Edward. *Stoic Philosophy and the Control Problem of AI Technology Caught in the Web*. Lanham, MD: Rowman & Littlefield, 2021.

Starr, Chester. "Epictetus and the Tyrant." *Classical Philology* 44 (1949) 20–29.

Stephens, William. "Epictetus on Beastly Vices and Animal Virtues." In *Epictetus: His Continuing Influence and Contemporary Relevance*, edited by Dane Gordon and David Suits, 207–39. New York: RIT Press, 2014.

——. *Marcus Aurelius: A Guide for the Perplexed*. London: Continuum, 2012.

——. *Stoic Ethics: Epictetus and Happiness as Freedom*. London: Continuum, 2007.

——. "Stoic Naturalism, Rationalism, and Ecology." *Environmental Ethics* 16 (1994) 275–86.

Striker, Gisela. *Essays on Hellenistic Epistemology and Ethics.* Cambridge: Cambridge University Press, 1996.

Thom, Johan Carl. *Cleanthes' Hymn to Zeus: Text, Translation, and Commentary.* Studien und Texte zu Antike und Christentum 33. Tübingen: Mohr Sieback, 2005.

Tieleman, Teun. *Galen and Chrysippus on the Soul: Argument and Refutation in the "De Placitis," Books II–III.* Philosophia Antiqua 68. Leiden: Brill, 1996.

Todd, Robert. "Monism and Immanence: The Foundations of Stoic Physics." In *The Stoics,* edited by John Rist, 137–60. Berkeley: University of California Press, 1978.

UNESCO. *A New Generation: 25 Years of Efforts for Gender Equality in Education.* https://unesdoc.unesco.org/ark:/48223/pf0000374514.

Weaver, P. R. C. "Epaphroditus, Josephus, and Epictetus." *Classical Quarterly* 44 (1994) 468–79.

White, Nicholas. "The Basis of Stoic Ethics." *Harvard Studies in Classical Philology* 83 (1979) 143–78.

———. *Individual and Conflict in Greek Ethics.* Oxford: Clarendon, 2002.

Whiting, Kai, and Leonidas Konstantakos. "Stoic Theology: Revealing or Redundant." *Religions* 10 (2019) 1–18.

Whiting, Kai, et al. "Sustainable Development, Wellbeing and Material Consumption: A Stoic Perspective." *Sustainability* 10 (2018) 1–20.

Wilson, Emily. *The Greatest Empire: A Life of Seneca.* Oxford: Oxford University Press, 2014.

www.ingramcontent.com/pod-product-compliance
Lightning Source LLC
Chambersburg PA
CBHW060339100426
42812CB00003B/1052